OXFORD POLITICAL THEORY

Series Editors: David Miller and Alan Ryan

MULTICULTURAL CITIZENSHIP

OXFORD POLITICAL THEORY

Oxford Political Theory presents the best new work in contemporary political theory. It is intended to be broad in scope, including original contributions to political philosophy, and also work in applied political theory. The series will contain works of outstanding quality with no restriction as to approach or subject matter.

OTHER TITLES IN THIS SERIES

Justice as Impartiality
Brian Barry

Real Freedom for All: What (if Anything) Can Justify Capitalism?
Philippe Van Parijs

Justificatory Liberalism: An Essay on Metaphysics and Political Theory
Gerald Gaus

The Politics of Presence: Democracy and Group Representation
Anne Phillips

On Nationality
David Miller

MULTICULTURAL CITIZENSHIP

A LIBERAL THEORY OF MINORITY RIGHTS

WILL KYMLICKA

CLARENDON PRESS · OXFORD
1995

Oxford University Press, Walton Street, Oxford OX2 6DP
Oxford New York
Athens Auckland Bangkok Bombay
Calcutta Cape Town Dar es Salaam Delhi
Florence Hong Kong Istanbul Karachi
Kuala Lumpur Madras Madrid Melbourne
Mexico City Nairobi Paris Singapore
Taipei Tokyo Toronto
and associated companies in
Berlin Ibadan

Oxford is a trade mark of Oxford University Press

Published in the United States
by Oxford University Press Inc., New York

British Library Cataloguing in Publication Data
Data available

Library of Congress Cataloging in Publication Data
Kymlicka, Will.
Multicultural citizenship: a liberal theory of minority rights /
Will Kymlicka.
(Oxford political theory)
Includes bibliographical references.
1. Minorities—Civil rights. 2. Ethnic groups—Civil rights.
3. Liberalism. 4. Multiculturalism.
I. Title. II. Series.
JF1061.K96 1995 323.1—dc20 95–5110
ISBN 0–19–827949–3

1 3 5 7 9 10 8 6 4 2

Typeset by Hope Services (Abingdon) Ltd.
Printed in Great Britain
on acid-free paper by
Biddles Ltd,
Guildford & King's Lynn

ACKNOWLEDGEMENTS

My greatest debt, as always, is to Susan Donaldson. Virtually everything I write is first read by Sue, and every idea in this book has been shaped by our discussions. When Novalis said 'It is certain any conviction gains infinitely the moment another soul will believe in it,' he could have been talking about my reliance on Sue's advice and opinions.

Over the last few years, as this book has taken shape, I have been moving back and forth between academic and government employment, both of which I enjoy in small doses. My ability to maintain this peripatetic lifestyle has depended on the support of a wide range of people and institutions, including Peter Heap and Leslie Seidle at the Institute for Research on Public Policy, Greg Gauld at Multiculturalism and Citizenship Canada, Barry Hoffmaster at the Westminster Institute for Ethics, Judith Nolté at the Royal Commission on New Reproductive Technologies, John Leyden at Carleton University, and Hilliard Aronovitch at the University of Ottawa. I am grateful to each for the interesting work they have sent my way, and for sparing me from the work I wished to avoid. I would also like to thank the Social Sciences and Humanities Research Council of Canada for funding.

My affiliation with the University of Ottawa has been loose, but none the less very rewarding. As a bilingual university with a mandate to serve both the anglophone and francophone communities in Canada, it is ideally suited for research on minority rights. I would like to thank Wayne Norman and Donald Lenihan, my colleagues in the philosophy department, for many hours of discussion on these topics. I owe a special debt to Wayne, who has provided thorough comments on this book. Chapter 9 is based on some work we co-authored. I also learned a great deal from the students in a graduate seminar I taught at the University in the spring of 1994, who cheerfully pointed out many problems with an earlier draft of this book.

I would also like to thank Brian Anderson, Lisa Charlebois, and Patricia Ivan for excellent research assistance; Beverley Slopen, Dominic Byatt, and Tim Barton for smoothing the publishing process; and many, many friends and colleagues for their comments, discussions, and papers, including Roberto Alejandro, Michael Asch, Judith Baker, Daniel Bell, Allen Buchanan, Alan Cairns, Joseph Carens,

G. A. Cohen, Raphael Cohen-Almagor, David Dyzenhaus, Avigail Eisenberg, Leslie Green, Amy Gutmann, Moshe Halbertal, Robert Howse, Tom Hurka, Jane Jenson, Dave Knott, Chandran Kukathas, Guy Laforest, Brian Langille, Jacob Levy, Dominique Leydet, Michael McDonald, Stephen Macedo, Patrick Macklem, Colin Macleod, Andrew Mason, David Miller, Tariq Modood, Margaret Moore, Glyn Morgan, James Nickel, Susan Moller Okin, Michael Oliver, Tom Palmer, Bhikhu Parekh, Filimon Peonidis, Anne Phillips, Robert Post, Kurt Priensberg, Maurice Rickard, Arthur Ripstein, John Russell, Alan Ryan, Sibyl Schwarzenbach, Michel Seymour, Michael Smith, Andrew Stark, John Tomasi, Mark Tunick, Mary Ellen Turpel, Jeremy Waldron, Peter G. White, Melissa Williams, and Iris Marion Young.

I would like to give special thanks to my parents. They have always supported my work, and have taken a particular interest in this project, which touches closely on their own lives.

Finally, I would like to thank Codie and Luke. Like most dogs, they are baffled, and sometimes exasperated, by the amount of time humans spend poring over the printed word. But they kept me company on some long nights, and I am grateful for that.

Many of the arguments in this book have been worked out in a series of papers I have written over the last few years, although most have been extensively rewritten: 'Three Forms of Group-Differentiated Citizenship in Canada', in Seyla Benhabib (ed.), *Democracy and Difference: Changing Boundaries of the Political* (Princeton University Press, forthcoming) (Chapter 2); 'Individual and Community Rights', in Judith Baker (ed.), *Group Rights* (University of Toronto Press, 1994) (Chapter 3); 'Liberalism and the Politicization of Ethnicity', *Canadian Journal of Law and Jurisprudence*, 4/2 (1991) (Chapter 4); 'Dworkin on Freedom and Culture', in J. Burley (ed.), *Reading Dworkin* (Basil Blackwell, forthcoming) (Chapter 5); 'Group Representation in Canadian Politics', in L. Seidle (ed.), *Equity and Community: The Charter, Interest Advocacy, and Representation* (Institute for Research on Public Policy, 1993) (Chapter 7); 'Two Models of Pluralism and Tolerance', *Analyse und Kritik*, 14/1 (1992) and 'The Rights of Minority Cultures: Reply to Kukathas', *Political Theory*, 20/1 (1992) (Chapter 8); *Recent Work in Citizenship Theory* (Department of Multiculturalism and Citizenship, Government of Canada, 1992), and 'Return of the Citizen', *Ethics*, 104/2 (1994) (with W. J. Norman) (Chapter 9).

A Note on the Jacket Illustration

The jacket illustration is a painting called 'The Peaceable Kingdom', by Edward Hicks, painted around 1834. It illustrates the signing of a treaty in 1682 between a group of Quakers and three local Indian tribes, the Leeni Lenape, Susquehannock, and Shawnee, allowing for the establishment of a Quaker community in Pennsylvania. (The Quakers were one of the few groups to honour their treaty commitments.) Hicks, a devout Quaker, viewed this treaty as the beginning of the 'peaceable kingdom' prophesied in Isaiah, in which love will replace hostility and competition both amongst humans and in the natural world (e.g. 'the lion will lie down with the lamb').

I chose this painting because it portrays and celebrates a form of multiculturalism that we often ignore. Most discussions of 'multiculturalism', at least in North America, focus on the case of immigrants, and the accommodation of their ethnic and racial differences within the larger society. Less attention has been paid to the situation of indigenous peoples and other non-immigrant 'national minorities' whose homeland has been incorporated into the boundaries of a larger state, through conquest, colonization, or federation. Treaties are a common means of regulating the interaction between dominant groups and national minorities. They reflect the idea that the two nations in a multination state treat each other as equals, and respect each other's right to speak for and govern themselves. Many people view such treaties as outmoded or irrelevant, and they have generally been ignored or violated by the majority whenever they were inconvenient. However, I think the underlying ideal is worth studying, and celebrating, and may indeed be vital to creating a more peaceable kingdom in the modern world.

CONTENTS

CHAPTER 1

Introduction

1. The Issues

Most countries today are culturally diverse. According to recent estimates, the world's 184 independent states contain over 600 living language groups, and 5,000 ethnic groups. In very few countries can the citizens be said to share the same language, or belong to the same ethnonational group.[1]

This diversity gives rise to a series of important and potentially divisive questions. Minorities and majorities increasingly clash over such issues as language rights, regional autonomy, political representation, education curriculum, land claims, immigration and naturalization policy, even national symbols, such as the choice of national anthem or public holidays. Finding morally defensible and politically viable answers to these issues is the greatest challenge facing democracies today. In Eastern Europe and the Third World, attempts to create liberal democratic institutions are being undermined by violent nationalist conflicts. In the West, volatile disputes over the rights of immigrants, indigenous peoples, and other cultural minorities are throwing into question many of the assumptions which have governed political life for decades. Since the end of the Cold War, ethnocultural conflicts have become the most common source of political violence in the world, and they show no sign of abating.[2]

This book outlines a new approach to these problems. There are no simple answers or magic formulas to resolve all these questions. Some conflicts are intractable, even when the disputants are motivated by a sense of fairness and tolerance, which all too often is lacking. Moreover, every dispute has its own unique history and circumstances that need to be taken into account in devising a fair and workable solution. My aim is to step back and present a more general view of the landscape—to identify some key concepts and principles that need to be taken into account, and so clarify the basic building blocks for a liberal approach to minority rights.

The Western political tradition has been surprisingly silent on these issues. Most organized political communities throughout recorded history have been multiethnic, a testament to the ubiquity of both conquest and long-distance trade in human affairs. Yet most Western political theorists have operated with an idealized model of the polis in which fellow citizens share a common descent, language, and culture. Even when the theorists themselves lived in polyglot empires that governed numerous ethnic and linguistic groups, they have often written as if the culturally homogeneous city-states of Ancient Greece provided the essential or standard model of a political community.[3]

To achieve this ideal of a homogeneous polity, governments throughout history have pursued a variety of policies regarding cultural minorities. Some minorities were physically eliminated, either by mass expulsion (what we now call 'ethnic cleansing') or by genocide. Other minorities were coercively assimilated, forced to adopt the language, religion, and customs of the majority. In yet other cases, minorities were treated as resident aliens, subjected to physical segregation and economic discrimination, and denied political rights.

Various efforts have been made historically to protect cultural minorities, and to regulate the potential conflicts between majority and minority cultures. Early in this century, bilateral treaties regulated the treatment of fellow nationals in other countries. For example, Germany agreed to accord certain rights and privileges to ethnic Poles residing within its borders, so long as Poland provided reciprocal rights to ethnic Germans in Poland. This treaty system was extended, and given a more multilateral basis, under the League of Nations.

However, these treaties were inadequate. For one thing, a minority was only ensured protection from discrimination and oppression if there was a 'kin state' nearby which took an interest in it. Moreover, the treaties were destabilizing, because where such kin states did exist, they often used treaty provisions as grounds for invading or intervening in weaker countries. Thus Nazi Germany justified its invasion of Poland and Czechoslovakia on the grounds that these countries were violating the treaty rights of ethnic Germans on their soil.

After World War II, it was clear that a different approach to minority rights was needed. Many liberals hoped that the new emphasis on 'human rights' would resolve minority conflicts. Rather than protecting vulnerable groups directly, through special rights for the members of designated groups, cultural minorities would be protected indirectly, by guaranteeing basic civil and political rights to all individuals regardless of group membership. Basic human rights such as freedom of speech, association, and conscience, while attributed to individuals, are typically exercised in community with others, and so provide protection for group life. Where these individual rights are firmly protected, liberals assumed, no further rights needed to be attributed to the members of specific ethnic or national minorities:

> the general tendency of the postwar movements for the promotion of human rights has been to subsume the problem of national minorities under the broader problem of ensuring basic individual rights to all human beings, without reference to membership in ethnic groups. The leading assumption has been that members of national minorities do not need, are not entitled to, or cannot be granted rights of a special character. The doctrine of human rights has been put forward as a substitute for the concept of minority rights, with the strong implication that minorities whose members enjoy individual equality of treatment cannot legitimately demand facilities for the maintenance of their ethnic particularism. (Claude 1955: 211)

Guided by this philosophy, the United Nations deleted all references to the rights of ethnic and national minorities in its Universal Declaration of Human Rights.

The shift from group-specific minority rights to universal human rights was embraced by many liberals, partly because it seemed a natural extension of the way religious minorities were protected. In the sixteenth century, European states were being torn apart by conflict between Catholics and Protestants over which religion should rule the land. These conflicts were finally resolved, not by granting special rights to particular religious minorities, but by separating church and state, and entrenching each's individual freedom of religion. Religious minorities are protected indirectly, by guaranteeing individual freedom of worship, so that people can freely associate with other co-religionists, without fear of state discrimination or disapproval.

Many post-war liberals have thought that religious tolerance based on the separation of church and state provides a model for dealing with ethnocultural differences as well. On this view, ethnic identity, like religion, is something which people should be free to express in their private life, but which is not the concern of the state. The state does not oppose the freedom of people to express their particular cultural attachments, but nor does it nurture such expression—rather, to adapt Nathan Glazer's phrase, it responds with 'benign neglect' (Glazer 1975: 25; 1983: 124). The members of ethnic and national groups are protected against discrimination and prejudice, and they are free to try to maintain whatever part of their ethnic heritage or identity they wish, consistent with the rights of others. But their efforts are purely private, and it is not the place of public agencies to attach legal identities or disabilities to cultural membership or ethnic identity. This separation of state and ethnicity precludes any legal or governmental recognition of ethnic groups, or any use of ethnic criteria in the distribution of rights, resources, and duties.[4]

Many liberals, particularly on the left, have made an exception in the case of affirmative action for disadvantaged racial groups. But in a sense this is the exception that proves the rule. Affirmative action is generally defended as a temporary measure which is needed to move more rapidly towards a 'colour-blind' society. It is intended to remedy years of discrimination, and thereby move us closer to the sort of society that would have existed had we observed the separation of state and ethnicity from the beginning. Thus the UN Convention on Racial Discrimination endorses affirmative action programmes only where they have this temporary and remedial character. Far from abandoning the ideal of the separation of state and ethnicity, affirmative action is one method of trying to achieve that ideal.

Some liberals, particularly on the right, think it is counterproductive to pursue a 'colour-blind' society through policies that 'count by race'. Affirmative action, they argue, exacerbates the very problem it was intended to solve, by making people more conscious of group differences, and more resentful of other groups. This dispute amongst liberals over the need for remedial affirmative action programmes is a familiar one in many liberal democracies.[5]

But what most post-war liberals on both the right and left continue to reject is the idea of *permanent* differentiation in the rights or status of the members of certain groups. In particular, they reject the claim that group-specific rights are needed to accommodate enduring cultural differences, rather than remedy historical discrimination. As we will see in subsequent chapters, post-war liberals around the world have repeatedly opposed the idea that specific ethnic or national groups should be given a permanent political identity or constitutional status.[6]

However, it has become increasingly clear that minority rights cannot be subsumed under the category of human rights. Traditional human rights standards are simply unable to resolve some of the most important and controversial questions relating to cultural minorities: which languages should be recognized in the parliaments, bureaucracies, and courts? Should each ethnic or national group have publicly funded education in its mother tongue? Should internal boundaries (legislative districts, provinces, states) be drawn so that cultural minorities form a majority within a local region? Should governmental powers be devolved from the central level to more local or regional levels controlled by particular minorities, particularly on culturally sensitive issues of immigration, communication, and education? Should political offices be distributed in accordance with a principle of national or ethnic proportionality? Should the traditional homelands of indigenous peoples be reserved for their benefit, and so protected from encroachment by settlers and resource developers? What are the responsibilities of minorities to integrate? What degree of cultural integration can be required of immigrants and refugees before they acquire citizenship?

The problem is not that traditional human rights doctrines give us the wrong answer to these questions. It is rather that they often give no answer at all. The right to free speech does not tell us what an appropriate language policy is; the right to vote does not tell us how political boundaries should be drawn, or how powers should be distributed between levels of government; the right to mobility does not tell us what an appropriate immigration and naturalization policy is. These questions have been left to the usual process of majoritarian decision-making within each state. The result, I will argue, has been to render cultural minorities vulnerable to significant injustice at the hands of the majority, and to exacerbate ethnocultural conflict.

To resolve these questions fairly, we need to supplement traditional human rights principles with a theory of minority rights. The necessity for such a theory has become painfully clear in Eastern Europe and the former Soviet Union. Disputes over local autonomy, the drawing of boundaries, language rights, and naturalization policy have engulfed much of the region in violent conflict. There is little hope that stable peace will be restored, or that basic human rights will be respected, until these minority rights issues are resolved.

It is not surprising, therefore, that minority rights have returned to prominence in international relations. For example, the Conference on Security and Co-operation in Europe (CSCE) adopted a declaration on the Rights of National Minorities in 1991, and established a High Commissioner on National Minorities in 1993. The United Nations has been debating both a Declaration on the Rights of Persons Belonging to National or Ethnic, Religious and Linguistic Minorities (1993), and a Draft Universal Declaration on Indigenous Rights (1988). The Council of Europe adopted a declaration on minority language rights in 1992 (the European Charter for Regional or Minority Languages). Other examples could be given.[7]

However, these declarations remain controversial. Some were

adopted hastily, to help prevent the escalation of conflict in Eastern Europe. As a result, they are quite vague, and often seem motivated more by the need to appease belligerent minorities than by any clear sense of what justice requires. Both the underlying justification for these rights, and their limits, remain unclear.

I believe it is legitimate, and indeed unavoidable, to supplement traditional human rights with minority rights. A comprehensive theory of justice in a multicultural state will include both universal rights, assigned to individuals regardless of group membership, and certain group-differentiated rights or 'special status' for minority cultures.

Recognizing minority rights has obvious dangers. The language of minority rights has been used and abused not only by the Nazis, but also by apologists for racial segregation and apartheid. It has also been used by intolerant and belligerent nationalists and fundamentalists throughout the world to justify the domination of people outside their group, and the suppression of dissenters within the group. A liberal theory of minority rights, therefore, must explain how minority rights coexist with human rights, and how minority rights are limited by principles of individual liberty, democracy, and social justice. That is the aim of this book.

2. *Outline of the Book*

It is a commonplace to say that modern societies are increasingly 'multicultural'. However, this vague term often obscures important distinctions. The first part of Chapter 2 will consider various forms of cultural pluralism. In particular, I will distinguish between 'multination' states (where cultural diversity arises from the incorporation of previously self-governing, territorially concentrated cultures into a larger state) and 'polyethnic' states (where cultural diversity arises from individual and familial immigration). I will explore the differences between 'national minorities' (in multination states) and 'ethnic groups' (in polyethnic states), and discuss the relationship between race, ethnicity, and nationality.

The rest of Chapter 2 provides a typology of the different sorts of minority rights that ethnic and national groups may demand. In particular, I will distinguish:

- self-government rights (the delegation of powers to national minorities, often through some form of federalism);

- polyethnic rights (financial support and legal protection for certain practices associated with particular ethnic or religious groups); and
- special representation rights (guaranteed seats for ethnic or national groups within the central institutions of the larger state).

I will give examples of each from various countries, and explore some of the key differences between them, in terms of their institutional embodiment and constitutional protection.

These three forms of group-differentiated rights are often described as 'collective rights'. In Chapter 3 I explore the connection between collective rights and individual rights. Many liberals believe that collective rights are inherently in conflict with individual rights. I will argue that we need to distinguish between two meanings of 'collective' rights. Collective rights could refer to the right of a group to limit the liberty of its own individual members in the name of group solidarity or cultural purity ('internal restrictions'); or it could refer to the right of a group to limit the economic or political power exercised by the larger society over the group, to ensure that the resources and institutions on which the minority depends are not vulnerable to majority decisions ('external protections'). I will argue that the latter need not conflict with individual liberty. Indeed, what distinguishes a *liberal* theory of minority rights is precisely that it accepts some external protections for ethnic groups and national minorities, but is very sceptical of internal restrictions.

In Chapter 4, I trace the historical relationship between liberalism and minority rights. There was widespread support for minority rights amongst liberals in the nineteenth century, and between the two world wars. The reasons for the shift in post-war liberal theory are complicated, and I try to sort through some of them. Part of the explanation lies in the decline of the British Empire, and in the failure of the League of Nations. Another important factor is the increased influence throughout the world of the American conception of an ethnicity-blind constitution. I will argue that this American conception has been shaped by unique factors (e.g. racial desegregation; the scope of immigration) which are not necessarily applicable to other countries. Indeed, I will argue that the American belief in an ethnicity-blind constitution is not even valid for the United States, since it ignores the special status of American Indians, Puerto Ricans, and others.

In Chapter 5, I will explore the role of culture within liberal-democratic theory. I first defend a certain vision of liberalism—grounded in a commitment to freedom of choice and (one form of) personal autonomy. I will then explain why this liberal vision is not only consistent with, but even requires, a concern with cultural membership. I will argue that individual choice is dependent on the presence of a societal culture, defined by language and history, and that most people have a very strong bond to their own culture.

Drawing on this conception of liberalism, I explore three major arguments in favour of group-differentiated rights for ethnic groups and national minorities in Chapter 6. In particular, I distinguish between *equality-based* arguments, which aim to show that the minority is facing some sort of unfair disadvantage which can be rectified by a group-differentiated right; and various *history-based* arguments, which aim to show that the minority has some historical claim to the group-differentiated right, based on prior sovereignty, treaties, or some other historical agreement or precedent. I will also consider arguments which appeal to the intrinsic value of *cultural diversity*, and how this relates to both the equality and historical arguments.

Chapter 7 focuses on issues of political representation, particularly proposals to guarantee seats in the central legislature for the members of certain ethnic or national groups. I will discuss some of the practical and theoretical difficulties raised by such proposals, and consider alternative ways of ensuring a voice for minorities in political decision-making. I will also discuss the tension between self-government rights (demanding that power be delegated from the central government to the minority community) and representation rights (demanding guaranteed representation for minorities in the central government).

In Chapter 8, I will discuss how liberals should respond to situations where minorities demand the right to restrict the basic civil and political liberties of their own members. I have already stated that a liberal theory of minority rights cannot justify such 'internal restrictions'—that is, it cannot accept the idea that it is morally legitimate for a group to oppress its own members in the name of group solidarity, religious orthodoxy, or cultural purity. This violates the liberal commitment to individual autonomy. Yet it is clear that some minorities desire such internal restrictions, and do not share the liberal commitment to autonomy. Does it follow that liberal states should impose liberal norms on illiberal minorities? This raises complicated issues about the meaning of tolerance and its limits. I discuss the relationship between the values of tolerance and individual autonomy within liberal theory, and outline some of the factors which need to be taken into account in evaluating the legitimacy of imposing liberal values on illiberal minorities.

In Chapter 9, I address the worry that group-differentiated rights for minority cultures will inhibit the development of a shared identity necessary for stable social order. Many people worry that group-differentiated citizenship encourages groups to focus on their differences, rather than their shared purposes. Citizenship is supposed to serve an integrative function, but can it do this if citizenship is not a common legal and political identity? I will argue that representation rights and polyethnic rights are consistent with integrating minority groups, and indeed may assist in this integration. Self-government rights, on the other hand, do pose a serious threat to social unity, since they encourage the national minority to view itself as a separate people with inherent rights to govern themselves. However, denying self-government rights can also threaten social unity, by encouraging secession. Identifying the bases of social unity in multination states is, I believe, one of the most pressing tasks facing liberals today.

In the final chapter, I make some concluding speculations about the future of multicultural citizenship. Many people, of all political stripes, have hoped and assumed that ethnic and national identities were a transient phase of human history. These parochial allegiances were supposed to fade as the world becomes increasingly integrated both economically and politically. In reality, 'globalization' has often created more room for minorities to maintain a distinct identity and group life. Globalization has made the myth of a culturally homogeneous state even more unrealistic, and has forced the majority within each state to be more open to pluralism and diversity. The nature of ethnic and national identities is changing in a world of free trade and global communications, but the challenge of multiculturalism is here to stay.

CHAPTER 2

The Politics of Multiculturalism

Modern societies are increasingly confronted with minority groups demanding recognition of their identity, and accommodation of their cultural differences. This is often phrased as the challenge of 'multiculturalism'. But the term 'multicultural' covers many different forms of cultural pluralism, each of which raises its own challenges. There are a variety of ways in which minorities become incorporated into political communities, from the conquest and colonization of previously self-governing societies to the voluntary immigration of individuals and families. These differences in the mode of incorporation affect the nature of minority groups, and the sort of relationship they desire with the larger society.

Generalizations about the goals or consequences of multiculturalism can therefore be very misleading. Indeed, much of the public debate over multiculturalism suffers from this flaw. For example, opponents of multiculturalism often say that it ghettoizes minorities, and impedes their integration into mainstream society; proponents respond that this concern for integration reflects cultural imperialism. Both of these charges are over-generalizations which ignore differences amongst minority groups, and misinterpret their actual motivations.

In this chapter, I focus on two broad patterns of cultural diversity. In the first case, cultural diversity arises from the incorporation of previously self-governing, territorially concentrated cultures into a larger state. These incorporated cultures, which I call 'national minorities', typically wish to maintain themselves as distinct societies alongside the majority culture, and demand various forms of autonomy or self-government to ensure their survival as distinct societies.

In the second case, cultural diversity arises from individual and familial immigration. Such immigrants often coalesce into loose associations which I call 'ethnic groups'. They typically wish to integrate into the larger society, and to be accepted as full members of it. While they often seek greater recognition of their ethnic identity, their aim is not to become a separate and self-governing nation alongside the larger society, but to modify the institutions and laws of the mainstream society to make them more accommodating of cultural differences.

These are just general patterns, of course, not laws of nature. And each of these general categories will need further refinement and qualification as we go. But we cannot begin to understand and evaluate the politics of multiculturalism unless we see how the historical incorporation of minority groups shapes their collective institutions, identities, and aspirations. I will begin by describing the nature of these two broad categories (s. 1), and then consider the specific demands associated with each (s. 2).

1. *Multination States and Polyethnic States*

One source of cultural diversity is the coexistence within a given state of more than one nation, where 'nation' means a historical community, more or less institutionally complete, occupying a given territory or homeland, sharing a distinct language and culture. A 'nation' in this sociological sense is closely related to the idea of a 'people' or a 'culture'—indeed, these concepts are often defined in terms of each other. A country which contains more than one nation is, therefore, not a nation-state but a multination state, and the smaller cultures form 'national minorities'. The incorporation of different nations into a single state may be involuntary, as occurs when one cultural community is invaded and conquered by another, or is ceded from one imperial power to another, or when its homeland is overrun by colonizing settlers. But the formation of a multination state may also arise voluntarily, when different cultures agree to form a federation for their mutual benefit.

Many Western democracies are multinational. For example, there are a number of national minorities in the United States, including the American Indians, Puerto Ricans, the descendants of Mexicans (Chicanos) living in the south-west when the United States annexed Texas, New Mexico, and California after the Mexican War of 1846–8, native Hawaiians, the Chamorros of Guam, and various other Pacific Islanders. These groups were all involuntarily incorporated into the United States, through conquest or colonization. Had a different balance of power existed, these groups might have retained or established their own sovereign governments. And talk of independence occasionally surfaces in Puerto Rico or the larger Indian tribes. However, the historical preference of these groups has not been to leave the United States, but to seek autonomy within it.

As they were incorporated, most of these groups acquired a special political status. For example, Indian tribes are recognized as 'domestic dependent nations' with their own governments, courts, and treaty rights; Puerto Rico is a 'Commonwealth'; and Guam is a 'Protectorate'. Each of these peoples is federated to the American polity with special powers of self-government.

These groups also have rights regarding language and land use. In Guam and Hawaii, the indigenous language (Chamorro and Hawaiian) has equal status with English in schools, courts, and other dealings with government, while Spanish is the sole official language of Puerto Rico. Language rights were also guaranteed to Chicanos in the south-west under the 1848 Treaty of Guadelupe Hidalgo, although these were abrogated as soon as anglophone settlers formed a majority of the population. Native Hawaiians, Alaskan Eskimos, and Indian tribes also have legally recognized land claims, which reserve certain lands for their exclusive use, and which provide guaranteed representation on certain regulatory bodies. In short, national minorities in the United States have a range of rights intended to reflect and protect their status as distinct cultural communities, and they have fought to retain and expand these rights.[1]

Most of these groups are relatively small and geographically isolated. Together they constitute only a fraction of the overall American population. As a result, these groups have been marginal to the self-identity of Americans, and indeed the very existence of national minorities, and their self-government rights, is often denied or downplayed by American politicians and theorists.

In other countries the existence of national minorities is more obvious. Canada's historical development has involved the federation of three distinct national groups (English, French, and Aboriginals).[2] The original incorporation of the Québécois and Aboriginal communities into the Canadian political community was involuntary. Indian homelands were overrun by French settlers, who were then conquered by the English. While the possibility of secession is very real for the Québécois, the historical preference of these groups—as with the national minorities in the United States—has not been to leave the federation, but to renegotiate the terms of federation, so as to increase their autonomy within it.

Many of the pivotal moments in Canadian history have centred on these attempts to renegotiate the terms of federation between English, French, and Aboriginals. The terms of federation are laid out in a series of constitutionally protected documents, including treaties and land claims with the Aboriginals, and the 1867 Confederation agreement between the English- and French-speaking colonies of British North America.

The most recent effort at renegotiation ended in October 1992, when a proposal to amend the constitution (the Charlottetown Accord) was defeated in a national referendum. This Accord would have entrenched an 'inherent right of self-government' for Aboriginals, and would have accorded Quebec a special status as 'the only society with a majority French language and culture in Canada and in North America'.

Many other Western democracies are also multinational, either because they have forcibly incorporated indigenous populations (e.g. Finland; New Zealand), or because they were formed by the more or less voluntary federation of two or more European cultures (e.g. Belgium and Switzerland). In fact, many countries throughout the world are multinational, in the sense that their boundaries were drawn to include the territory occupied by pre-existing, and often previously self-governing, cultures. This is true of most countries throughout the former Communist bloc (e.g. Dreyer 1979; Connor 1984) and the Third World (Rothchild and Olorunsola 1983; Selassie 1993; B. Davidson 1992).

To say that these countries are 'multination' states is not to deny that the citizens view themselves for some purposes as a single people. For example, the Swiss have a strong sense of common loyalty, despite their cultural and linguistic divisions. Indeed, multination states cannot survive unless the various national groups have an allegiance to the larger political community they cohabit.

Some commentators describe this common loyalty as a form of national identity, and so consider Switzerland a nation-state. I think this is misleading. We should distinguish 'patriotism', the feeling of allegiance to a state, from national identity, the sense of membership in a national group. In Switzerland as in most multination states, national groups feel allegiance to the larger state only because the larger state recognizes and respects their distinct national existence. The Swiss are patriotic, but the Switzerland they are loyal to is defined as a federation of distinct peoples. For that reason, it is best seen as a multination state, and the feelings of common loyalty it engenders reflect a shared patriotism, not a common national identity.

The second source of cultural pluralism is immigration. A country will exhibit cultural pluralism if it accepts large numbers of individuals and families from other cultures as immigrants, and allows them to maintain some of their ethnic particularity. This has always been a vital part of life in Australia, Canada, and the United States, which have the three highest per capita rates of immigration in the world. Indeed, well over half of all legal immigration in the world goes into one of these three countries.

Prior to the 1960s, immigrants to these countries were expected to shed their distinctive heritage and assimilate entirely to existing cultural norms. This is known as the 'Anglo-conformity' model of immigration. Indeed, some groups were denied entry if they were seen as unassimilable (e.g. restrictions on Chinese immigration in Canada and the United States, the 'white-only' immigration policy in Australia). Assimilation was seen as essential for political stability, and was further rationalized through ethnocentric denigration of other cultures.

This shared commitment to Anglo-conformity is obscured by the popular but misleading contrast between the American 'melting-pot' and the Canadian 'ethnic mosaic'. While 'ethnic mosaic' carries the connotation of respect for the integrity of immigrant cultures, in practice it simply meant that immigrants to Canada had a choice of two dominant cultures to assimilate to. While Canada is binational, the 'uneasy tolerance which French and English were to show towards each other was not extended to foreigners who resisted assimilation or were believed to be unassimilable'.[3]

However, beginning in the 1970s, under pressure from immigrant groups, all three countries rejected the assimilationist model, and adopted a more tolerant and pluralistic policy which allows and indeed encourages immigrants to maintain various aspects of their ethnic heritage. It is now widely (though far from unanimously) accepted that immigrants should be free to maintain some of their old customs regarding food, dress, religion, and to associate with each other to maintain these practices. This is no longer seen as unpatriotic or 'unamerican'.

But it is important to distinguish this sort of cultural diversity from that of national minorities. Immigrant groups are not 'nations', and do not occupy homelands. Their distinctiveness is manifested primarily in their family lives and in voluntary associations, and is not inconsistent with their institutional integration. They still participate within the public institutions of the dominant culture(s) and speak the dominant language(s). For example, immigrants (except for the elderly) must learn English to acquire citizenship in Australia and the United

States, and learning English is a mandatory part of children's education. In Canada, they must learn either of the two official languages (French or English).

The commitment to ensuring a common language has been a constant feature of the history of immigration policy. Indeed, as Gerald Johnson said of the United States, 'It is one of history's little ironies that no polyglot empire of the old world has dared to be so ruthless in imposing a single language upon its whole population as was the liberal republic "dedicated to the proposition that all men are created equal".'[4] The rejection of Anglo-conformity has not meant a slackening in this commitment to ensuring that immigrants become anglophones, which is seen as essential if they are to be included in the mainstream of economic, academic, and political life of the country.

So while immigrant groups have increasingly asserted their right to express their ethnic particularity, they typically wish to do so within the public institutions of the English-speaking society (or French-speaking in Canada). In rejecting assimilation, they are not asking to set up a parallel society, as is typically demanded by national minorities. The United States and Australia, therefore, have a number of 'ethnic groups' as loosely aggregated subcultures within the larger English-speaking society, and so exhibit what I will call 'polyethnicity'. Similarly in Canada there are ethnic subcultures within both the English- and French-speaking societies.

It is possible, in theory, for immigrants to become national minorities, if they settle together and acquire self-governing powers. After all, this is what happened with English-speaking colonists throughout the British Empire, Spanish colonists in Puerto Rico, and French colonists in Quebec. These colonists did not see themselves as 'immigrants', since they had no expectation of integrating into another culture, but rather aimed to reproduce their original society in a new land. It is an essential feature of colonization, as distinct from individual emigration, that it aims to create an institutionally complete society. It would, in principle, be possible to allow or encourage immigrants today to view themselves as colonists, if they had extensive government support in terms of settlement, language rights, and the creation of new political units. But immigrants have not asked for or received such support. (Whether this is fair or not is a separate question, which I discuss in Chapter 5.)

There is a widespread perception that this 'polyethnic' model no longer applies to Hispanic immigrants to the United States. These immigrants are said to be uninterested in learning English, or in integrating into the anglophone society. This is a mistaken perception, which arises because people treat Hispanics as a single category, and so confuse the demands of Spanish-speaking national minorities (Puerto Ricans and Chicanos) with those of Spanish-speaking immigrants recently arrived from Latin America. Even within the category of recent arrivals, it is important to distinguish immigrants from two other Hispanic groups—Cuban refugees and illegal Mexican migrant workers.

The Cuban refugees living in Miami see themselves as exiles, not immigrants. When they arrived in the United States, they assumed that their return to Cuba was imminent. The American government encouraged this assumption, partly for political reasons during the Cold War. As a result, Cuban exiles have not had the incentive to integrate, and the larger society has not encouraged them to do so. (This is unlike refugees from Indo-China, many of whom plan to stay in America, and who therefore exhibit much the same pattern of integration as immigrants—Tollefson 1989.)

Similarly, Mexicans working illegally in the United States are always one step away from leaving the country. Since they are not able to apply for citizenship, and face a serious risk of being deported at any time, they too have not had the incentive or encouragement to integrate. Moreover, they lack access to the language instruction offered immigrants.

If we set aside these special cases, and look instead at Hispanic immigrants who come to the United States with the intention to stay and become citizens, the evidence suggests that they, as much as any other immigrants, are committed to learning English and participating in the mainstream society. Indeed, among Latino immigrants, 'assimilation to the English group occurs more rapidly now than it did one hundred years ago'.[5]

This shows that the category of 'Hispanic' should be used with caution. Since the 1960s, the US Census has treated 'Hispanic' as a common ethnic group or origin, but most Hispanics themselves view their ethnic or national identity in a more particular way—as Puerto Ricans, Chicanos, Cubans, Mexicans, Spaniards, or Guatemalans—reflecting the very different histories these groups have experienced in the United States. It will be interesting to see whether Hispanics develop a common identity and political agenda that transcends these differences. If they do, and if it takes the form of a separate national identity, then the issue of national minorities will move from the margins to the centre of American political debate. At present, however, 'Hispanic' is little more than a statistical category covering a range of national minorities, immigrants, and exiles, all with their own distinct identities and demands.[6]

Immigration is not only a 'New World' phenomenon. Many other countries also accept immigrants, although not in the same magnitude as the United States, Canada, and Australia. Since World War II, Britain and France have accepted immigrants from their former colonies. Other countries which accept few immigrants none the less accept refugees from throughout the world (e.g. Sweden). In yet other countries, 'guest-workers' who were originally seen as only temporary residents have become *de facto* immigrants. For example, Turkish guest-workers in Germany have become permanent residents, with their families, and Germany is often the only home known to their children (and now grandchildren). All these countries are exhibiting increasing 'polyethnicity'.[7]

Obviously, a single country may be both multinational (as a result of the colonizing, conquest, or confederation of national communities) and polyethnic (as a result of individual and familial immigration). Indeed, all of these patterns are present in Canada—the Indians were overrun by French settlers, the French were conquered by the English, although the current relationship between the two can be seen as a voluntary federation, and both the English and French have accepted immigrants who are allowed to maintain their ethnic identity. So Canada is both multinational and polyethnic, as is the United States.

Those labels are less popular than the term 'multicultural'. But that term can be confusing, precisely because it is ambiguous between multinational and polyethnic. This ambiguity has led to unwarranted criticisms of the Canadian government's 'multiculturalism' policy, which is the term the government uses for its post-1970 policy of promoting polyethnicity rather than assimilation for immigrants. Some French Canadians have opposed the 'multiculturalism' policy because they think it reduces their claims of nationhood to the level of immigrant ethnicity.[8] Other people had the opposite fear that the policy was intended to treat immigrant groups as nations, and hence support the development of institutionally complete cultures alongside the French and English. In fact, neither fear was justified, since 'multiculturalism' is a policy of supporting polyethnicity within the national institutions of the English and French cultures (Burnet 1975: 36). Since 'multicultural' invites this sort of confusion, I will use the terms 'multinational' and 'polyethnic' to refer to the two main forms of cultural pluralism.

Some people use 'multicultural' in an even broader way, to

encompass a wide range of non-ethnic social groups which have, for various reasons, been excluded or marginalized from the mainstream of society. This usage is particularly common in the United States, where advocates of a 'multicultural' curriculum are often referring to efforts to reverse the historical exclusion of groups such as the disabled, gays and lesbians, women, the working class, atheists, and Communists.[9]

This points out the complexity of the term 'culture'. Many of these groups do have a distinct culture in one common sense of that word—that is, where 'culture' refers to the distinct customs, perspectives, or ethos of a group or association, as when we talk about a 'gay culture', or even a 'bureaucratic culture'. This is perhaps the most localized meaning of 'a culture'. At the other extreme, using 'culture' in the widest sense, we can say that all of the Western democracies share a common 'culture'—that is, they all share a modern, urban, secular industrialized civilization, in contrast to the feudal, agricultural, and theocratic world of our ancestors.

These two non-ethnic senses of culture are captured by the OED's definition of culture as the 'customs' or 'civilization' of a group or people. If culture refers to the 'customs' of a group, then the various lifestyle enclaves, social movements, and voluntary associations which can be found in any modern society all have their own 'cultures'. Defined this way, even the most ethnically homogeneous state, like Iceland, would none the less be 'multicultural', since it contains a diverse array of associations and groups based on class, gender, sexual orientation, religion, moral belief, and political ideology.

If culture refers to the 'civilization' of a people, then virtually all modern societies share the same culture. Defined this way, even the most multinational country like Switzerland, or the most polyethnic country like Australia, is not very 'multicultural', in so far as the various national and ethnic groups all participate in the same modern industrialized form of social life.

I am using culture (and 'multicultural') in a different sense. My focus will be on the sort of 'multiculturalism' which arises from national and ethnic differences. As I said earlier, I am using 'a culture' as synonymous with 'a nation' or 'a people'—that is, as an intergenerational community, more or less institutionally complete, occupying a given territory or homeland, sharing a distinct language and history. And a state is multicultural if its members either belong to different nations (a multination state), or have emigrated from different nations (a polyethnic state), and if this fact is an important aspect of personal identity and political life.

This is simply my stipulative definition of 'culture' and 'multicultural', although I think it corresponds with one common usage of these terms. I am not including the sorts of lifestyle enclaves, social movements, and voluntary associations which others include within the ambit of multiculturalism. This is not because I think the issues raised by these groups and movements are unimportant. On the contrary, I take it as given that accommodating ethnic and national differences is only part of a larger struggle to make a more tolerant and inclusive democracy.

The marginalization of women, gays and lesbians, and the disabled cuts across ethnic and national lines—it is found in majority cultures and homogeneous nation-states as well as national minorities and ethnic groups—and it must be fought in all these places. An adequate theory of the rights of cultural minorities must therefore be compatible with the just demands of disadvantaged social groups, and I hope to show that my theory meets this test. Moreover, as I will discuss, there are important analogies between the claims of justice made by these social movements and the claims of ethnic groups, since both have been excluded and marginalized in virtue of their 'difference'.

Given these analogies, some people are tempted to say that these social groups form distinct 'cultures' or 'subcultures', and that the struggle against their oppression is a struggle for 'multiculturalism'.[10] And there is a sense in which gays and lesbians, women, and the disabled form separate cultures within the larger society. But this is very different from the sense in which the Québécois form a separate culture within Canada, and it is important to keep these different senses of culture (and 'multiculturalism') in mind.

For the purposes of this book, I will not describe all of these groups as 'cultures' or 'subcultures'; nor will I use 'multiculturalism' as an umbrella term for every group-related difference in moral perspective or personal identity, although I recognize that this may be an appropriate usage in other contexts. What matters is not the terminology we use, but that we keep certain distinctions in mind. I believe, as I will argue throughout the book, that it is important to distinguish national minorities (distinct and potentially self-governing societies incorporated into a larger state) from ethnic groups (immigrants who have left their national community to enter another society). We can distinguish both of these from what are often called 'new social movements'—that is, associations and movements of gays, women, the poor, the disabled—who have been marginalized within their own national society or ethnic group. Each raises its own distinctive issues, and must be examined on its own merits. My focus in this book will be on the first two, although I will try show how they connect in various ways to the third.

This distinction between national minorities and ethnic groups is surprisingly neglected amongst political theorists. One of the few contemporary theorists to discuss it is Michael Walzer, although he redescribes the distinction as one between 'New World' and 'Old World' ethnic diversity. According to Walzer, cultural pluralism in the Old World consisted of 'intact and rooted communities', of nations that 'were established on lands they had occupied for many centuries' (1982: 9). When attempts were made to deprive these national communities of their language and culture, it gave rise to calls for 'national liberation'.

In the New World, however, pluralism 'originated in individual and familial migration', involving people who were 'susceptible to cultural change, for they were not only uprooted; they had uprooted themselves. Whatever the pressures that had driven them to the New World, they had chosen to come, while others like themselves, in their own families, had chosen to remain.' As a result, 'the Old World call for self-determination had no resonance' in the New World. Having uprooted themselves, immigrants had no reason for secession, or for rejecting English as the public language. And while they did resist Anglo-conformity, 'their resistance took a new form. It was not a demand that politics follow nationality, but rather that politics be separated from nationality—as it was already separated from religion. It was not a demand for national liberation, but for ethnic pluralism' (Walzer 1982: 6–11; 1983*b*: 224).

Similarly, Nathan Glazer distinguishes between Old World countries which are 'a federation of peoples', and New World countries which are composed of 'dispersed, mixed, assimilated [and] integrated' immigrant groups (Glazer 1983: 227). Because immigrants uproot themselves with the expectation of entering another national society, they 'rarely put forward concrete ethnic demands of the type we might see in nations where ethnic groups formed more compact, self-conscious, culture-maintaining entities', such as 'the right to use their language in a state's government, or to establish institutions reflecting their distinctive ethnic culture, or to secede'. Unlike in the Old World, there was 'an absence . . . of ethnic concentrations that could claim national rights on the basis of settlement on American territories before they became part of the United States' (Glazer 1983: 276–83).

I think this way of talking about 'New World' and 'Old World' diversity is a dangerous over-simplification. It is true that a greater proportion of the cultural diversity in the New World comes from immigration than in Europe. But national minorities are found in the New World, just as immigration occurs in the Old World. (There is also the special situation of African-Americans which, as I discuss below, does not fit either category.) It is simply not true that there were no 'intact and rooted communities . . . established on lands they had occupied for many centuries' in the New World (Walzer), or that there were no 'compact, self-conscious, culture-maintaining entities' that 'could claim national rights on the basis of settlement on American territories before they became part of the United States' (Glazer). This ignores the existence of American Indians, Puerto Ricans, native Hawaiians, the Chamorros of Guam, amongst others. As Stephen Thernstrom puts it, 'there are sizeable numbers of people whose ancestors did not come to the United States either voluntarily or involuntarily. Instead, the United States came to them in the course of its relentless expansion across the continent and into the Caribbean and Pacific' (Thernstrom 1983: 248).

Walzer and Glazer are in fact aware of the existence of these national minorities in the United States and other New World countries. Perhaps they were simply making a very rough generalization. Yet this is not a harmless over-simplification, confined to a few academic writings. It reflects and perpetuates a long history of denying the rights, even the very existence, of national minorities throughout North and South America on the grounds that these countries are 'immigrant countries'.

Representatives of the United States at the League of Nations and the United Nations, as well as representatives of various South American countries, Australia, and New Zealand, have consistently argued that they are immigrant countries, and hence have no national minorities. When the United Nations adopted measures to protect these minorities (Article 27 of the International Covenant on Civil and Political Rights), various 'New World' countries insisted that a clause be added saying that the Article only applied in those states in which minorities exist, and proclaimed that the Article was therefore inapplicable to them.[11]

This posture has, until very recently, shielded New World countries from international scrutiny of their treatment of indigenous peoples. As a result, the rights of indigenous peoples in the Americas, New Zealand, and Australia have been violated with virtual impunity. Brazil has been particularly insistent in its claims that it has no national minorities, and the decimation of its Indian tribes is dangerously close to making that claim true.

In fact, the history of ignoring national minorities in the New World is inextricably tied up with European beliefs about the inferiority of the indigenous peoples who occupied the land before European settlement. Until recently, they were seen as 'wards' or 'subject races', lacking the political development to qualify as nations, incapable of self-government, and needing the paternalistic protection of their white 'superiors'. Traditional international law did not regard indigenous populations as subjects of international law, and treaties signed with them were not viewed as treaties according to international law, but unilateral acts pertaining to domestic law. These racist attitudes are slowly fading, but they have often been replaced, not with the recognition that indigenous peoples are distinct nations, but with the assumption that they are a disadvantaged 'racial minority' or 'ethnic group' for whom progress requires integration into the mainstream of society. While government policy toward Indians has run the gamut of genocide, expulsion, segregation, and assimilation, the one constant is that governments have never 'genuinely recognized Aboriginal peoples as distinct Peoples with cultures different from, but not inferior to, their own'.[12]

It is wrong, therefore, to say that the New World lacks national minorities—even as a rough generalization. The historical genesis of that claim lies in racist attitudes towards the indigenous peoples, and it continues to perpetuate the invisibility of their claims of justice.

Most countries in the Americas are both multinational and polyethnic, as are most countries in the world. Yet very few countries are prepared to recognize these facts. In the USA, there is ample recognition that the country is polyethnic, but difficulty accepting that the country is also multinational, and that national minorities have special claims of cultural rights and self-government. Countries like Belgium and Switzerland, on the other hand, have long recognized that they contain national minorities whose language rights and self-government claims must be respected. But they have trouble admitting that they are increasingly polyethnic, and, as a result, their traditional conceptions of citizenship cannot fully accommodate immigrants. Canada, with its policy of 'multiculturalism within a bilingual framework' and its recognition of Aboriginal rights to self-government, is one of the few countries which has officially recognized and endorsed both polyethnicity and multinationality.

It is important to note that national groups, as I am using that term, are not defined by race or descent. This is obvious in the case of the majority anglophone society in both the United States and Canada. In both countries, there have been high rates of immigration for over a century, first from northern Europe, then from southern and eastern Europe, and now mostly from Asia and Africa. As a result, anglophone Americans or Canadians who are of solely Anglo-Saxon descent are a (constantly shrinking) minority.

But the same is true of national minorities as well. The level of immigration into French Canada was low for many years, but is now as high as English Canada or the United States, and Quebec actively seeks francophone immigrants from West Africa and the Caribbean. There have also been high rates of intermarriage between the indigenous peoples of North America and the English, French, and Spanish populations. As a result, all of these national groups are racially and ethnically mixed. The number of French Canadians who are of solely Gallic descent, or American Indians who are of solely Indian descent, is also constantly shrinking, and will soon be a minority in each case.[13]

In talking about national minorities, therefore, I am not talking about racial or descent groups, but about cultural groups.[14] Of course, some national groups define themselves in terms of blood. The most obvious case is Germany. Membership in the German nation is determined by descent, not culture. As a result, ethnic Germans who have lived their whole lives in Russia, and who do not speak a word of German, are automatically entitled to German citizenship, while ethnic Turks who have lived their whole lives in Germany and who are completely assimilated to German culture are not allowed to gain citizenship.

The Afrikaners in South Africa also have a descent-based conception of their nation. They sought to prohibit mixed-race marriages, and excluded the children of such marriages (the 'Coloureds') from their neighbourhoods and organizations, even though the language and culture of the Coloureds are essentially identical to their own. (These residency restrictions, which were allegedly aimed to protect the Afrikaner culture, were never applied to white anglophones who do not speak a word of Afrikaans.)

Such descent-based approaches to national membership have obvious racist overtones, and are manifestly unjust. It is indeed one of the tests of a liberal conception of minority rights that it defines national membership in terms of integration into a cultural community, rather than descent. National membership should be open in principle to anyone, regardless of race or colour, who is willing to learn the language and history of the society and participate in its social and political institutions.

Some people suggest that a truly liberal conception of national membership should be based solely on accepting political principles of democracy and rights, rather than integration into a particular culture. This non-cultural conception of national membership is often said to be what distinguishes the 'civic' or 'constitutional' nationalism of the United States from illiberal 'ethnic' nationalism. But, as I noted earlier, this is mistaken. Immigrants to the United States must not only pledge allegiance to democratic principles, they must also learn the language and history of their new society. What distinguishes 'civic' nations from 'ethnic' nations is not the absence of any cultural component to national identity, but rather the fact that anyone can integrate into the common culture, regardless of race or colour.[15]

Immigration and the incorporation of national minorities are the two most common sources of cultural diversity in modern states. These two broad categories are applicable to other countries, and most cultural groups can be located within one or other of these camps. But of course not all ethnocultural groups fit neatly into them. In particular, the situation of African-Americans is quite distinct. They do not fit the voluntary immigrants pattern, not only because they were brought to America involuntarily as slaves, but also because they were prevented (rather than encouraged) from integrating into the institutions of the majority culture (e.g. racial segregation; laws against miscegenation and the teaching of literacy). Nor do they fit the national minority pattern, since they do not have a homeland in America or a common historical language. They came from a variety of African cultures, with different languages, and no attempt was made to keep together those with a common ethnic background. On the contrary, people from the same culture (even from the same family) were typically split up once in America. Moreover, they were legally prohibited from trying to recreate their own culture (e.g. all forms of black association, except churches, were illegal).

The situation of African-Americans, therefore, is very unusual.[16] They were not allowed to integrate into the mainstream culture; nor were they allowed to maintain their earlier languages and cultures, or to create new cultural associations and institutions. They did not have their own homeland or territory, yet they were physically segregated.

Various attempts have been made to redefine African-Americans as either an immigrant group or a national minority. Some African-Americans, sceptical of the possibility of integration, adopted the language of nationalism, and sought a form of territorial self-government. The idea of creating a 'black state' in the South had some support in the 1930s (it was even endorsed by the American Communist Party), and resurfaced briefly in the 1960s. But that idea was never realistic, not only because blacks and whites are intermingled throughout the South, but also because African-Americans are no longer concentrated in the South, having migrated throughout the country. As a result, there is no state where African-Americans form a majority.

In any event, most blacks do not have or want a distinct national identity. They see themselves as entitled to full membership in the American nation, even if whites unjustly deny them that birthright, and so have fought for full and equal participation within the mainstream society. To achieve this, many American liberals have hoped that the immigrant model of integration can be made to work for African-Americans, and this was the underlying presupposition of the civil rights movement. But that too has proven unrealistic, given the profound historical differences between voluntary immigrants and African-Americans, and it is increasingly accepted that some new model of integration will have to be worked out.[17]

So we should not expect policies which are appropriate for either voluntary immigrants or national minorities to be appropriate for African-Americans, or vice versa. On the contrary, it would be quite surprising if the same measures were appropriate for all these contexts. Yet, as I discuss in Chapter 4, a surprising number of post-war American political theorists have made this assumption.

There are other cultural groups which do not fit neatly into either the national minority or voluntary immigrant category. For example, there are refugees who, like immigrants, have come as individuals or families, but did not do so voluntarily. There are also immigrant groups which have come voluntarily, but only because they had been promised that they would be allowed to re-create their own separate and self-governing community (e.g. the Hutterites in Canada). Conversely, some national minorities have, over time, become dispersed or disempowered, and so lost the capacity for self-government. I discuss these and other hard cases in Chapters 5 and 8.

Given these hard cases and grey areas, it might seem misguided to try to develop a theory of minority rights which attaches any weight to the distinction between ethnic groups and national minorities. Perhaps we should instead think of all these groups as falling on a continuum. But there are many clear cases of voluntary immigrants and national minorities. Indeed, a recent survey of ethnonational conflict throughout the world concluded that most groups involved fall into the two basic patterns I have outlined.[18] Moreover, a theory of minority rights is also forward-looking. The hard cases which exist today have often arisen as a result of past injustices and inconsistencies. I believe that a fairer and more consistent immigration policy will work, over time, to prevent such hard cases. I return to this point in Chapter 5.

2. Three Forms of Group-Differentiated Rights

Virtually all liberal democracies are either multinational or polyethnic, or both. The 'challenge of multiculturalism' is to accommodate these national and ethnic differences in a stable and morally defensible way (Gutmann 1993). In this section, I will discuss some of the most important ways in which democracies have responded to the demands of national minorities and ethnic groups.

In all liberal democracies, one of the major mechanisms for accommodating cultural differences is the protection of the civil and political rights of individuals. It is impossible to overstate the importance of freedom of association, religion, speech, mobility, and political organization for protecting group difference. These rights enable individuals to form and maintain the various groups and associations which constitute civil society, to adapt these groups to changing circumstances, and to promote their views and interests to the wider population. The protection afforded by these common rights of citizenship is sufficient for many of the legitimate forms of diversity in society.

Various critics of liberalism—including some Marxists, communitarians, and feminists—have argued that the liberal focus on individual rights reflects an atomistic, materialistic, instrumental, or conflictual view of human relationships. I believe that this criticism is profoundly mistaken, and that individual rights can be and typically are used to sustain a wide range of social relationships. Indeed, the most basic liberal right—freedom of conscience—is primarily valuable for the protection it gives to intrinsically social (and non-instrumental) activities.[19]

However, it is increasingly accepted in many countries that some forms of cultural difference can only be accommodated through special legal or constitutional measures, above and beyond the common rights of citizenship. Some forms of group difference can only be accommodated if their members have certain group-specific rights—what Iris Young calls 'differentiated citizenship' (I. Young 1989: 258).

For example, a recent government publication in Canada noted that:

> In the Canadian experience, it has not been enough to protect only universal individual rights. Here, the Constitution and ordinary laws also protect other rights accorded to individuals as members of certain communities. This

accommodation of both types of rights makes our constitution unique and reflects the Canadian value of equality that accommodates difference. The fact that community rights exist alongside individual rights goes to the very heart of what Canada is all about. (Government of Canada 1991*a*: 3)

It is quite misleading to say that Canada is unique in combining universal individual rights and group-specific 'community rights'. Such a combination exists in many other federal systems in Europe, Asia, and Africa. As I noted earlier, even the constitution of the United States, which is often seen as a paradigm of individualism, allows for various group-specific rights, including the special status of American Indians and Puerto Ricans.

It is these special group-specific measures for accommodating national and ethnic differences that I will focus on. There are at least three forms of group-specific rights: (1) self-government rights; (2) polyethnic rights; and (3) special representation rights. I will say a few words about each, before considering some of the issues they raise for liberal-democratic theory in subsequent chapters.

1. *Self-government rights*. In most multination states, the component nations are inclined to demand some form of political autonomy or territorial jurisdiction, so as to ensure the full and free development of their cultures and the best interests of their people. At the extreme, nations may wish to secede, if they think their self-determination is impossible within the larger state.

The right of national groups to self-determination is given (limited) recognition in international law. According to the United Nations' Charter, 'all peoples have the right to self-determination'. However, the UN has not defined 'peoples', and it has generally applied the principle of self-determination only to overseas colonies, not internal national minorities, even when the latter were subject to the same sort of colonization and conquest as the former. This limitation on self-determination to overseas colonies (known as the 'salt-water thesis') is widely seen as arbitrary, and many national minorities insist that they too are 'peoples' or 'nations', and, as such, have the right of self-determination. They demand certain powers of self-government which they say were not relinquished by their (often involuntary) incorporation into a larger state.[20]

One mechanism for recognizing claims to self-government is federalism, which divides powers between the central government and regional subunits (provinces/states/cantons). Where national minorities are regionally concentrated, the boundaries of federal subunits can be drawn so that the national minority forms a majority in one of the subunits. Under these circumstances, federalism can provide extensive self-government for a national minority, guaranteeing its ability to make decisions in certain areas without being outvoted by the larger society.

For example, under the federal division of powers in Canada, the province of Quebec (which is 80 per cent francophone) has extensive jurisdiction over issues that are crucial to the survival of the French culture, including control over education, language, culture, as well as significant input into immigration policy. The other nine provinces also have these powers, but the major impetus behind the existing division of powers, and indeed behind the entire federal system, is the need to accommodate the Québécois. At the time of Confederation, most English Canadian leaders were in favour of a unitary state, like Britain, and agreed to a federal system primarily to accommodate French Canadians.

One difficulty in a federal system is maintaining the balance between centralization and decentralization. While most Quebecers want an even more decentralized division of powers, most English Canadians favour a stronger central government. One of the challenges facing Canada, therefore, is finding an acceptable form of 'asymmetrical federalism' which grants Quebec powers not given to other provinces. Other federal states face a similar problem.[21]

Federalism is often used to accommodate national diversity, and so some commentators include the rights and powers attached to federal units amongst the 'collective rights' of national minorities (e.g. F. Morton 1985: 77; Van Dyke 1982: 24–31). Of course, many federal systems arose for reasons quite unrelated to cultural diversity. Federalism is often simply a form of administrative decentralization (as in Germany), or the result of historical accidents of colonization (as in Australia). There is no inherent connection between federalism and cultural diversity. But federalism is one common strategy of accommodating national minorities. It is not surprising that countries which are 'a federation of peoples' should also form a political federation.[22]

In the United States, however, a deliberate decision was made not to use federalism to accommodate the self-government rights of national minorities. It would have been quite possible in the nineteenth century to create states dominated by the Navaho, for example, or by Chicanos, Puerto Ricans, and native Hawaiians. At the time these groups were incorporated into the United States, they formed majorities in their homelands. However, a deliberate decision was made not to accept any territory as a state unless these national groups were outnumbered. In some cases, this was achieved by drawing boundaries so that Indian tribes or Hispanic groups were outnumbered (Florida). In other cases, it was achieved by delaying statehood until anglophone settlers swamped the older inhabitants (e.g. Hawaii; the south-west). In cases where the national minority was not likely to be outnumbered, a new type of non-federal political unit was created, such as the 'commonwealth' of Puerto Rico, or the 'Protectorate' of Guam.[23]

As a result, none of the fifty states can be seen as ensuring self-government for a national minority, the way that Quebec ensures self-government for the Québécois. Self-government is instead achieved through political institutions located inside existing states (e.g. Indian reservations), or entirely outside the federal system (e.g. Puerto Rico, Guam). This has tended to make national minorities in the United States more vulnerable, since their self-government powers do not have the same constitutional protection as states' rights. On the other hand, it has provided greater flexibility in redefining those powers so as to suit the needs and interests of each minority. It is much easier to negotiate new self-government provisions for the Navaho or Puerto Ricans than to modify the powers of individual states.

Federalism can only serve as a mechanism for self-government if the national minority forms a majority in one of the federal subunits, as the Québécois do in Quebec. This is not true of most indigenous peoples in North America, who are fewer in number and whose communities are often dispersed across state/provincial lines. Moreover, with few exceptions (such as the Navaho), no redrawing of the boundaries of these federal subunits would create a state, province, or territory with an indigenous majority. It would have been possible to create a state or province dominated by an Indian tribe in the nineteenth century, but, given the massive influx of settlers since then, it is now virtually inconceivable.

One exception concerns the Inuit in the north of Canada, who wish to divide the Northwest Territories into two, so that they will form the majority in the eastern half (to be called 'Nunavut'). This redrawing of federal boundaries is seen as essential to the implementation of the Inuit's right of self-government, and has recently been approved by the federal government.

For the other indigenous peoples in North America, however, self-government has been primarily tied to the system of reserved lands (known as tribal 'reservations' in the United States, and band 'reserves' in Canada). Substantial powers have been devolved from the federal government to the tribal/band councils which govern each reserve. Indian tribes/bands have been acquiring increasing control over health, education, family law, policing, criminal justice, and resource development. They are becoming, in effect, a third order of government, with a collection of powers that is carved out of both federal and state/provincial jurisdictions.[24] However, the administrative difficulties are daunting. Indian tribes/bands differ enormously in the sorts of powers they desire. Moreover, they are territorially located within existing states/provinces, and must co-ordinate their self-government with state/provincial agencies. The exact scope and mechanisms of indigenous self-government in Canada and the United States therefore remain unclear.

Similar systems of self-government exist, or are being sought, by many other indigenous peoples. A recent international declaration regarding the rights of indigenous peoples emphasizes the importance of political self-government. In many parts of the world, however, the hope for political powers is almost utopian, and the more immediate goal is simply to secure the existing land base from further erosion by settlers and resource developers. Indeed, a recent study showed that the single largest cause of ethnic conflict in the world today is the struggle by indigenous peoples for the protection of their land rights.[25]

Self-government claims, then, typically take the form of devolving political power to a political unit substantially controlled by the members of the national minority, and substantially corresponding to their historical homeland or territory. It is important to note that these claims are not seen as a temporary measure, nor as a remedy for a form of oppression that we might (and ought) someday to eliminate. On the contrary, these rights are often described as 'inherent', and so permanent (which is one reason why national minorities seek to have them entrenched in the constitution).

2. *Polyethnic rights*. As I noted earlier, immigrant groups in the last thirty years have successfully challenged the 'Anglo-conformity' model which assumed that they should abandon all aspects of their ethnic heritage and assimilate to existing cultural norms and customs. At first, this challenge simply took the form of demanding the right freely to express their particularity without fear of prejudice or discrimination in the mainstream society. It was the demand, as Walzer put it, that 'politics be separated from nationality—as it was already separated from religion' (Walzer 1982: 6–11).

But the demands of ethnic groups have expanded in important directions. It became clear that positive steps were required to root out discrimination and prejudice, particularly against visible minorities. For this reason, anti-racism policies are considered part of the 'multiculturalism' policy in Canada and Australia, as are changes to the education curriculum to recognize the history and contribution of minorities. However, these policies are primarily directed at ensuring the effective exercise of the common rights of citizenship, and so do not really qualify as group-differentiated citizenship rights.

Some ethnic groups and religious minorities have also demanded various forms of public funding of their cultural practices. This includes the funding of ethnic associations, magazines, and festivals. Given that most liberal states provide funding to the arts and museums, so as to preserve the richness and diversity of our cultural resources, funding for ethnic studies and ethnic associations can be seen as falling under this heading. Indeed, some people defend this funding simply as a way of ensuring that ethnic groups are not discriminated against in state funding of art and culture. Some people believe that public funding agencies have traditionally been biased in favour of European-derived forms of cultural expression, and programmes targeted at ethnic groups remedy this bias. A related demand—discussed at length in Chapter 5—is for the provision of immigrant language education in schools.

Perhaps the most controversial demand of ethnic groups is for exemptions from laws and regulations that disadvantage them, given their religious practices. For example, Jews and Muslims in Britain have sought exemption from Sunday closing or animal slaughtering legislation; Sikh men in Canada have sought exemption from motorcycle helmet laws and from the official dress-codes of police forces, so that they can wear their turban; Orthodox Jews in the United States have sought the right to wear the yarmulka during military service; and Muslim girls in France have sought exemption from school dress-codes so that they can wear the *chador*.[26]

These group-specific measures—which I call 'polyethnic rights'—are intended to help ethnic groups and religious minorities express their cultural particularity and pride without it hampering their success in the economic and political institutions of the dominant society. Like self-government rights, these polyethnic rights are not seen as temporary, because the cultural differences they protect are not something we seek to eliminate. But, as I discuss in Chapters 5 and 9, unlike self-government rights, polyethnic rights are usually intended to promote integration into the larger society, not self-government.

3. *Special representation rights*. While the traditional concern of national minorities and ethnic groups has been with either self-government or polyethnic rights, there has been increasing interest by

these groups, as well as other non-ethnic social groups, in the idea of special representation rights.

Throughout the Western democracies, there is increasing concern that the political process is 'unrepresentative', in the sense that it fails to reflect the diversity of the population. Legislatures in most of these countries are dominated by middle-class, able-bodied, white men. A more representative process, it is said, would include members of ethnic and racial minorities, women, the poor, the disabled, etc. The under-representation of historically disadvantaged groups is a general phenomenon. In the United States and Canada, women, racial minorities, and indigenous peoples all have under one-third of the seats they would have based on their demographic weight. People with disabilities and the economically disadvantaged are also significantly under-represented.[27]

One way to reform the process is to make political parties more inclusive, by reducing the barriers which inhibit women, ethnic minorities, or the poor from becoming party candidates or party leaders; another way is to adopt some form of proportional representation, which has historically been associated with greater inclusiveness of candidates.

However, there is increasing interest in the idea that a certain number of seats in the legislature should be reserved for the members of disadvantaged or marginalized groups. During the debate in Canada over the Charlottetown Accord, for example, a number of recommendations were made for the guaranteed representation of women, ethnic minorities, official language minorities, and Aboriginals.

Group representation rights are often defended as a response to some systemic disadvantage or barrier in the political process which makes it impossible for the group's views and interests to be effectively represented. In so far as these rights are seen as a response to oppression or systemic disadvantage, they are most plausibly seen as a temporary measure on the way to a society where the need for special representation no longer exists—a form of political 'affirmative action'. Society should seek to remove the oppression and disadvantage, thereby eliminating the need for these rights.

However, the issue of special representation rights for groups is complicated, because special representation is sometimes defended, not on grounds of oppression, but as a corollary of self-government. A minority's right to self-government would be severely weakened if some external body could unilaterally revise or revoke its powers, without consulting the minority or securing its consent. Hence it would seem to be a corollary of self-government that the national minority be guaranteed representation on any body which can interpret or modify its powers of self-government (e.g. the Supreme Court). Since the claims of self-government are seen as inherent and permanent, so too are the guarantees of representation which flow from it (unlike guarantees grounded on oppression).[28]

This is just a brief sketch of three mechanisms used to accommodate cultural differences, all of which will be examined in more detail in subsequent chapters. Virtually every modern democracy employs one or more of these mechanisms. Obviously, these three kinds of rights can overlap, in the sense that some groups can claim more than one kind of right. For example, indigenous groups may demand both special representation in the central government, in virtue of their disadvantaged position, and various powers of self-government, in virtue of their status as a 'people' or 'nation'. But these rights need not go together. An oppressed group, like the disabled, may seek special representation, but have no basis for claiming either self-government or polyethnic rights. Conversely, an economically successful immigrant group may seek polyethnic rights, but have no basis for claiming either special representation or self-government, etc.

I have not yet said anything in defence of these rights. I will try to provide a (qualified) defence of them in Chapters 5 and 6. But we must first address certain confusions about the relationship between individual rights and collective rights, which is the subject of the next chapter.

CHAPTER 3

Individual Rights and Collective Rights

A liberal democracy's most basic commitment is to the freedom and equality of its individual citizens. This is reflected in constitutional bills of rights, which guarantee basic civil and political rights to all individuals, regardless of their group membership. Indeed, liberal democracy emerged in part as a reaction against the way that feudalism defined individuals' political rights and economic opportunities by their group membership.

How then can liberals accept the demand for group-differentiated rights by ethnic and national minorities? Why should the members of certain groups have rights regarding land, language, representation, etc. that the members of other groups do not have? To many people, the idea of group-differentiated rights seems to rest on a philosophy or world-view opposite to that of liberalism. It seems more concerned with the status of groups than with that of individuals. Moreover, it seems to treat individuals as the mere carriers of group identities and objectives, rather than as autonomous personalities capable of defining their own identity and goals in life. Group-differentiated rights, in short, seem to reflect a collectivist or communitarian outlook, rather than the liberal belief in individual freedom and equality.

This is a misperception. It rests on a number of confusions which I hope to sort out over the next few chapters. I will try to show that many forms of group-differentiated citizenship are consistent with liberal principles of freedom (Ch. 5) and equality (Ch. 6). But we first need to clear up some popular misunderstandings about the nature of group-differentiated rights.

The various forms of group-differentiated citizenship outlined in Chapter 2 are often described, by both proponents and critics, as 'collective rights'. This terminology can be quite misleading. For one thing, the category of collective rights is large and heterogeneous. It includes the rights of trade unions and corporations; the right to bring class-action suits; the right of all citizens to clean air, etc. These rights have little in common, and it is important not to lump the idea of group-differentiated citizenship with the myriad of other issues that arise under the heading of 'collective rights'.

More importantly, the terminology of collective rights encourages people to make erroneous assumptions about the relationship between group-differentiated citizenship and individual rights. It is natural to assume that collective rights are rights exercised by collectivities, as opposed to rights exercised by individuals, and that the former conflict with the latter. As we will see, these assumptions do not apply to many forms of group-differentiated citizenship. The relationship between group-differentiated citizenship and individual rights is in fact quite complicated, and we need to find a vocabulary that can capture all its nuances.

1. *Internal Restrictions and External Protections*

Many liberals fear that the 'collective rights' demanded by ethnic and national groups are, by definition, inimical to individual rights. This view has been popularized in Canada by former Prime Minister Pierre Trudeau, who explained his opposition to self-government rights for Quebec by saying that he believed in 'the primacy of the individual', and that 'only the individual is the possessor of rights' (Trudeau 1990: 363–4).

However, this rhetoric about individual versus collective rights is unhelpful. We need to distinguish two kinds of claims that an ethnic or national group might make. The first involves the claim of a group against its own members; the second involves the claim of a group against the larger society. Both kinds of claims can be seen as protecting the stability of national or ethnic communities, but they respond to different sources of instability. The first kind is intended to protect the group from the destabilizing impact of *internal dissent* (e.g. the decision of individual members not to follow traditional practices or customs), whereas the second is intended to protect the group from the impact of *external decisions* (e.g. the economic or political decisions of the larger society). To distinguish these two kinds of claims, I will call the first 'internal restrictions', and the second 'external protections'.

Both of these get labelled as 'collective rights', but they raise very different issues. Internal restrictions involve *intra-group* relations—the ethnic or national group may seek the use of state power to restrict the liberty of its own members in the name of group solidarity. This raises the danger of individual oppression. Critics of 'collective rights' in this sense often invoke the image of theocratic and patriarchal cultures where women are oppressed and religious orthodoxy legally enforced as an example of what can happen when the alleged rights of the collectivity are given precedence over the rights of the individual.

Of course, all forms of government and all exercises of political authority involve restricting the liberty of those subject to the authority. In all countries, no matter how liberal and democratic, people are required to pay taxes to support public goods. Most democracies also require people to undertake jury duty, or to perform some amount of military or community service, and a few countries require people to vote (e.g. Australia). All governments expect and sometimes require a minimal level of civic responsibility and participation from their citizens.

But some groups seek to impose much greater restrictions on the liberty of their members. It is one thing to require people to do jury duty or to vote, and quite another to compel people to attend a particular church or to follow traditional gender roles. The former are intended to uphold liberal rights and democratic institutions, the latter restrict these rights in the name of cultural tradition or religious orthodoxy. For the purposes of this discussion, I will use 'internal restrictions' to refer only to the latter sort of case, where the basic civil and political liberties of group members are being restricted.[1]

External protections involve *inter*-group relations—that is, the ethnic or national group may seek to protect its distinct existence and identity by limiting the impact of the decisions of the larger society. This too raises certain dangers—not of individual oppression within a group, but of unfairness between groups. One group may be marginalized or segregated in the name of preserving another group's distinctiveness. Critics of 'collective rights' in this sense often cite the apartheid system in South Africa as an example of what can happen when a minority group demands special protections from the larger society.

However, external protections need not create such injustice. Granting special representation rights, land claims, or language rights to a minority need not, and often does not, put it in a position to dominate other groups. On the contrary, as I discuss in Chapter 6, such rights can be seen as putting the various groups on a more equal footing, by reducing the extent to which the smaller group is vulnerable to the larger.

Notice that internal restrictions can and do exist in culturally homogeneous countries. The desire to protect cultural practices from internal dissent exists to some extent in every culture, even homogeneous nation-states. External protections, however, can only arise in multinational or polyethnic states, since they protect a particular ethnic or national group from the destabilizing impact of the decisions of the larger society.[2]

The two kinds of claims need not go together. Some ethnic or national groups seek external protections against the larger society without seeking to impose legally enforceable internal restrictions on their own members. Other groups do not claim any external protection against the larger community, but seek wide powers over the behaviour of their own members. Yet other groups make both kinds of claims. These variations lead to fundamentally different conceptions of minority rights, and it is important to determine what sort of claim a group is making. To foreshadow the conclusions of the next three chapters, I will argue that liberals can and should endorse certain external protections, where they promote fairness between groups, but should reject internal restrictions which limit the right of group members to question and revise traditional authorities and practices.

If a group demands one of the three kinds of group-differentiated rights I discussed in Chapter 2 (self-government rights, polyethnic rights, and special representation rights), are they seeking to impose internal restrictions or gain external protections? It depends. These group-differentiated rights can serve both aims, depending on the circumstances. I will start by showing how they can provide external protections, and then consider how they can impose internal restrictions.

All three types of group-differentiated citizenship can be used to provide external protections. That is, each type helps protect a minority from the economic or political power of the larger society, although each responds to different external pressures in different ways:

- Special group representation rights within the political institutions of the larger society make it less likely that a national or ethnic minority will be ignored on decisions that are made on a countrywide basis.
- Self-government rights devolve powers to smaller political units, so that a national minority cannot be outvoted or outbid by the

majority on decisions that are of particular importance to their culture, such as issues of education, immigration, resource development, language, and family law.

- Polyethnic rights protect specific religious and cultural practices which might not be adequately supported through the market (e.g. funding immigrant language programmes or arts groups), or which are disadvantaged (often unintentionally) by existing legislation (e.g. exemptions from Sunday closing legislation or dress codes that conflict with religious beliefs).

Each of these three forms of group-differentiated rights helps reduce the vulnerability of minority groups to the economic pressures and political decisions of the larger society. Some national and ethnic minorities seek group-differentiated rights solely for this sort of external protection. Such groups are concerned with ensuring that the larger society does not deprive them of the conditions necessary for their survival, not with controlling the extent to which their own members engage in untraditional or unorthodox practices.

Under these circumstances, there is no necessary conflict between external protections and the individual rights of group members. The existence of such external protections tells us about the relationship between the majority and minority groups; it does not yet tell us about the relationship between the ethnic or national group and its own members. Groups which have these external protections may fully respect the civil and political rights of their own members. Indeed, I will argue in Chapter 5 that these measures are not only consistent with the liberty of individual members, but may actually promote it.[3]

Other groups, however, are concerned with controlling internal dissent, and seek group-differentiated rights in order to impose internal restrictions on their members. Both self-government rights and polyethnic rights can, under some circumstances, be used to limit the rights of the members of the minority group.

This possibility has often been raised in the context of claims for self-government by indigenous peoples. For example, as part of their self-government, tribal councils in the United States have historically been exempted from the usual constitutional requirement to respect the rights listed in the American Bill of Rights. Under the 1968 Indian Civil Rights Act, tribal governments are now required to respect most (but not all) of these individual rights. However, there are still limits on the judicial review of the actions of tribal councils. If a member of an Indian tribe feels her rights have been violated by her tribal council, she can seek redress in a tribal court, but she cannot (except under exceptional circumstances) seek redress from the Supreme Court.

Similarly, Indian bands in Canada have argued that their self-governing band councils should not be subject to judicial review under the Canadian Charter of Rights and Freedoms. They do not want their members to be able to challenge band decisions in the courts of the mainstream society.

These limits on the application of constitutional bills of rights create the possibility that individuals or subgroups within Indian communities could be oppressed in the name of group solidarity or cultural purity. For example, concern has been expressed that Indian women in the United States and Canada might be discriminated against under certain systems of self-government, if these are exempt from the usual constitutional requirement of sexual equality. Indeed, the Native Women's Association of Canada, worried about the danger of sexual discrimination on their reserves, has demanded that the decisions of Aboriginal governments be subject to the Canadian Charter.[4]

On the other hand, many Indians insist that this fear of sexual oppression reflects misinformed or prejudiced stereotypes about their cultures. They argue that Indian self-government needs to be exempt from the Bill/Charter of Rights, not in order to restrict the liberty of women within Indian communities, but to defend the *external* protections of Indians *vis-à-vis* the larger society. Their special rights to land, or to hunt, or to group representation, which help reduce their vulnerability to the economic and political decisions of the larger society, could be struck down as discriminatory under the Bill/Charter of Rights.[5]

Also, Indian leaders fear that white judges on the Supreme Court may interpret certain rights in culturally biased ways. For example, traditional Indian forms of consensual political decision-making could be seen as denying democratic rights. These traditional procedures do not violate the underlying democratic principle of the constitution—namely, that legitimate authority requires the consent of the governed, subject to periodic review. However, they do not use the particular method for securing the consent of the governed envisioned by the constitution—namely, periodic election of representatives. Rather, they rely on certain time-honoured procedures for ensuring consensual decision-making. Indian leaders worry that white judges will impose their own culturally specific form of democracy, without considering whether traditional Indian practices are an equally valid interpretation of democratic principles.

Hence many Indian leaders seek exemption from the Bill/Charter of Rights, but at the same time affirm their commitment to the basic human rights and freedoms which underlie these constitutional documents. They endorse the principles, but object to the particular institutions and procedures that the larger society has established to enforce these principles.[6] Hence they seek to create or maintain their own procedures for protecting human rights, specified in tribal/band constitutions, some of which are based on the provisions of international protocols on human rights. Some Indian groups have also accepted the idea that their governments, like all sovereign governments, should be accountable to international human rights tribunals (e.g. the United Nations' Human Rights Commission). What they object to is the claim that their self-governing decisions should be subject to the federal courts of the dominant society—courts which, historically, have accepted and legitimized the colonization and dispossession of Indian peoples and lands.

In short, many Indian groups—even those who object to federal judicial review of their self-government—do not seek to impose internal restrictions. There are, however, some important exceptions. One relatively clear case of internal restrictions amongst self-governing indigenous groups involves the Pueblo, an American Indian tribe, and freedom of religion. Because they are not subject to the Bill of Rights, tribal governments are not required to obey its strict separation of church and state. The Pueblo have, in effect, established a theocratic government that discriminates against those members who do not share the tribal religion. For example, housing benefits have been denied to those members of the community who have converted to Protestantism. In this case, there is little question that self-government powers are being used to limit the freedom of members to question and revise traditional practices.[7]

It is often difficult for outsiders to assess the likelihood that self-government for an indigenous or national minority will lead to the suppression of basic individual rights. The identification of oppression requires sensitivity to the specific situation, particularly when dealing with other cultures. I will return to this, and to questions of judicial review, in Chapter 8.

It is also possible for polyethnic rights to be used to impose internal restrictions. Immigrant groups and religious minorities could, in principle, seek the legal power to impose traditional cultural practices on their members. Ethnic groups could demand the right to take their children out of school before the legally prescribed age, so as to reduce the chances that the child will leave the community; or the right to continue traditional customs such as clitoridectomy or compulsory arranged marriages that violate existing laws regarding informed consent. There have been cases of husbands who have beaten their wives because they took a job outside the home, and who have then used the fact that wife assault is acceptable practice in their original homeland as a legal defence. More generally, there are fears that 'multiculturalism taken to its logical extreme' could justify allowing each ethnic group to impose its own legal traditions on its members, even when these traditions conflict with basic human rights and constitutional principles (Abu-Laban and Stasiulus 1992: 379).

The threat to individual rights from such internal restrictions is real enough. But it is a mistake to suggest that allowing such oppressive practices is the 'logical' extension of current 'multiculturalism' policies in the major immigrant countries. Existing policies are intended to enable immigrants to express their ethnic identity, if they so desire, and to reduce some of the external pressures on them to assimilate. It is perfectly logical to accept that aim, while denying that groups are entitled to impose practices on members who do not wish to maintain them. The model of polyethnicity underlying public policy in Canada, Australia, and the United States supports the ability of immigrants to choose for themselves whether to maintain their ethnic identity. There is no suggestion that ethnic groups should have any ability to regulate individuals' freedom to accept or reject that identity. As such, public policy (quite consistently) endorses some external protections, while rejecting internal restrictions (Government of Canada 1991*b*: 11).

Moreover, there is little support for the imposition of internal restrictions amongst the members of minority groups themselves. Very few of the mainstream immigrant organizations within Western democracies have sought such policies.[8] Most demands for polyethnic rights are defended in terms of, and take the form of, external protections against the larger community.

Of course, some groups do demand internal restrictions. This is particularly true of religious communities, rather than immigrant groups *per se*. For example, the United States exempts the Amish, a centuries-old Christian sect, from laws regarding the mandatory education of children. Canada provides a similar exemption to a number of other long-standing Christian sects (Mennonites, Doukhobours, Hutterites). Members of these sects can withdraw their children from schools before the legal age of 16, and are also not required to teach the usual school curriculum. Parents worry that if their children received this broader education, they would be tempted to leave the sect and join the wider society. These groups may also put severe restrictions on the ability of group members to leave their group.[9]

It is worth noting that these internal restrictions are not the result of the recent shift toward a more 'polyethnic' immigration policy. The legal exemptions accorded Christian sects long pre-date that policy, and recent immigrant groups have not received such exemptions. For example, Western democracies have firmly rejected the idea that immigrants from Arab or Asian countries should be able to continue traditional practices which involve restricting the basic rights of their own members, such as compulsory arranged marriages, or sexual discrimination in education or family law. The idea that Muslim law regarding family status should be legally recognized is occasionally floated, particularly by Muslim leaders in Britain. But there has been no movement towards giving legal recognition to *talaq* divorces, or towards exempting Muslims from civil laws regarding the equitable division of marital property.[10]

So there are some cases of ethnic and national groups demanding internal restrictions. In these cases, a group has sought the legal power to restrict the liberty of its own members so as to preserve its traditional religious practices. These groups are seeking to establish or maintain a system of group-differentiated rights which protects communal practices, not only from decisions made outside the group, but also from internal dissent, and this often requires exemption from the constitutional or legislative requirements of the larger society.[11]

I return to these demands in Chapter 8, and discuss whether liberal states should be more 'tolerant' of them. But for now, it is important to note that such demands are rare, and rarely successful. Most of the demands for group-specific rights made by ethnic and national groups in Western democracies are for external protections. Those few groups which have demanded the power to impose internal restrictions have generally been rebuffed. While most liberal democracies have, over the last twenty years, made some efforts to accommodate ethnic and national differences, this shift towards a more 'multicultural' public policy has almost entirely been a matter of accepting certain external protections, not internal restrictions.

This distinction between internal restrictions and external protections, like the distinction between nations and ethnic groups, is not always easy to draw. Measures designed to provide external protection often have implications for the liberty of members within the community. Minimally, these measures often cost money to administer, and so may require increased taxation of members. But sometimes the implications can be more serious.

For example, the Salman Rushdie affair has led some British Muslims to propose group-libel laws that would provide the same protection to religious groups that hate-speech laws provide to racial groups. In the case of hate-speech laws, the motivation was to provide a form of external protection—that is, to protect blacks and Jews from racist elements in the larger society. Group-libel laws are often similarly defended as a way of protecting Muslims from the virulent 'Islamophobia' of Western countries. But group-libel laws can also be used to restrict the spread of blasphemy or apostasy within a religious community. Indeed, as the example of Rushdie himself suggests, there is reason to think that some Muslim leaders seek such laws primarily to control apostasy within the Muslim community, rather than to control the expression of non-Muslims.[12] Laws that are justified in terms of external protection can open the door to internal restrictions.

Another example involves indigenous land rights. The survival of indigenous cultures throughout the world is heavily dependent on protection of their land base, and indigenous peoples have fought tenaciously to maintain their land. Indeed, as I noted earlier, indigenous struggles over land are the single largest cause of ethnic conflict in the world (Gurr 1993: viii). But this land base is vulnerable to the greater economic and political power of the larger society. History has shown that the most effective way to protect indigenous communities from this external power is to establish reserves where the land is held in common and/or in trust, and cannot be alienated without the consent of the community as a whole. This is consistent with traditional notions regarding land amongst indigenous peoples, but one of the most common strategies that European settlers used for breaking open indigenous lands for settlement was to replace traditional communal ownership with individualized title, against the will of the indigenous peoples themselves. Once land is divided and alienable, it becomes possible for the wealthier members of the larger society to buy up the land and other resources on which the community depends. Moreover, individualized alienable land is also more vulnerable to expropriation by governments.

So the establishment of reserved land provides protection against the economic and political power of the larger society to buy out or expropriate indigenous land. Yet one by-product of common ownership of reserved land is that individual members of an indigenous community have less ability to borrow money, since they have less alienable property to use as collateral. While this is not a violation of a basic civil or political right, it is a significant restriction on the liberty of individual members. Unfortunately, it seems to be a natural by-product of the external protection provided by indigenous land holdings.[13]

In so far as internal restrictions are present, they are often defended in this way as unavoidable by-products of external protections, rather than as desirable in and of themselves.[14] There is little enthusiasm for what we might call 'pure' internal restrictions—that is, protecting the historical customs or religious character of an ethnic or national group through limitations on the basic civil liberties of its members.

This distinction between internal restrictions and external protections is often ignored by both proponents and critics of group-differentiated rights. Thus we find liberal critics who assume that all forms of group-differentiated citizenship are 'affected by an inherent deficiency in that they place the group over and above the individual' (Tomuschat 1983: 978–9). While this is a relevant objection to internal restrictions, it is not valid for external protections, which do not 'place the group over and above the individual'.

The same mistake is also made by proponents of group-differentiated citizenship. For example, some Aboriginals in Canada have argued that their right to external protections against the larger society entails the right to limit the basic liberties of their own members. This was evident in two recent court cases in Canada. The first case involved the special fishing rights of Aboriginal peoples, which are a form of external protection. Fishing is an important aspect of some Aboriginal cultures, and guaranteed fishing rights ensure that they are not outbid or outvoted by the larger society on decisions regarding access to fishing. These external protections were upheld by the Canadian Supreme Court. The second case involved an Indian man who was literally kidnapped by members of his band and forced to undergo an initiation ceremony which involved assault, battery, and unlawful imprisonment. The defendants argued that the earlier Supreme Court decision supporting group-specific Aboriginal fishing rights proved that the 'collective rights' of Aboriginal peoples take precedence over individual rights in the Canadian constitution. The Court rejected this reasoning, and rightly so, since there is no reason to assume that external protections and internal restrictions stand or fall together.[15]

Rather than granting an unqualified priority to collective over individual rights, or vice versa, we should instead distinguish external protections and internal restrictions. Far from standing together, I will argue in Chapter 5 that the very reasons we have to support external protections are also reasons to oppose internal restrictions.

2. *The Ambiguity of 'Collective Rights'*

We can now see why the term 'collective rights' is so unhelpful as a label for the various forms of group-differentiated citizenship. The problem is partly that the term is too broad, and partly that it fails to distinguish internal restrictions from external protections. But a deeper problem is that it suggests a false dichotomy with individual rights.

On one natural interpretation, 'collective rights' refer to the rights accorded to and exercised by collectivities, where these rights are distinct from, and perhaps conflicting with, the rights accorded to the individuals who compose the collectivity. This is not the only possible definition of collective rights—indeed there are hundreds of definitions in the literature—but almost everyone agrees that collective rights are, by definition, not individual rights.

Yet many forms of group-differentiated citizenship are in fact exercised by individuals. Group-differentiated rights can be accorded to the individual members of a group, or to the group as a whole, or to a federal state/province within which the group forms the majority.[16]

Consider minority language rights. The right of francophones in Canada to use French in federal courts is a right accorded to and exercised by individuals. The right of francophones to have their children educated in French schools is slightly different: it is exercised by individuals but only 'where numbers warrant'. The special hunting and fishing rights of indigenous peoples, on the other hand, are usually exercised by the tribe/band. For example, an Indian tribal/band council will determine what hunting will occur. An Indian whose hunting is restricted by her council cannot claim that this is a denial of her rights, because Indian hunting rights are not accorded to individuals. The right of the Québécois to preserve and promote their culture, affirmed in the existing system of federalism, is yet a fourth case: it is exercised by the province of Quebec, whose citizens are predominantly Québécois, but also include many non-francophones.[17] These are all group-differentiated rights, since they are accorded on the basis of cultural membership. But some are accorded to individuals, some to the group, some to a province or territory, and some where numbers warrant.

The fact that certain minority language rights are exercised by individuals has led to a large (and largely sterile) debate about whether they are really 'collective rights' or not. This debate is sterile because the question of whether the right is (or is not) collective is morally unimportant. The real issue in evaluating language rights is why they are group-specific—that is, why francophones should be able to demand court proceedings or education in their mother-tongue at public expense when Greek- or Swahili-speakers cannot. The answer, I have suggested, is that language rights are one component of the national rights of the French Canadians. Since immigrant groups are not national minorities, they are not accorded similar language rights. (I discuss whether this is justified or not in Chs. 5–6.)

The fact that French Canadians are a national minority is essential to understanding why individual francophones have a right to a trial in French, and why a group of francophone parents can demand a French school where numbers warrant, and why the province of Quebec has jurisdiction over education under the federal division of powers. These variations in who actually exercises the right are largely a matter of administrative convenience which does not affect the underlying justification based on the recognition of the French as a national minority. Since Greeks, for example, are not a national minority in Canada, they are not granted either individual or collective rights regarding the official recognition of their mother tongue.

The case of Indian hunting rights also shows that what matters is not whether the right is 'collective' (as opposed to individual), but that it is group-differentiated. Many non-Indians in the United States, Canada, and Australia object to the fact that Indians have special hunting and fishing rights. But they would not be appeased if these rights were accorded to individual Indians rather than to the band. They object to the fact that rights are accorded on the basis of group membership, thereby giving Indians special rights and special status. Whether these group-specific rights are attributed to individual Indians or Indian bands/tribes is, for critics, largely irrelevant.[18]

So describing group-differentiated citizenship in the language of collective rights is doubly misleading. Some group-differentiated rights are in fact exercised by individuals, and in any event the question of whether the rights are exercised by individuals or collectives is not the fundamental issue. The important issue is why certain rights are group-differentiated—that is, why the members of certain groups should have rights regarding land, language, representation, etc. that the members of other groups do not have.[19]

This conflation of group-differentiated citizenship with collective rights has had a disastrous effect on the philosophical and popular debate. Because they view the debate in terms of collective rights, many people assume that the debate over group-differentiated citizenship is essentially equivalent to the debate between individualists and collectivists over the relative priority of the individual and the community. Individualists argue that the individual is morally prior to the community: the community matters only because it contributes to the well-being of the individuals who compose it. If those individuals no longer find it worthwhile to maintain existing cultural practices, then the community has no independent interest in preserving those practices, and no right to prevent individuals from modifying or rejecting them. Hence individualists reject the idea that ethnic and national groups have any collective rights.

Collectivists, by contrast, deny that a community's interests are reducible to the interests of the members who compose it. They put collective rights on a par with individual rights, and defend them in a parallel way. Theories of individual rights begin by explaining what an individual is, what interests she has *qua* individual, and then derive a set of individual rights that protect those interests. Similarly, collectivists begin by explaining what a community is, what interests it has *qua* community, and then derive a set of community rights that protect those interests. Just as certain individual rights flow from each individual's interest in personal liberty, so certain community rights flow from each community's interest in self-preservation. These community rights must then be weighed against the rights of the individuals who compose the community.

This debate over the reducibility of community interests to individual interests dominates the literature on collective rights.[20] But it is irrelevant to most group-differentiated rights issues in liberal democracies. The claim that communities have interests independently of their members is relevant to internal restrictions—it might explain why members of a community are obliged to maintain cultural practices. But it cannot explain external restrictions—that is, why some rights are unequally distributed between groups, why the members of one group have claims against the members of another group. The idea that groups are prior to individuals, even if true, cannot by itself explain this asymmetry between groups.

Collectivists and individualists disagree about whether communities can have rights or interests independently of their individual members. This argument over the primacy of the individual or the community is an old and venerable one in political philosophy. But it should be clear, I hope, how unhelpful it is for evaluating most group-differentiated rights in Western democracies. Most such rights are not about the primacy of communities over individuals. Rather, they are based upon the idea that justice between groups requires that the members of different groups be accorded different rights.

Does justice between the members of different groups require group-differentiated citizenship? I believe it does, and Chapters 5 and 6 will explain why. Before we explore these arguments, however, I want to fill in some of the historical background. My arguments will challenge some deeply rooted liberal beliefs about freedom and equality, and so it is important to see how those views became so deeply rooted in the first place.

CHAPTER 4

Rethinking the Liberal Tradition

We now have a clearer idea, I hope, of the types of groups and the types of claims which underlie the 'politics of multiculturalism'. How should liberals respond to these claims? Contemporary liberal thinkers are of little help in answering this question. Few contemporary theorists have explicitly discussed the rights of ethnic and national minorities, or developed any principles for evaluating claims to language rights, for example, or federal autonomy.

It was not always this way. For most of the nineteenth century and the first half of the twentieth, the rights of national minorities were continually discussed and debated by the great liberal statesmen and theorists of the age. As I will show, they disagreed about how best to respond to multination states, but they all took it for granted that liberalism needed some or other theory of the status of national minorities.

Contemporary liberals, by contrast, have been surprisingly silent about these issues. There are very few discussions of the differences between nation-states and polyethnic or multination states, or of the demands associated with each form of ethnic or national diversity. And when contemporary liberals have addressed these issues—often in brief pronouncements or parenthetical asides—they have tended to recite simplistic formulas about 'non-discrimination' or 'benign neglect', formulas that cannot do justice to the complexities involved.

In this chapter, I will trace the origin of contemporary liberal attitudes towards minority rights. I will first explore some of the historical debates about national minorities (s. 1), then consider some of the reasons why this issue virtually disappeared from view after World War II (ss. 2–4), and conclude with a brief discussion of the role of minority rights in the socialist tradition (s. 5).

In the process, I hope to correct some common mistakes about the liberal tradition. It is widely believed that liberals have always opposed the political recognition and support of ethnicity and nationality, and that demands for group-differentiated rights for cultural groups are a recent and illiberal deviation from long-established liberal practice.[1]

This is simply not true. Minority rights were an important part of liberal theory and practice in the nineteenth century and between the world wars. If anything, it is the idea of 'benign neglect' which is a recent arrival in the liberal tradition. Moreover, its emergence can be traced to a series of contingent factors, including ethnocentric denigration of non-European cultures, fears about international peace and security, and the influence of racial desegregation decisions in the United States. These factors have had a profound but often distorting effect on liberal thinking. Issues and arguments that were relevant in one set of circumstances have been mistakenly generalized to other cases where they do not apply. Once we sort out these confusions, it should become clear that minority rights are a legitimate component of the liberal tradition.

1. The History of Liberal Views on National Minorities

The liberal tradition contains a striking diversity of views on the rights of minority cultures. At one end of the spectrum, there have been strong proponents of minority rights. Indeed, there have been times in the last two centuries when endorsement of minority rights was considered a clear sign of one's liberal credentials.

For example, it was a common tenet of nineteenth-century liberalism that national minorities were treated unjustly by the multination empires of Europe, such as the Habsburg, Ottoman, and tsarist empires. The injustice was not simply the fact that the minorities were denied individual civil and political liberties, since that was true of the members of the dominant nation in each empire as well. The injustice was rather the denial of their national rights to self-government, which were seen as an essential complement to individual rights, since 'the cause of liberty finds its basis, and secures its roots, in the autonomy of a national group' (Barker 1948: 248; cf. Mazzini 1907: 51–2, 176–7; Humboldt 1988: 21, 41–3, 153). The promotion of national autonomy 'offers a realization of the ideal of an "area of liberty", or in other words, of a free society for free men' (Hoernlé 1939: 181).

The precise connection between individual freedom and nationality is not always clear in these theorists. In some cases, it was simply the assumption that multination states were inherently unstable, and so liable to authoritarianism (I discuss this claim below). But in other theorists, such as Wilhelm von Humboldt and Giuseppe Mazzini, the claim is that the promotion of individuality and the development of human personality is intimately tied up with membership in one's national group, in part because of the role of language and culture in enabling choice.[2]

This liberal commitment to some form of national self-government was so common that George Bernard Shaw once quipped that 'A Liberal is a man who has three duties: a duty to Ireland, a duty to Finland, and a duty to Macedonia.'[3] (All three nations were incorporated into multination empires at the time.) Notice that the liberal aim was not to grant individual rights to all citizens of these multination empires, but rather to grant political powers to the constituent nations within each empire. Liberals predicted (accurately) that these empires would fall apart because of their reluctance to grant 'any system of autonomy under which the various nations could have enjoyed the position of quasi-States' (Barker 1948: 254).

It may seem odd that a liberal could ever have been defined (even in a jest) by a commitment to national rights rather than individual rights. But we find the same linkage between liberalism and support for the rights of national minorities between the world wars. Leonard Hobhouse, for example, said that 'the more liberal statesmanship' of his day had recognized the necessity of minority rights to ensure 'cultural equality' (Hobhouse 1966: 297, 299). There is more than one way to meet the legitimate demands of national minorities, he thought, but 'clearly it is not achieved by equality of franchise. The smaller nationality does not merely want equal rights with others. It stands out for a certain life of its own' (Hobhouse 1928: 146–7). One manifestation of this liberal commitment was the minority protection scheme set up under the League of Nations for various European national minorities, which provided both universal individual rights and certain group-specific rights regarding education, local autonomy, and language.

Again, the precise connection between equality and minority rights was rarely spelled out. But the general idea was clear enough. A multination state which accords universal individual rights to all its citizens, regardless of group membership, may appear to be 'neutral' between the various national groups. But in fact it can (and often does) systematically privilege the majority nation in certain fundamental ways—for example, the drawing of internal boundaries; the language of schools, courts, and government services; the choice of public holidays; and the division of legislative power between central and local governments. All of these decisions can dramatically reduce the political power and cultural viability of a national minority, while enhancing that of the majority culture. Group-specific rights regarding education, local autonomy, and language help ensure that national minorities are not disadvantaged in these decisions, thereby enabling the minority, like the majority, to sustain 'a life of its own'.

We have here the two major claims which, I believe, underlie a liberal defence of minority rights: that individual freedom is tied in some important way to membership in one's national group; and that group-specific rights can promote equality between the minority and majority. I think these two ideas are essentially correct, and I try to develop and expand on them in Chapters 5 and 6 respectively.

These two claims were widely accepted by many nineteenth- and early twentieth-century liberals. To be sure, some liberals opposed various demands for minority rights. But not because of a commitment to the principle of 'benign neglect'. Rather, they believed, with John Stuart Mill, that free institutions are 'next to impossible' in a multination state:

> Among a people without fellow-feelings, especially if they read and speak different languages, the united public opinion necessary to the workings of representative institutions cannot exist . . . [It] is in general a necessary condition of free institutions that the boundaries of governments should coincide in the main with those of nationalities. (Mill 1972: 230, 233)

For liberals like Mill, democracy is government 'by the people', but self-rule is only possible if 'the people' are 'a people'—a nation. The members of a democracy must share a sense of political allegiance, and common nationality was said to be a precondition of that allegiance. Thus T. H. Green argued that liberal democracy is only possible if people feel bound to the state by 'ties derived from a common dwelling place with its associations, from common memories, traditions and customs, and from the common ways of feeling and thinking which a common language and still more a common literature embodies' (T. Green 1941: 130–1; cf. Rich 1987: 155). According to this stream of liberal thought, since a free state must be a nation-state, national minorities must be dealt with by coercive assimilation or the redrawing of boundaries, not by minority rights.

The alleged need for a common national identity is an important issue which, as we will see, has been raised again and again throughout the liberal tradition. Some liberals support the need for a common national identity, others deny its necessity. Moreover, some liberals deny that a multination state even has the capacity to promote a common national identity which will displace or take precedence over the existing identity of a national minority. I discuss these questions at length in Chapter 9.

However, in the nineteenth century, the call for a common national identity was often tied to an ethnocentric denigration of smaller national groups. It was commonplace in nineteenth-century thought to distinguish the 'great nations', such as France, Italy, Poland, Germany, Hungary, Spain, England, and Russia, from smaller 'nationalities', such as the Czechs, Slovaks, Croats, Basques, Welsh, Scots, Serbians, Bulgarians, Romanians, and Slovenes. The great nations were seen as civilized, and as the carriers of historical development. The smaller nationalities were primitive and stagnant, and incapable of social or cultural development. So some nineteenth-century liberals endorsed national independence for great nations, but coercive assimilation for smaller nationalities.

Thus Mill insisted that it was undeniably better for a Scottish Highlander to be part of Great Britain, or for a Basque to be part of France, 'than to sulk on his own rocks, the half-savage relic of past times, revolving in his own little mental orbit, without participation or interest in the general movement of the world' (Mill 1972: 363–4). Mill was hardly alone in this view. As I discuss later in this chapter, nineteenth-century socialists shared this ethnocentric view, which was also invoked to justify the coerced assimilation of indigenous peoples throughout the British Empire.[4]

Other liberals argued the opposite position, that true liberty was only possible in a multination state. For example, Lord Acton argued, against Mill, that the divisions between national groups and their desire for an internal life of their own serves as a check against the aggrandizement and abuse of state power (Acton 1922: 285–90). This debate was revisited by British liberals during and after World War I. For example, Alfred Zimmern defended Acton's claim that a multination state checks the abuse of state power (Zimmern 1918), while Ernest Barker defended Mill's belief that a nation-state can best sustain free institutions (Barker 1948). Here again very different views about the status of national minorities were defended, yet each side claimed that it represented the truly liberal view.

So there is a considerable range of views on minority rights within the liberal tradition. Notice also that none of these earlier positions endorses the idea—championed by many contemporary liberals—that the state should treat cultural membership as a purely private matter. On the contrary, liberals either endorsed the legal recognition of minority cultures, or rejected minority rights not because they rejected the idea of an official culture, but precisely because they believed there should only be *one* official culture.[5]

This is just a quick sketch of the way many earlier liberals viewed nationality. A fuller account would probably reveal an even greater range of views, since it was a prominent theme in most major liberal writings of the era. What explains this remarkable level of interest and debate in one era, and its subsequent virtual disappearance in post-war liberal thought? It is partly related to the rise and fall of the British Empire. From the early 1800s to the beginning of decolonization after World War II, English liberals were constantly confronted with the issue of how to export liberal institutions to their colonies. The desire to transplant liberal institutions was fuelled by a somewhat contradictory combination of old-fashioned imperialism (expanding England's domain by setting up little Englands overseas), and a universalistic liberal faith in the 'rights of man', which viewed liberal institutions in the colonies as the first step towards their freedom and independence from English power.

But whatever the motives, English liberals were constantly confronted with the fact that liberal institutions which worked in England did not work in multination states. It quickly became clear that many English liberal institutions were as much English as liberal—that is, they were only appropriate for a (relatively) ethnically and racially homogeneous society such as England. As Lord Balfour put it, while 'constitutions are easily copied', the successful working of English institutions 'may be difficult or impossible' if national divisions in the colonies are 'either too numerous or too profound'. English institutions presupposed 'a people so fundamentally at one that they can afford to bicker' (Hancock 1937: 429).

According to W. Hancock, who studied national conflicts within the Empire, British colonial policy was at first shaped by 'abstract universalizers of liberal doctrine' who possessed 'an irresistible propensity to generalize the Englishman's "principles" at large, without realizing that in so doing they [were] taking for granted the whole rich and stable background of English history'. They tried to 'assert their "principles" in the Empire without realizing that what they [were] really seeking [was] to impose their own national forms, regardless of the historic life and culture and needs of some quite different community'. In short, they 'thought it sufficient to transplant, where the need was to translate' (Hancock 1937: 496).

As a result, liberals who went to administer or study British colonies found that the liberalism they learned in England simply did not address some of the issues of cultural diversity they faced. An early example of this was Lord Durham, one of John Stuart Mill's circle, who was sent to Canada to head an inquiry into the causes of the Rebellions of 1837. On the surface, the rebellions in English and French Canada were about demands for more responsible and democratic government (like the American Revolution), and this was how British liberals initially interpreted them. But, as Durham put it in his report, 'I expected to find a contest between a government and a people: I found two nations warring in the bosom of a single state.' He also found that existing liberal theory was not much help in resolving this sort of dispute. His solution, endorsed by J. S. Mill and adopted by the British government, was the more or less forcible assimilation of the French, so as to create a homogeneous English nation-state. He had no sympathy for the 'vain endeavour' of the French Canadians to maintain their 'backward' culture (Craig 1963: 146–50).[6]

However, Durham's policy was a complete failure, as French-Canadian resistance to assimilation led to a paralysis in colonial government. Most subsequent liberals, therefore, proposed accommodating national divisions in the colonies. Indeed, many liberals believed that developing a theory of national rights was the greatest challenge facing English liberalism if its appeal was to move beyond the boundaries of its (culturally homogeneous) homeland (e.g. Hoernlé 1939: 123–5, 136–8; Hobhouse 1928: 146; Hancock 1937: 429–31, 495–6; Clarke 1934: 7–8).

My guess is that the same story was repeated a hundred times throughout the British Empire, from the early 1800s to the beginning of decolonization. There must have been generations of English thinkers who learned the essentials of liberal theory at universities in England, and who went overseas with the hope of transplanting those principles, but who were then faced with a set of issues regarding minority rights that they were unprepared to deal with. It would be interesting to have a proper study of the ways English liberals adapted their principles to deal with the existence of minority cultures in their various colonies. Problems of nationality arose throughout the Commonwealth—from Canada and the Caribbean to Africa, Palestine, and India—and the colonial experience led to a wealth of experimentation regarding communal representation, language rights, treaties and other historical agreements between national groups, federalism, land rights, and immigration policy. With the decline of the Empire, however, liberals stopped thinking about these issues, and little of this experience was fed back into British liberal theory.[7]

The issue of minority rights was raised not only in the colonies, but also by events on the Continent. Nationalist conflicts in Europe were a constant threat to international peace before World War II, and this too encouraged liberals to attend to the rights of national minorities. Yet this factor also disappeared after World War II, as nationalist conflicts in Europe were replaced by Cold War conflicts over ideology.[8]

So the ushering in of the post-war era relieved British liberals of the two major reasons for thinking about national minorities—governing overseas colonies, and responding to nationalist conflicts on the Continent. Perhaps as a result, many theorists have reverted to being 'abstract liberal universalizers' who cannot distinguish the core principles of liberalism from its particular institutional manifestations in uninational states like England.

American liberals during the nineteenth and early twentieth centuries were less involved in this debate. They did not have to deal with the existence of colonies, and they were some distance from Europe. As a result, they were not forced to develop a more generalized or comparative view about the application of liberal principles to multination states. Two American liberals who did talk about minority rights were Randolph Bourne and Horace Kallen (Bourne 1964; H. Kallen 1924). But they were almost exclusively concerned with the status of white immigrant groups in the USA, and ignored the claims of territorially concentrated and historically settled national minorities, of the sort we find in Europe, Quebec, and the Third World.

Post-war American liberalism exhibits the same neglect of national minorities. As I discuss later, virtually all American political theorists treat the United States as a polyethnic nation-state, rather than a truly multination state. Perhaps this is because national minorities in the United States are relatively small and isolated (e.g. Puerto Ricans, American Indians, native Hawaiians, Alaskan Eskimos). These groups are virtually invisible in American political theory. If they are mentioned at all, it is usually as an afterthought. This has had a profound effect on liberal thought around the world, since American theorists have become the dominant interpreters of liberal principles since World War II.[9]

These factors—the fall of the British Empire, the rise of Cold War conflict, and the prominence of American theorists within post-war liberalism—help explain why the heated debate about national minorities amongst pre-war liberals has given way to a virtual silence. But these factors do not explain why contemporary liberals in practice have become so hostile to minority rights. Why, even in the absence of theoretical discussions, have liberals not intuitively supported minority rights—as many did before the war—and seen them as promoting liberal values of individual freedom and social equality? Why have they instead adopted the idea of 'benign neglect'?

I believe this is the result of the convergence of a number of post-war political changes. Three features of the post-war world have conspired to lead liberals to adopt a misplaced antagonism towards the recognition of national rights: (1) disillusionment with the minority rights scheme of the League of Nations, (2) the American racial desegregation movement, and (3) the 'ethnic revival' amongst immigrant groups in the United States. I will discuss each of these in turn, to see how they have helped shape the new liberal distrust of minority rights.

2. *The Failure of the Minority Treaties*

The first important change in liberal views came with the failure of the League of Nations's minority protection scheme, and its role in the outbreak of World War II. The scheme gave international recognition to the German-speaking minorities in Czechoslovakia and Poland, and the Nazis encouraged them to make demands and lodge complaints against their governments. When the Polish and Czech governments were unwilling or unable to meet the escalating demands of their German minorities, the Nazis used this as a pretext for aggression. This Nazi manipulation of the League scheme, and the co-operation of the German minorities in it, created 'a strong reaction against the concept of international protection of [national minorities] . . . the hard fact was that statesmen, generally backed by a public opinion which was deeply impressed by the perfidy of irredentist and disloyal minorities, were disposed to curtail, rather than to expand, the rights of minorities' (Claude 1955: 57, 69). This curtailing of minority rights was done, not in the interest of justice, but by people 'within whose frame of reference the interests of the national state ranked as supreme values . . . [The majority nationality] has an interest in making the national state secure, and its institutions stable, even at the cost of obliterating minority cultures and imposing enforced homogeneity upon the population' (Claude 1955: 80–1).

This 'frame of reference' is similar to the earlier liberal view that freedom requires cultural homogeneity, although it differs in emphasis. Whereas Mill and Green were concerned with domestic stability, post-war statesmen were primarily concerned with international peace. But the effect was the same—questions about the fairness of minority rights were subordinated to the higher demands of stability.

There was an explicit desire to leave the issue of minority rights off the United Nations agenda, and the UN has only recently agreed to reconsider the legitimacy of minority rights claims (Sohn 1981; Thornberry 1980; 1991). The fear that national minorities will be disloyal (or simply apathetic) continues to inhibit discussion of the justice of these claims, both internationally and in the domestic politics of many countries.[10]

Recent events in the former Yugoslavia show that the threat to international peace from irredentist minorities is still a very real one. The likelihood of violence is dramatically increased when a minority is seen (or sees itself) as belonging to an adjacent 'mother country' which proclaims itself as the legitimate protector of the minority. The government of Hungary has declared itself the protector of ethnic Hungarians in Slovakia and Romania; leaders in Russia and Serbia have made similar declarations about ethnic Russians in the Baltics and ethnic Serbs in Bosnia and Croatia. Protecting the rights of a national minority under these circumstances can become a pretext for territorial aggression by the self-proclaimed protector state. This shows the necessity of developing truly international mechanisms for protecting national minorities that do not rely on the destabilizing threat of intervention by kin states.

The problem of irredentism is much greater in Europe than in North America. Indigenous peoples in North America have no protector state to appeal to, and it has been over 100 years since anyone has viewed France as the protector of the Québécois in Canada. It has been almost as long since anyone viewed Spain as the protector of the Puerto Ricans. In these contexts, while minority rights may affect domestic stability, they pose little threat to international peace.

3. *Racial Desegregation in the United States*

The modern liberal rejection of minority rights began with worries about political stability, but it acquired the mantle of justice when it was linked to racial desegregation. In *Brown* v. *Board of Education*, the American Supreme Court struck down the system of segregated educational facilities for black and white children in the South. This decision, and the civil rights movement generally, had an enormous influence on American views of racial equality. The new model of racial justice was 'colour-blind laws', replacing 'separate but equal treatment', which was now seen as the paradigm of racial injustice.

But the influence of *Brown* was soon felt in areas other than race relations, for it seemed to lay down a principle which was equally applicable to relations between ethnic and national groups. According to this principle, injustice is a matter of arbitrary exclusion from the dominant institutions of society, and equality is a matter of non-discrimination and equal opportunity to participate. Viewed in this light, legislation providing separate institutions for national minorities seems no different from the segregation of blacks. The natural extension of *Brown*, therefore, was to remove the separate status of minority cultures, and encourage their equal participation in mainstream society.

This reasoning underlay the Canadian government's 1969 proposal to remove the special constitutional status of Indians. Drawing on the language of *Brown*, the government said that 'separate but equal services do not provide truly equal treatment', and that 'the ultimate aim of removing the specific references to Indians from the constitution . . . is a goal to be kept constantly in view'.[11] Similarly, the Canadian Supreme Court invoked *Brown* when striking down a law which gave group-specific status to Indians.[12]

Brown's formula for racial justice has also been invoked against the rights of American Indians, native Hawaiians, and the rights of national minorities in international law. Under the influence of *Brown*, these national groups have been treated as a 'racial minority', and their autonomous institutions have been struck down as forms of 'racial segregation' or 'racial discrimination'.[13]

But the actual judgement in *Brown* does not support this application of the colour-blind formula to the rights of national minorities. The Court was simply not addressing the issue of national rights, like the right of a culture to the autonomous institutions needed to be able to develop itself freely within a multination state. Segregationists were not claiming that whites and blacks formed different cultures, with different languages and literatures. On the contrary, the whole burden of their case was that the education received by blacks in their segregated facilities was *identical* to that of whites. The question was whether racial groups could be given separate facilities, so long as the facilities were identical. And the Court ruled that, *under those circumstances*, segregation was inherently unequal, since it would be seen as a 'badge of inferiority', as a sign of racism.

Nothing in the judgement warrants the claim that national rights are incompatible with liberal equality. Indeed, the judgement, examined more closely, may argue *for* the recognition of national rights. Consider the situation of American Indians, whose separate institutions came under attack after *Brown*. As Michael Gross notes,

> Where blacks have been forcibly *excluded* (segregated) from white society by law, Indians—aboriginal peoples with their own cultures, languages, religions and territories—have been forcibly *included* (integrated) into that society by law. That is what [is] meant by coercive assimilation—the practice of compelling, through submersion, an ethnic, cultural and linguistic minority to shed its uniqueness and identity and mingle with the rest of society. (Gross 1973: 244)

Integrated education for the Indians, like segregated education for the blacks, is a 'badge of inferiority' for it fails 'to recognize the importance and validity of the Indian community'. In fact, the 'integration of Indian children in white-dominated schools had the same negative educational and emotional effects which segregation was held to have in *Brown*. Hence the 'underlying principle' which struck down the segregation of blacks—namely, that racial classifications harmful to a minority are prohibited—should also strike down legislated integration of Indians (Gross 1973: 242–8).

The point is not that Indians do not need protection against racism. But whereas racism against blacks comes from the denial by whites that blacks are full members of the community, racism against Indians comes primarily from the denial by whites that Indians are distinct peoples with their own cultures and communities. Unfortunately, the centrality of the civil rights movement for African-Americans has prevented people from seeing the distinctive issues raised by the existence of national minorities.

In one sense, it is paradoxical that *Brown* has been taken as a model for all ethnic and national groups. As I noted in Chapter 2, the historical situation and present circumstances of African-Americans are virtually unique in the world, and there is no reason to think that policies which are appropriate for them would be appropriate for either national minorities or voluntary immigrants (or vice versa). But in another sense, this extension of *Brown* is understandable. The history of slavery and segregation represents one of the greatest evils of modern times, and its legacy is a society with very deep racial divisions. It is not surprising that the American government and courts, and public opinion generally, should wish to eliminate anything which even remotely resembles racial segregation. While separate and self-governing institutions for Indians or native Hawaiians have only a superficial resemblance to racial segregation, this has been enough to expose them to legal assault. While understandable, this over-generalization of *Brown* is unfortunate, and unjust. There is no reason why justice for African-Americans should come at the price of injustice for indigenous peoples and other national minorities.

4. Polyethnicity and the American Ethnic Revival

The belief that minority rights are unfair and divisive was confirmed, for many liberals, by the ethnic revival which rocked the United States and elsewhere in the 1960s and 1970s. As I discussed earlier (Ch. 2, s. 1), this revival began with the claim that it was legitimate (not 'unamerican') for ethnic groups to express their distinctive characteristics (as opposed to the 'Anglo-conformity' model of immigration). But it soon moved on to new demands. For example, one result of the more open expression of ethnic identity was that ethnic groups became more conscious of their status as a group. It became common to measure the distribution of income or occupations amongst ethnic groups, and some of those groups which were faring less well demanded group-based ameliorative action, such as quotas in education and employment. They also wanted their heritage recognized in the school curriculum and government symbols.

American liberals have had an ambiguous relationship to this ethnic revival. Most liberals accepted the initial demand by ethnic groups for the abandonment of the Anglo-conformity model.[14] But as demands escalated, liberal support diminished. In fact, the increasing politicization of immigrant groups profoundly unsettled American liberals, for it affected the most basic assumptions and self-conceptions of American political culture. And this anxiety has had important repercussions for their attitude toward national minorities.

As I noted earlier, most American political theorists think of the United States as an immigrant country. Indeed, it is the original immigrant country. The idea of building a country through polyethnic immigration was quite unique in history, and many people thought it untenable. There were no historical precedents to show that an ethnically mixed country of immigrants would be stable. What would bind people together when they came from such different backgrounds, including every conceivable race, religion, language group, sharing virtually nothing in common?

The answer, of course, was that immigrants would have to integrate into the existing anglophone society, rather than forming separate and distinct nations with their own homelands inside the United States. There was no hope for the long-term survival of the country if the Germans, Swedes, Dutch, Greeks, Italians, Poles, and so on each viewed themselves as separate and self-governing peoples, rather than as members of a single (polyethnic) American people. As John Higham puts it, the English settlers conceived of themselves as 'the formative population' of the American colonies/states, and 'theirs was the polity, the language, the pattern of work and settlements, and many of the mental habits to which the immigrants would have to adjust' (Higham 1976: 6; cf. Steinberg 1981: 7).

Immigrants would not only have the right to integrate into the mainstream anglophone society (and so would be protected against discrimination and prejudice); they also had the obligation to integrate (and so would be required to learn English in schools, and English would be the language of public life). The commitment to integrating immigrants was not just evidence of intolerance or ethnocentrism on the part of WASPs (although it was that in part), it was also an understandable response to the uncertainty about whether a country built through polyethnic immigration would be viable.

It was fundamental then, that immigrants view themselves as ethnic groups, not as national minorities. For a long time, immigrants seemed content with this arrangement. But the ethnic revival challenged this traditional model. As the ethnic revival escalated, some immigrant associations in the United States adopted the language and attitudes of colonized 'nations' or 'peoples' (Glazer 1983: 110–11). They labelled social pressures for integration as 'oppression', and demanded their right to 'self-determination', including state recognition of their mother tongue, and state support for separate ethnic institutions.

As I discuss below, these sorts of demands represented only a minor element amongst American immigrant groups. However, they caused serious anxiety amongst liberals. Most liberals viewed the adoption of nationalist rhetoric by immigrant groups not only as a threat to social unity, but also as morally unjustified. Liberals argued that immigrants had no legitimate basis to claim such national rights. After all, they had come voluntarily, knowing that integration was expected of them. When they chose to leave their culture and come to America, they voluntarily relinquished their national membership, and the national rights which go with it.

This attitude toward the ethnic revival is clearly expressed in the writings of Michael Walzer, a leading American political theorist (and editor of the left-liberal journal *Dissent*), and Nathan Glazer, a leading American sociologist (and editor of the right-liberal journal *Public Interest*). According to Glazer, immigrants

> had come to this country not to maintain a foreign language and culture but with the intention . . . to become Americanized as fast as possible, and this meant English language and American culture. They sought the induction to a new language and culture that the public schools provided—as do many present-day immigrants, too—and while they often found, as time went on,

that they regretted what they and their children had lost, this was *their* choice, rather than an imposed choice. (Glazer 1983: 149)

Similarly, Walzer argues that because the immigrants 'had come voluntarily', the 'call for self-determination' had no basis here. Nor was there any basis or reason for rejecting English as the public language (Walzer 1982: 6–7,10; 1983*b*: 224).

Both Glazer and Walzer emphasize how the process of integrating voluntary immigrants differs from the assimilation of conquered or colonized national minorities in the multination states of Europe. In the latter case, it is wrong to deprive 'intact and rooted communities' that 'were established on lands they had occupied for many centuries' of mother-tongue education or local autonomy. Under these conditions, integration is an 'imposed choice' which national minorities typically (and justifiably) have resisted. The integration of immigrants, by contrast, 'was aimed at peoples far more susceptible to cultural change, for they were not only uprooted; they had uprooted themselves. Whatever the pressures that had driven them to the New World, they had chosen to come, while others like themselves, in their own families, had chosen to remain' (Walzer 1982: 9; cf. Glazer 1983: 227, 283). Demands for national rights by immigrant groups are not only unjustified. They are also divisive, since each group will resent any special rights given to other groups, and impracticable, since American ethnic groups are too 'dispersed, mixed, assimilated and integrated' to exercise collective autonomy. Indeed, any attempt to turn ethnic groups into the 'compact, self-conscious, culture-maintaining entities' necessary for collective autonomy would require coercion, since many immigrants prefer to integrate into the mainstream society, both culturally and geographically. Implementing the extensive new demands of the ethnic revival would, therefore, be unjust, impracticable, divisive, and coercive (Glazer 1983: 227, 124).

I think that Glazer and Walzer are right to emphasize the difference between immigrants and national minorities, and to focus on the fact that (in most cases) the decision to emigrate was voluntary. This fact does, I believe, affect the legitimacy of their claims. As I discuss in Chapter 5, while voluntary immigrants can legitimately assert certain polyethnic rights, they have no claim of justice to national self-government.[15]

Given the centrality of immigration to American society, it is not surprising that liberals have been so hostile to any signs of latent nationalism amongst immigrant groups. In a country built primarily on immigration, with immigrants from virtually every linguistic and cultural group around the world, any serious attempt to redefine ethnic groups as national minorities would undermine the very fabric of society.

What is perhaps more surprising is that liberals have been so hostile to self-government claims by the few national minorities which do exist in the United States. Having emphasized the difference between immigrants and national minorities, one might have expected Walzer and Glazer to endorse the self-government demands of American Indians, Puerto Ricans, native Hawaiians, etc. These groups, after all, really are conquered and colonized peoples, like the national minorities in Europe.

Glazer recognizes that these groups 'possess much more in the way of national characteristics' (1983: 283–4), and that they are demanding national rights on just the grounds that he emphasizes are inapplicable to immigrant groups:

> Both blacks and the Spanish-speaking point to a distinctive political situation: the blacks were brought as slaves, and the Mexicans and Puerto Ricans were conquered. The American Indians were also conquered. The white ethnic groups, however, came as free immigrants. Thus the blacks, the Spanish-speaking groups, the American Indians, and perhaps some other groups can make stronger claims for public support of their distinctive cultures than can European groups. (Glazer 1983: 118)

Glazer accepts that 'there is a good deal of weight' in their demands for national rights (Glazer 1983: 119). Similarly, the logic of Walzer's argument suggests these national minorities should not be forced to accept an approach which is 'not primarily the product of their experience', but rather is 'adapted to the needs of immigrant communities' (Walzer 1982: 6, 27).

Yet liberals in the United States have not endorsed the rights of national minorities. Some liberals simply ignore the existence of such groups. While Glazer and Walzer recognize their existence, they none the less insist that 'benign neglect' is appropriate for them as well as immigrants. Thus Glazer expresses his hope that 'these groups, with proper public policies to stamp out discrimination and inferior status and to encourage acculturation and assimilation, will become not very different from the European and Asian ethnic groups, the ghost nations, bound by nostalgia and sentiment and only occasionally coalescing around distinct interests' (Glazer 1983: 284). Similarly, Walzer hopes that the policies which have worked for immigrants can 'successfully be extended to the racial minorities now asserting their own group claims' (Walzer 1982: 27; cf. Ogbu 1988: 164–5).

Why do Glazer and Walzer reject the implications of their own argument? At one point, Walzer suggests that Indians do not really want national rights: 'Racism is the great barrier to a fully developed pluralism and as long as it exists American Indians and blacks, and perhaps Mexican Americans as well, will be tempted' by national rights. These national rights claims would not be tempting if national minorities had the 'same opportunities for group organization and cultural expression' available to immigrant groups (Walzer 1982: 27).

But there is no evidence that Indians, for example, only desire national rights because they have been prevented from becoming an ethnic group. Indeed, this is completely at odds with the history of Indian tribes in America or Canada. Indians have often been pressured to become 'just another ethnic group', but they have resisted that pressure and fought to protect their distinct status. As I noted earlier, Indians are indeed subject to racism, but the racism they are most concerned with is the racist denial that they are distinct peoples with their own cultures and communities.[16]

In the end, the main reason why Glazer and Walzer reject self-government claims for national minorities is that these claims are, in effect, 'unamerican'. According to Glazer, there

> is such a thing as a state ideology, a national consensus, that shapes and determines what attitude immigrant and minority groups will take toward the alternative possibilities of group maintenance and group rights on the one hand, or individual integration and individual rights on the other . . . The United States, whatever the realities of discrimination and segregation, had as a national ideal a unitary and new ethnic identity, that of American. (Glazer 1978: 100)

Although minority rights are not inherently unfair, they are none the less incompatible with America's 'national consensus' and 'state ideology'.

Similarly, Walzer says that the question of national rights within a multination state 'must itself be worked out politically, and its precise character will depend upon understandings shared among the citizens about the value of cultural diversity, local autonomy, and so on. It is to these understandings that we must appeal when we make our arguments' (Walzer 1983*a*: 29). And in America, the larger political community sees national rights as 'inconsistent with our historical traditions and shared understandings—inconsistent, too, with contemporary living patterns, deeply and bitterly divisive' (Walzer 1983*a*: 151).[17]

This appeal to a 'state ideology' or 'shared understandings' is puzzling. For one thing, their description of the alleged consensus is biased. Walzer and Glazer say the state must either give political recognition to both ethnic and national groups, or deny political recognition to both sorts of groups. But why can the national consensus not emphasize what they themselves emphasize—the difference between the coerced assimilation of minority nations and the voluntary assimilation of immigrants? Why can the national consensus not recognize that national minorities have legitimate claims which voluntary immigrants do not?

Indeed, this is the actual practice in both the USA and Canada. Indians, Inuit, French Canadians, native Hawaiians, and Puerto Ricans all have a special political status that ethnic groups do not have. This has been a long-standing arrangement, and it is not clear why both countries could not continue to support self-government for national minorities but not for ethnic groups.

Walzer and Glazer apparently think that this arrangement is unstable. After asserting that the 'proper' policy is to assimilate national minorities, Glazer goes on to note 'a final complication':

> If the public policy gets turned around to the point where, rather than trying to suppress or ignore the existence of the ethnic group as a distinctive element in American society and polity, it acknowledges a distinctive status for some groups and begins to attach rights in public law to membership in them, will that not react on the others, halfway toward assimilation, and will they not begin to reassert themselves so that they will not be placed at a disadvantage? (1983: 284)

Here is the crux of the matter for Glazer. National minorities who desire recognition of their national rights may have both justice and established practice on their side, but

> Our problem is that we are not a federation of peoples (like Canada or the Soviet Union) but of states, and our ethnic groups are already too dispersed, mixed, assimilated, integrated to permit without confusion a policy that separates out some for special treatment. But if we try, then many other groups will join the queue, or try to, and the hope of a larger fraternity of all Americans will have to be abandoned . . . In a multiethnic society, such a policy can only encourage one group after another to raise claims to special treatment for its protection . . . The demand for special treatment will lead to animus against other groups that already have it, by those who think they should have it and don't. (Glazer 1983: 227–9)

In other words, recognizing the legitimate demands of Indians or Puerto Ricans would make European and Asian ethnic groups demand illegitimate and divisive benefits, and thereby jeopardize the 'larger fraternity of all Americans'.[18]

This is yet another version of Mill's argument about the need for a common identity to ensure stability in a democracy. But it adds a new twist to that argument. Unlike Mill, Glazer is not concerned about the destabilizing impact of the national minorities themselves on domestic stability. In the United States, these groups are too small and geographically isolated to jeopardize the overall stability of the country. And, unlike post-war statesmen, Glazer is not concerned about the potential for national minorities to create international conflict. National minorities in the United States are not irredentist.

Instead, Glazer is concerned about the ripple effect of national minorities on immigrant groups. He is worried that according self-government rights to national minorities will encourage immigrant groups to make similar claims. Is this a realistic fear? I think not. The idea that immigrant groups are looking to establish themselves as national minorities is, I believe, based on a misreading of the 'ethnic revival'. The ethnic revival is not a repudiation of integration into the mainstream society. Even the most politicized ethnic groups are not interested in reconstituting themselves as distinct societies or self-governing nations alongside the mainstream society.

On the contrary, the ethnic revival is essentially a matter of self-identity and self-expression, disconnected from claims for the revival or creation of a separate institutional life. People want to identify themselves in public as members of an ethnic group, and to see others with the same identity in prominent positions of respect or authority (e.g. in politics and the media, or in textbooks and government documents). They are demanding increased recognition and visibility within the mainstream society. The ethnic revival, in other words, involves a revision in the terms of integration, not a rejection of integration (see Ch. 5, s. 5).

Where then did Walzer and Glazer get the idea that ethnic groups were demanding national rights? In retrospect, it may simply be the fact that the ethnic revival amongst American immigrants arose at the same time as nationalist movements resurfaced in Europe and Quebec. But as John Stone notes, this 'coincidence in time' does not mean that the two developments 'were part of the same political process' (Stone 1985: 101).

Some commentators point to demands for affirmative action programmes as evidence of a desire to be treated as a national minority. But that is a mistake. Demands for affirmative action within the mainstream economy are evidence of a desire to integrate into the institutions of the larger society, not a desire for separate and self-governing institutions. And there is no reason to think that accommodating the legitimate demands of national minorities will change this aspiration of immigrants.[19]

In any event, it is worth pointing out how, here again, justice is being sacrificed to stability. Neither Glazer nor Walzer suggests there is anything unfair or illiberal about self-government for national minorities.[20] On the contrary, both give good arguments why national minorities should, in principle, have special political status. Moreover, they admit that the 'national consensus' which rejects such rights was defined by settler groups to suit their own distinctive circumstances, and that national minorities do not share its aims. Like Mill and post-war statesmen, however, they feel that rights for national minorities are inconsistent with political unity, and that the latter takes precedence over the former.

This concludes my overview of the history of minority rights within the liberal tradition. I have noted the striking diversity of views about such rights within the tradition, from strong support to deep anxiety. But what is equally striking is that few if any liberals, until very recently, have supposed that such rights are inherently illiberal. Even those liberals who objected to minority rights did so on grounds of stability, not freedom or justice, and indeed they have often conceded that they are purchasing stability at the price of injustice.

Yet somehow many contemporary liberals have acquired the belief that minority rights are inherently in conflict with liberal principles. Liberals today insist that the liberal commitment to individual liberty precludes the acceptance of collective rights, and that the liberal commitment to universal (colour-blind) rights precludes the acceptance of group-specific rights. But these bald statements are no part of the liberal tradition. Few if any liberals, until very recently, supposed that liberal principles allowed only universal individual rights. What contemporary liberals take to be well-established liberal principles are in fact novel additions to the liberal canon.

Moreover, these new 'principles' are primarily the result of confusions and over-generalizations. I have looked at three factors in the development of the post-war liberal consensus against group-differentiated rights for ethnic and national groups: a *realpolitik* fear about international peace, a commitment to racial equality, and a worry about the escalating demands of immigrant groups. Underlying each is a legitimate concern. But each has also been over-generalized. Certain arguments against the demands of particular groups, based on localized factors (irredentism, racial segregation, voluntary immigration), have been mistakenly generalized to all cases of cultural pluralism. And the combined effect of all three has been a distortion of liberal thinking on minority rights. Out of this mixture has arisen the belief that minority rights are inherently unjust, a betrayal of liberal equality. But these influences, examined more closely, argue the opposite—the first concedes the fairness of minority rights, and the second and third argue against separate political institutions for racial and immigrant groups on grounds that are consistent with, and indeed support, the legitimacy of national rights.

In fact, none of these factors challenges the two basic claims which, I suggested earlier, underlie a liberal defence of minority rights: namely, that individual freedom is tied to membership in one's national group; and that group-specific rights can promote equality between the minority and majority.

In the next two chapters, I will outline a new theory that builds on these two claims. First, however, I want to examine the history of minority rights in the socialist tradition. There are important parallels between the two traditions, and this comparison will further show, I think, the extent to which historical contingencies have shaped (and distorted) modern attitudes towards minority rights.

5. *Minority Rights in the Socialist Tradition*

One might expect socialists to have been hospitable to the idea of rights for cultural communities, since community or fraternity is a key principle of socialism. In fact, however, socialists have traditionally felt hostile towards minority rights, for a variety of reasons.

First, socialism was tied to a particular theory of social evolution. According to many nineteenth-century socialists, socialism was part of (if not the culmination of) a theory of historical development. And development, on this view, involves expansion. Evolution was often defined in terms of expansion in the size of human social units from family and tribe to the local, regional, national, and eventually the global. Smaller cultural communities, therefore, must give way to larger ones.

Marx and Engels, for example, accepted the right of 'the great national subdivisions of Europe' to independence. Hence they supported the unification of France, Italy, Poland, Germany; and the independence of Hungary, Spain, England, and Russia. But they rejected the idea that the smaller 'nationalities' had any such right, such as the Czechs, Croats, Basques, Welsh, Bulgarians, Romanians, and Slovenes. The great nations, with their highly centralized political and economic structures, were the carriers of historical development. The smaller nationalities were backward and stagnant, their continued existence 'nothing more than a protest against a great historical driving power'. Attempts to maintain minority languages were misguided, for the German language was 'the language of liberty' for the Czechs in Bohemia, just as French was the language of liberty for the Bretons.[21]

Hence these smaller 'nationalities' were expected to assimilate to one of the 'great nations', without the benefit of any minority rights, whether it be language rights, or national autonomy. On the contrary, the great nations were entitled to use 'iron ruthlessness' in subduing and assimilating these 'remains of nations'. It was not only the right of the German nation to 'subdue, absorb, and assimilate' smaller nationalities, but also its historical 'mission', and a sign of its historical 'vitality'. As Engels put it, 'By the same right under which France took Flanders, Lorrain and Alsace, and will sooner or later take Belgium—by that same right Germany takes over Schleswig; it is the right of civilisation as against barbarism, of progress as against stability . . . [This] is the right of historical evolution.'

As I discussed earlier, Marx and Engels were not alone in this view. Recall Mill's claim that it is better for the Basque to assimilate to the French than to 'sulk on his own rocks, the half-savage relic of past times, revolving in his own little mental orbit' (Mill 1972: 363–4). Indeed, Hobsbawm says it is 'sheer anachronism' to criticize Marx or Mill for this view, 'which was shared by every impartial mid-nineteenth century observer' (Hobsbawm 1990: 35).

Socialists today have jettisoned this ethnocentric conception of a 'right of historical evolution'. They are now more likely to see ever-increasing centralization as evidence of economic imperialism which subverts local democracy, and which is insensitive to the needs of people for community on a smaller scale. Indeed, whereas Marx thought that bigger was better, many socialists (and environmentalists) now think that small is beautiful. Certain kinds of community and collective action are only possible in smaller groups. Membership in these groups can give a sense of belonging and participation. For that reason, many socialists now seek to decentralize power as much as possible to the municipal or regional level of government.

Some socialists have assumed that decentralization will help meet the needs of ethnic and national minorities. But this is not necessarily the case. Decentralization may actually work to the disadvantage of minority groups. Consider the claims of indigenous peoples in

Brazil's Amazon region. Devolving powers from the federal to the state or local level has hurt the Indian tribes there, since non-indigenous settlers constitute the overwhelming majority at the state and local level. The governors of the states which include the Amazonian Indians favour greater settlement and development, and have bitterly opposed the plans of the federal government to create large native reserves.[22] This is a problem facing indigenous peoples around the world. The greatest opposition to their claims often comes not from the central government, but from the local and state governments in their area, and decentralization has proved disastrous for them.

Decentralization only meets the needs of national minorities if it increases the capacity of the group for self-government. This depends on many factors, including how boundaries are drawn, and how powers are distributed. For example, decentralization to the territorial level in Canada will only help the Inuit if territorial boundaries are redrawn so that they form a majority in the new territory (see Ch. 2). Similarly, decentralization to the municipal level will only help Indian bands if they are given special powers over resource development and social policy not given to (or desired by) city or county councils. The general idea of decentralization, or of empowering local communities, cannot by itself accommodate these demands of cultural groups.[23]

In short, self-government requires, not a general decentralization of power, but the explicit recognition of national groups, through such things as language rights, land claims, an asymmetric distribution of powers, and the redrawing of political boundaries. Generally speaking, socialist proponents of decentralization have not accepted these demands by national groups. Indeed, they have been as reluctant to accord political status to national minorities as the earlier proponents of centralization.

One reason for this reluctance is that socialists have tended to view cultural differences from a narrowly political standpoint, asking only whether cultural identities promote or retard the political struggle for socialism. And most socialists have assumed that ethnic and national identities are a political hindrance. As Garth Stevenson puts it, the left 'has always argued the essential political differences to be those of class, and that politics essentially involves attempts to reconcile class differences. The left has always been suspicious that cultural criteria—whether they be religious, linguistic, ethnic or simply geographic—are devices exploited by the economically powerful to divide people, to prevent them from defining themselves in terms of common class experiences' (Stevenson 1986: 142). National consciousness is seen as precluding and displacing class-consciousness.

In practice, socialists have often appealed to cultural identity where this was helpful in gaining or maintaining power. When the Bolsheviks acquired power in Russia, they realized that they had to accommodate minority cultures, notwithstanding Marx's strictures. They imposed elaborate systems of language rights and national autonomy for minorities in their Eastern European satellites, and became known as ardent defenders of minority rights in the United Nations (Sigler 1983: 186–8). And they supported nationalist movements in non-Communist countries, in the hope of destabilizing Western countries or Western allies in the Third World.

However, these strategic attempts at accommodating cultural communities were developed without any underlying theory regarding the value of cultural identity. There is little sustained reflection within the socialist tradition about why or whether membership in a national minority has any value beyond its strategic role in the struggle for socialism. There are few discussions of what human needs are being met or frustrated by maintaining or losing one's cultural membership.[24] As a result, socialist attempts at accommodating diversity have been largely *ad hoc* and ultimately incoherent.

For example, Lenin was convinced that it was entirely consistent to promote equality for national minorities through language rights and limited forms of local autonomy, yet suppress the religion and literature of a culture, and rewrite its history. National identity, for Lenin, had nothing to do with a shared history, or the value of participating in and revising cultural traditions. It was simply an empty vessel that could be filled up with Communist content. (Stalin later summarized this doctrine as 'national in form, socialist in content'.) Needless to say, this strategy was a failure in terms of both promoting socialism and respecting minority cultures.[25]

Some socialists have opposed minority rights because national differences inhibit the sense of solidarity needed to achieve social justice. The viability of socialism, with its traditional principle of distribution according to need, presupposes that the citizens of a country be willing to make sacrifices for each other. Some socialists believe that this is only possible where citizens share the same national identity.

According to David Miller, for example, egalitarian justice is only possible if citizens are bound to each other by 'common ties', by a strong sense of 'common membership' and 'common identity' which 'must exist at a national level'. Since 'subcultures threaten to undermine the overarching sense of identity', the state must promote 'a common identity as citizens that is stronger than [people's] separate identities as members of ethnic or other sectional groups'. In so far as national minorities view themselves as a distinct people, rather than simply one part of the polyethnic make-up of a common nation, their claims cannot be accommodated. They must either secede or assimilate (Miller 1989: 237, 279, 284, 288).

This is yet another version of Mill's position. Just as Mill thought that 'the united public opinion' necessary for the working of liberal institutions is impossible without a common language and national identity (Mill 1972: 230), so Miller thinks that the 'common purpose' necessary for socialist institutions is only possible in a nation-state (Miller 1988–9).[26]

Whether there is likely to be genuine solidarity in a multination state which allows its component nations to be self-governing is an important question, to which I return in Chapter 9. But it is worth noting that Miller's position assumes that assimilation is a viable option—that is, that the state has the capacity to promote a common national identity amongst all citizens which will displace or take precedence over the existing identity of a national minority. But as I argue in Chapters 5 and 9, it is not clear that this will work. If people's bonds to their own language and culture are sufficiently deep, then attempting to suppress the cultural identity and self-government claims of national minorities may simply aggravate the level of alienation and division. (In this respect, Mill was perhaps more realistic in accepting that creating a common national identity within a multination state may require the coercive assimilation of national minorities.)

For a variety of reasons, then, the socialist tradition has generally opposed minority rights. This is often explained in terms of the Marxian and utopian socialist commitment to 'internationalism'—that is, the claim that workers of the world will unite, and that a classless society will transcend national divisions.

This is an unhelpful explanation. Indeed, it makes the same mistake as those who explain liberal hostility to minority rights in terms of liberalism's 'abstract individualism'. Critics of liberalism often argue that liberals conceive of the individual as a solitary atom who is independent of, and prior to, her cultural environment, and that this is why liberals oppose minority rights.[27]

Neither of these explanations is helpful, since neither can account for the nature and historical development of the views actually adopted by socialists and liberals over the years.[28] The fact is that most socialists (like many liberals) have operated with a model of the nation-state. They have not tried to transcend all national divisions, but rather have assumed that a socialist state should contain and promote a single national identity. As I have discussed, there are a variety of reasons for this—an ethnocentric denigration of smaller cultures, a strategic assessment of the conditions for the acquiring and maintaining of Communist power, and a concern about the development of an effective sense of justice. The result of these factors has been a pronounced tendency to seek the assimilation of minority cultures (or 'nationalities') into larger cultures ('great nations').

Explaining socialist opposition to group-differentiated rights in terms of 'internationalism', or explaining liberal opposition in terms of 'abstract individualism', obscures the real situation. The fact is that both liberals and socialists have accepted the existence of national groups, and the value of national identities. Both recognize that their principles presuppose the existence of national groups between the abstract individual and universal humanity. The problem is that they have often supported the existence and identity of majority nations, while neglecting or denigrating national minorities. References to socialist internationalism and liberal individualism are of no help in understanding this disparity. Indeed, they render this disparity invisible, by pretending that socialists and liberals neglect all cultural groups equally.

I believe that the demands of national minorities and ethnic groups raise a deep challenge to all Western political traditions. All of these traditions have been shaped, implicitly or explicitly, by the same historical influences which have shaped liberal thinking. They have all been guilty of ethnocentric assumptions, or of over-generalizing particular cases, or of conflating contingent political strategy with enduring moral principle. The task of developing a consistent and principled theory of minority rights is not one that liberals face alone.

CHAPTER 5

Freedom and Culture

This book aims to develop a distinctively liberal approach to minority rights. This is not the same as developing the traditional liberal approach, for there is no single traditional approach. There has been a striking diversity of views within the liberal tradition, most of which have been shaped by historical contingencies and political exigencies. To identify a distinctly liberal approach, therefore, we need to start all over again. We need to lay out the basic principles of liberalism, and then see how they bear on the claims of ethnic and national minorities.

The basic principles of liberalism, of course, are principles of individual freedom. Liberals can only endorse minority rights in so far as they are consistent with respect for the freedom or autonomy of individuals. In this chapter, I will show that minority rights are not only consistent with individual freedom, but can actually promote it. I will defend the idea—common in earlier liberal theorists—that 'the cause of liberty' often 'finds its basis in the autonomy of a national group' (Barker 1948: 248).

Of course, some ethnic and national groups are deeply illiberal, and seek to suppress rather than support the liberty of their members. Under these circumstances, acceding to the demands of minority groups may result in gross violations of the most basic liberties of individuals. But in other cases, respecting minority rights can enlarge the freedom of individuals, because freedom is intimately linked with and dependent on culture. My aim in this chapter is to trace this connection between freedom and culture.

I will begin by describing the sort of 'culture' which I think is particularly relevant to individual freedom (s. 1). The modern world is divided into what I will call 'societal cultures', whose practices and institutions cover the full range of human activities, encompassing both public and private life. These societal cultures are typically associated with national groups. I will then try to explain why individual freedom is intimately tied up with membership in these cultures. This will require a brief discussion of the conception of freedom which is central to the liberal tradition (s. 2). I will then show how this freedom is dependent on the presence of a societal culture (s. 3), and why it matters that national minorities have access to their own culture (s. 4). I will also discuss whether immigrant groups should be given the rights and resources necessary to sustain a distinct societal culture, and how liberals should respond to cultures which are illiberal (s. 5).

My aim is to show that the liberal value of freedom of choice has certain cultural preconditions, and hence that issues of cultural membership must be incorporated into liberal principles. This will set up the discussion in the next chapter about how group-differentiated rights for ethnic and national minorities fit within a larger theory of liberal justice.

1. Defining Cultures

As I noted in Chapter 2, the term 'culture' has been used to cover all manner of groups, from teenage gangs to global civilizations. The sort of culture that I will focus on, however, is a *societal* culture—that is, a culture which provides its members with meaningful ways of life across the full range of human activities, including social, educational, religious, recreational, and economic life, encompassing both public and private spheres. These cultures tend to be territorially concentrated, and based on a shared language.[1]

I have called these 'societal cultures' to emphasize that they involve not just shared memories or values, but also common institutions and practices. Ronald Dworkin has said that the members of a culture have 'a shared vocabulary of tradition and convention' (Dworkin 1985: 231). But that gives us an abstract or ethereal picture of cultures. In the case of a societal culture, this shared vocabulary is the everyday vocabulary of social life, embodied in practices covering most areas of human activity. And in the modern world, for a culture to be embodied in social life means that it must be institutionally embodied—in schools, media, economy, government, etc.

Such 'societal cultures' did not always exist, and their creation is intimately linked with the process of modernization (Gellner 1983). Modernization involves the diffusion throughout a society of a common culture, including a standardized language, embodied in common economic, political, and educational institutions. This occurs for a variety of reasons. It is a functional requirement of a modern economy, with its need for a mobile, educated, and literate work-force. Second, it reflects the need for a high level of solidarity within modern democratic states. The sort of solidarity essential for a welfare state requires that citizens have a strong sense of common identity and common membership, so that they will make sacrifices for each other, and this common identity is assumed to require (or at least be facilitated by) a common language and history. Third, the diffusion of a common culture seems required by the modern commitment to equality of opportunity. The provision of standardized public education throughout a society, for example, has been seen as essential to ensure equality of opportunity for people from different classes, races, and regions of the society.

Most contemporary liberals write as if this process of building a common culture extends throughout the entire country, so that there is just one such culture in each country. For example, Dworkin suggest that the United States contains a single 'cultural structure' based on a 'shared language' (Dworkin 1985: 232–3; 1989: 488).

The claim that all Americans share a common culture based on the English language is clearly false. Yet there is a kernel of truth in it. The United States has integrated an extraordinary number of people from very different backgrounds into a common culture. The vast majority of Americans do in fact participate in the same societal culture, based on the English language. At other times and places, differences in ethnicity, race, region, class, gender, and religion were often assumed to preclude the possibility of a common culture. But in the United States and other modern societies, the common culture is capacious, integrating a rich array of groups.

If there is not a single culture in the United States, there is a dominant culture that incorporates most Americans, and those who fall outside it belong to a relatively small number of minority cultures. To understand the impressive integrative power of this common culture, but also its limits, it is worth examining how immigrants and national minorities relate to the dominant American culture.

When immigrants come to the United States, they bring their language and historical narratives with them. But they have left behind the set of institutionalized practices, conducted in their mother tongue, which actually provided culturally significant ways of life to people in their original homeland. They bring with them a 'shared vocabulary of tradition and convention', but they have uprooted themselves from the social practices which this vocabulary originally referred to and made sense of.

Some immigrants might hope to re-create these practices in their entirety in their new country. But that is effectively impossible without significant government support, which is rarely if ever provided. On the contrary, as we saw in Chapters 2 and 3, immigration policy in the United States is intended to integrate immigrants within the existing English-speaking culture. Immigrants come as individuals or families, rather than entire communities, and settle throughout the country, rather than forming 'homelands'. They are expected to learn the English language and American history, and to speak English in public life—e.g. at school, work, and when interacting with governments and other public agencies. (I discuss whether this is legitimate or not below.)

Immigrants are no longer expected to assimilate entirely to the norms and customs of the dominant culture, and indeed are encouraged to maintain some aspects of their ethnic particularity. But this commitment to 'multiculturalism' or 'polyethnicity' is a shift in *how* immigrants integrate into the dominant culture, not whether they integrate. The rejection of 'Anglo-conformity' primarily has involved affirming the right of immigrants to maintain their ethnic heritage in the private sphere—at home, and in voluntary associations. To a lesser extent, it also involved reforming the public institutions of the dominant culture so as to provide some recognition or accommodation of their heritage. But it has not involved the establishment of distinct and institutionally complete societal cultures alongside the anglophone society. (By 'institutionally complete', I mean containing a full range of social, educational, economic, and political institutions, encompassing both public and private life.)

Under these conditions, the immigrants' mother tongue is often spoken at home, and passed on to the children, but by the third generation English has become the mother tongue, and the original language is increasingly lost. This process is speeded up, of course, by the fact that public schooling is only provided in English. In fact, it is very difficult for languages to survive in modern industrialized societies unless they are used in public life. Given the spread of standardized education, the high demands for literacy in work, and widespread interaction with government agencies, any language which is not a public language becomes so marginalized that it is likely to survive only amongst a small élite, or in a ritualized form, not as a living and developing language underlying a flourishing culture.[2]

So while there are many aspects of their heritage that immigrants will maintain and cherish, this will take the form not of re-creating a separate societal culture, but rather of contributing new options and perspectives to the larger anglophone culture, making it richer and more diverse. For the third generation, if not sooner, learning the original mother tongue is not unlike learning a foreign language. Learning the old language may be rewarding as a hobby or business skill, but for the children of immigrants, it is the anglophone culture which defines their options, not the culture from which their parents uprooted themselves.[3]

The situation of national minorities in the United States—i.e. groups whose homeland has been incorporated through conquest, colonization, or federation—is very different. At the time of their incorporation, each group constituted an ongoing societal culture, separate from the anglophone culture. They did not have to re-create their culture in a new land, since their language and historical narratives were already embodied in a full set of social practices and institutions, encompassing all aspects of social life. These practices and institutions defined the range of socially meaningful options for their members.

These groups have fought to retain their existence as distinct societal cultures, although not all have been accorded the language and self-government rights necessary to do so. Indeed, some groups have faced enormous pressures to assimilate. In the case of many Indian tribes, for example, there have been prohibitions on the use of their mother tongue, and attempts to break open their lands for settlement so that they have become minorities in their historical homelands. Yet they have persisted, and their status as self-governing 'domestic dependent nations' is now more firmly recognized. The determination they have shown in maintaining their existence as distinct cultures, despite these enormous economic and political pressures, shows the value they attach to retaining their cultural membership.

So the typical situation of immigrant groups and national minorities is very different. Of course, I have over-simplified the contrast. The extent to which immigrant groups have been allowed or encouraged to integrate varies considerably, as does the extent to which national minorities have been able to maintain a separate culture (see below.)

But, as a general rule, both in the United States and in other Western democracies, dominant cultures have had far less success accommodating national groups than ethnic groups. In multination states, national minorities have resisted integration into the common culture, and instead sought to protect their separate existence by consolidating their own societal cultures. American Indian tribes and Puerto Ricans, like the Aboriginal peoples and Québécois in Canada, are not just subgroups within a common culture, but genuinely distinct societal cultures.

In short, for a culture to survive and develop in the modern world, given the pressures towards the creation of a single common culture in each country, it must be a societal culture.[4] Given the enormous significance of social institutions in our lives, and in determining our options, any culture which is not a societal culture will be reduced to ever-decreasing marginalization. The capacity and motivation to form and maintain such a distinct culture is characteristic of 'nations' or 'peoples' (i.e. culturally distinct, geographically concentrated, and institutionally complete societies). Societal cultures, then, tend to be national cultures.

This connection is confirmed from another direction, by studies of nationalism. Most analysts of nationalism have concluded that the defining feature of nations is that they are 'pervasive cultures', 'encompassing cultures', or 'organizational cultures' (e.g. A. Smith 1986: 2; Margalit and Raz 1990: 444; Tamir 1993; Poole 1993). In short, just as societal cultures are almost invariably national cultures, so nations are almost invariably societal cultures.

2. *Liberalism and Individual Freedom*

I believe that societal cultures are important to people's freedom, and that liberals should therefore take an interest in the viability of societal cultures. To show this, however, I need briefly to consider the nature of freedom, as it is conceived within the liberal tradition.[5]

The defining feature of liberalism is it that ascribes certain fundamental freedoms to each individual. In particular, it grants people a very wide freedom of choice in terms of how they lead their lives. It allows people to choose a conception of the good life, and then allows them to reconsider that decision, and adopt a new and hopefully better plan of life.

Why should people be free to choose their own plan of life? After all, we know that some people will make imprudent decisions, wasting their time on hopeless or trivial pursuits. Why then should the government not intervene to protect us from making mistakes, and to compel us to lead the truly good life? There are a variety of reasons why this is not a good idea: governments may not be trustworthy; some individuals have idiosyncratic needs which are difficult for even a well-intentioned government to take into account; supporting controversial conceptions of the good may lead to civil strife. Moreover, paternalistic restrictions on liberty often simply do not work—lives do not go better by being led from the outside, in accordance with values the person does not endorse. Dworkin calls this the 'endorsement constraint', and argues that 'no component contributes to the value of a life without endorsement . . . it is implausible to think that someone can lead a better life against the grain of his profound ethical convictions than at peace with them' (Dworkin 1989: 486).[6]

However, the fact that we can get it wrong is important, because (paradoxically) it provides another argument for liberty. Since we can be wrong about the worth or value of what we are currently doing, and since no one wants to lead a life based on false beliefs about its worth, it is of fundamental importance that we be able rationally to assess our conceptions of the good in the light of new information or experiences, and to revise them if they are not worthy of our continued allegiance.[7]

This assumption that our beliefs about the good life are fallible and revisable is widely endorsed in the liberal tradition—from John Stuart Mill to the most prominent contemporary American liberals, such as John Rawls and Ronald Dworkin. (Because of their prominence, I will rely heavily on the works of Rawls and Dworkin in the rest of this chapter.) As Rawls puts it, individuals 'do not view themselves as inevitably tied to the pursuit of the particular conception of the good and its final ends which they espouse at any given time'. Instead, they are 'capable of revising and changing this conception'. They can 'stand back' from their current ends to 'survey and assess' their worthiness (Rawls 1980: 544; cf. Mill 1982: 122; Dworkin 1983).

So we have two preconditions for leading a good life. The first is that we lead our life from the inside, in accordance with our beliefs about what gives value to life. Individuals must therefore have the resources and liberties needed to lead their lives in accordance with their beliefs about value, without fear of discrimination or punishment. Hence the traditional liberal concern with individual privacy, and opposition to 'the enforcement of morals'. The second precondition is that we be free to question those beliefs, to examine them in light of whatever information, examples, and arguments our culture can provide. Individuals must therefore have the conditions necessary to acquire an awareness of different views about the good life, and an ability to examine these views intelligently. Hence the equally traditional liberal concern for education, and freedom of expression and association. These liberties enable us to judge what is valuable, and to learn about other ways of life.

It is important to stress that a liberal society is concerned with both of these preconditions, the second as much as the first. It is all too easy to reduce individual liberty to the freedom to pursue one's conception of the good. But in fact much of what is distinctive to a liberal state concerns the forming and revising of people's conceptions of the good, rather than the pursuit of those conceptions once chosen.

Consider the case of religion. A liberal society not only allows individuals the freedom to pursue their existing faith, but it also allows them to seek new adherents for their faith (proselytization is allowed), or to question the doctrine of their church (heresy is allowed), or to renounce their faith entirely and convert to another faith or to atheism (apostasy is allowed). It is quite conceivable to have the freedom to pursue one's current faith without having any of these latter freedoms. There are many examples of this within the Islamic world. Islam has a long tradition of tolerating other monotheistic religions, so that Christians and Jews can worship in peace. But proselytization, heresy, and apostasy are generally prohibited. This was true, for example, of the 'millet system' of the Ottoman Empire, which I will look at in more depth in Chapter 8. Indeed, some Islamic states have said the freedom of conscience guaranteed in the Universal Declaration of Human Rights should not include the freedom to change religion (Lerner 1991: 79–80). Similarly, the clause in the Egyptian constitution guaranteeing freedom of conscience has been interpreted so as to exclude freedom of apostasy (Peters and de Vries 1976: 23). In such a system, freedom of conscience means there is no forced conversion, but nor is there voluntary conversion.

A liberal society, by contrast, not only allows people to pursue their current way of life, but also gives them access to information about other ways of life (through freedom of expression), and indeed requires children to learn about other ways of life (through mandatory education), and makes it possible for people to engage in radical revision of their ends (including apostasy) without legal penalty. These aspects of a liberal society only make sense on the assumption that revising one's ends is possible, and sometimes desirable, because one's current ends are not always worthy of allegiance. A liberal society does not compel such questioning and revision, but it does make it a genuine possibility.

3. *Societal Cultures as Context of Choice*

I have just outlined what I take to be the predominant liberal conception of individual freedom. But how does this relate to membership in societal cultures? Put simply, freedom involves making choices amongst various options, and our societal culture not only provides these options, but also makes them meaningful to us.

People make choices about the social practices around them, based on their beliefs about the value of these practices (beliefs which, I have noted, may be wrong). And to have a belief about the value of a practice is, in the first instance, a matter of understanding the meanings attached to it by our culture.

I noted earlier that societal cultures involve 'a shared vocabulary of tradition and convention' which underlies a full range of social practices and institutions (Dworkin 1985: 231). To understand the meaning of a social practice, therefore, requires understanding this 'shared vocabulary'—that is, understanding the language and history which constitute that vocabulary. Whether or not a course of action has any significance for us depends on whether, and how, our language renders vivid to us the point of that activity. And the way in which language renders vivid these activities is shaped by our history, our 'traditions and conventions'. Understanding these cultural narratives is a precondition of making intelligent judgements about how to lead our lives. In this sense, our culture not only provides options, it also 'provides the spectacles through which we identify experiences as valuable' (Dworkin 1985: 228).[8]

What follows from this? According to Dworkin, we must protect our societal culture from 'structural debasement or decay' (1985: 230).[9] The survival of a culture is not guaranteed, and, where it is threatened with debasement or decay, we must act to protect it. Cultures are valuable, not in and of themselves, but because it is only through having access to a societal culture that people have access to a range of meaningful options. Dworkin concludes his discussion by saying, 'We inherited a cultural structure, and we have some duty, out of simple justice, to leave that structure at least as rich as we found it' (1985: 232–3).

In this passage and elsewhere, Dworkin talks about 'cultural structures'. This is a potentially misleading term, since it suggests an overly formal and rigid picture of what (as I discuss below) is a very diffuse and open-ended phenomenon. Cultures do not have fixed centres or precise boundaries. But his main point is, I think, sound enough. The availability of meaningful options depends on access to a societal culture, and on understanding the history and language of that culture—its 'shared vocabulary of tradition and convention' (Dworkin 1985: 228, 231).[10]

This argument about the connection between individual choice and culture provides the first step towards a distinctively liberal defence of certain group-differentiated rights. For meaningful individual choice to be possible, individuals need not only access to information, the capacity to reflectively evaluate it, and freedom of expression and association. They also need access to a societal culture. Group-differentiated measures that secure and promote this access may, therefore, have a legitimate role to play in a liberal theory of justice.[11]

Of course, many details remain to be filled in, and many objections need to be answered. In particular, this connection between individual choice and societal cultures raises three obvious questions: (1) is individual choice tied to membership in one's *own* culture, or is it sufficient for people to have access to some or other culture? (2) if (as I will argue) people have a deep bond to their own culture, should immigrant groups be given the rights and resources necessary to re-create their own societal cultures? and (3) what if a culture is organized so as to preclude individual choice—for example, if it assigns people a specific role or way of life, and prohibits any questioning or revising of that role? I will start answering these questions in the rest of the chapter, although a full answer will only emerge in later chapters.

4. *The Value of Cultural Membership*

I have tried to show that people's capacity to make meaningful choices depends on access to a cultural structure. But why do the members of a national minority need access to their *own* culture?[12] Why not let minority cultures disintegrate, so long as we ensure their members have access to the majority culture (e.g. by teaching them the majority language and history)? This latter option would involve a cost to minorities, but governments could subsidize it. For example, governments could pay for the members of national minorities to learn about the majority language and history.

This sort of proposal treats the loss of one's culture as similar to the loss of one's job. Language training for members of a threatened culture would be like worker retraining programmes for employees of a dying industry. We do not feel obliged to keep uncompetitive industries afloat in perpetuity, so long as we help employees to find employment elsewhere, so why feel obliged to protect minority cultures, so long as we help their members to find another culture?

This is an important question. It would be implausible to say that people are never able to switch cultures. After all, many immigrants function well in their new country (although others flounder, and many return home). Waldron thinks that these examples of successful 'cosmopolitan' people who move between cultures disprove the claim that people are connected to their own culture in any deep way. Suppose, he says, that

> a freewheeling cosmopolitan life, lived in a kaleidoscope of cultures, is both possible and fulfilling. . . . Immediately, one argument for the protection of minority cultures is undercut. It can no longer be said that all people need their rootedness in the particular culture in which they and their ancestors were reared in the way that they need food, clothing, and shelter . . . Such immersion may be something that particular people like and enjoy. But they no longer can claim that it is something that they need. . . . The collapse of the Herderian argument based on distinctively human *need* seriously undercuts any claim that minority cultures might have to special support or assistance or to extraordinary provision or forbearance. At best, it leaves the right to culture roughly on the same footing as the right to religious freedom. (Waldron 1992*a*: 762)

Because people do not need their own culture, minority cultures can ('at best') claim the same negative rights as religious groups—that is, the right to non-interference, but not to state support.

I think Waldron is seriously overstating the case here. For one thing, he vastly overestimates the extent to which people do in fact move between cultures, because (as I discuss below) he assumes that cultures are based on ethnic descent. On his view, an Irish-American who eats Chinese food and reads her child *Grimms' Fairy-Tales* is thereby 'living in a kaleidoscope of cultures' (e.g. Waldron 1992*a*: 754). But this is not moving between societal cultures. Rather it is enjoying the opportunities provided by the diverse societal culture which characterizes the anglophone society of the United States.

Of course, people do genuinely move between cultures. But this is rarer, and more difficult. In some cases, where the differences in social organization and technological development are vast, successful integration may be almost impossible for some members of the minority. (This seems to be true of the initial period of contact between European cultures and indigenous peoples in some parts of the world.)

But even where successful integration is possible, it is rarely easy. It is a costly process, and there is a legitimate question whether people should be required to pay those costs unless they voluntarily choose to do so. These costs vary, depending on the gradualness of the process, the age of the person, and the extent to which the two cultures are similar in language and history.[13] But even where the obstacles to integration are smallest, the desire of national minorities to retain their cultural membership remains very strong (just as the members of the majority culture typically value their cultural membership).

In this sense, the choice to leave one's culture can be seen as analogous to the choice to take a vow of perpetual poverty and enter a religious order. It is not impossible to live in poverty. But it does not follow that a liberal theory of justice should therefore view the desire for a level of material resources above bare subsistence simply as 'something that particular people like and enjoy' but which 'they no longer can claim is something that they need' (Waldron 1992*a*: 762). Liberals rightly assume that the desire for nonsubsistence resources is so normal—and the costs of forgoing them so high for most people's way of life—that people cannot reasonably be *expected* to go without such resources, even if a few people voluntarily choose to do so. For the purposes of determining people's claims of justice, material resources are something that people can be assumed to want, whatever their particular conception of the good. Although a small number of people may choose to forgo non-subsistence resources, this is seen as forgoing something to which they are entitled.

Similarly, I believe that, in developing a theory of justice, we should treat access to one's culture as something that people can be expected to want, whatever their more particular conception of the good. Leaving one's culture, while possible, is best seen as renouncing something to which one is reasonably entitled. This is a claim, not about the limits of human possibility, but about reasonable expectations.

I think that most liberals have implicitly accepted this claim about people's legitimate expectation to remain in their culture. Consider Rawls's argument about why the right to emigrate does not make political authority voluntary:

> normally leaving one's country is a grave step: it involves leaving the society and culture in which we have been raised, the society and culture whose language we use in speech and thought to express and understand ourselves, our aims, goals, and values; the society and culture whose history, customs, and conventions we depend on to find our place in the social world. In large part, we affirm our society and culture, and have an intimate and inexpressible knowledge of it, even though much of it we may question, if not reject. The government's authority cannot, then, be freely accepted in the sense that the bonds of society and culture, of history and social place of origin, begin so early to shape our life and are normally so strong that the right of emigration (suitably qualified) does not suffice to make accepting its authority free, politically speaking, in the way that liberty of conscience suffices to make accepting ecclesiastical authority free. (Rawls 1993*a*: 222)

Because of these bonds to the 'language we use in speech and thought to express and understand ourselves', cultural ties 'are normally too strong to be given up, and this fact is not to be deplored'. Hence, for the purposes of developing a theory of justice, we should assume that 'people are born and are expected to lead a complete life' within the same 'society and culture' (Rawls 1993*a*: 277).

I agree with Rawls's view about the difficulty of leaving one's culture.[14] Yet his argument has implications beyond those which he himself draws. Rawls presents this as an argument about the difficulty of leaving one's political community. But his argument does not rest on the value of specifically political ties (e.g. the bonds to one's government and fellow citizens). Rather it rests on the value of cultural ties (e.g. bonds to one's language and history). And cultural boundaries may not coincide with political boundaries. For example, someone leaving East Germany for West Germany in 1950 would not be breaking the ties of language and culture which Rawls emphasizes, even though she would be crossing state borders. But a francophone leaving Quebec City for Toronto, or a Puerto Rican leaving San Juan for Chicago, would be breaking those ties, even though she is remaining within the same country.

According to Rawls, then, the ties to one's culture are normally too strong to give up, and this is not to be regretted. We cannot be expected or required to make such a sacrifice, even if some people voluntarily do so. It is an interesting question why the bonds of language and culture are so strong for most people. It seems particularly puzzling that people would have a strong attachment to a liberalized culture. After all, as a culture is liberalized—and so allows members to question and reject traditional ways of life—the resulting cultural identity becomes both 'thinner' and less distinctive. That is, as a culture becomes more liberal, the members are less and less likely to share the same substantive conception of the good life, and more and more likely to share basic values with people in other liberal cultures.

The Québécois provide a nice illustration of this process. Before the Quiet Revolution, the Québécois generally shared a rural, Catholic, conservative, and patriarchal conception of the good. Today, after a rapid period of liberalization, most people have abandoned this traditional way of life, and Québécois society now exhibits all the diversity that any modern society contains—e.g. atheists and Catholics, gays and heterosexuals, urban yuppies and rural farmers, socialists and conservatives, etc. To be a 'Québécois' today, therefore, simply means being a participant in the francophone society of Quebec. And francophones in Quebec no more agree about conceptions of the good than anglophones in the United States. So being a 'Québécois' seems to be a very thin form of identity.

Moreover, the process of liberalization has also meant that the Québécois have become much more like English Canadians in their basic values. Liberalization in Quebec over the last thirty years has been accompanied by a pronounced convergence in personal and political values between English- and French-speaking Canadians, so that it would now be 'difficult to identify consistent differences in attitudes on issues such as moral values, prestige ranking of professions, role of the government, workers' rights, aboriginal rights, equality between the sexes and races, and conception of authority' (Dion 1992: 99; cf. Dion 1991: 301; Taylor 1991: 54).[15]

In short, liberalization in Quebec has meant both an increase in differences amongst the Québécois, in terms of their conceptions of the good, and a reduction in differences between the Québécois and the members of other liberal cultures. This is not unique to Quebec. The same process is at work throughout Europe. The modernization and liberalization of Western Europe has resulted both in fewer commonalities within each of the national cultures, and greater commonalities across these cultures. As Spain has liberalized, it has become both more pluralistic internally, and more like France or Germany in terms of its modern, secular, industrialized, democratic, and consumerist civilization.

This perhaps explains why so many theorists have assumed that liberalization and modernization would displace any strong sense of national identity. As cultures liberalize, people share less and less with their fellow members of the national group, in terms of traditional customs or conceptions of the good life, and become more and more like the members of other nations, in terms of sharing a common civilization. Why then would anyone feel strongly attached to their own nation? Such an attachment seems, to many commentators, like the 'narcissism of minor differences' (Ignatieff 1993: 21; Dion 1991).

Yet the evidence is overwhelming that the members of liberal cultures *do* value their cultural membership. Far from displacing national identity, liberalization has in fact gone hand in hand with an increased sense of nationhood. Many of the liberal reformers in Quebec have been staunch nationalists, and the nationalist movement grew in strength throughout the Quiet Revolution and afterwards. The same combination of liberalization and a strengthened national identity can be found in many other countries. For example, in Belgium, the liberalization of Flemish society has been accompanied by a sharp rise in nationalist sentiment (Peterson 1975: 208). The fact that their culture has become tolerant and pluralistic has in no way diminished the pervasiveness or intensity of people's desire to live and work in their own culture. Indeed, Walker Connor goes so far as to suggest that few if any examples exist of recognized national groups in this century having voluntarily assimilated to another culture, even though many have had significant economic incentives and political pressures to do so (Connor 1972: 350–1; 1973: 20).

Why are the bonds of language and culture so strong for most people? Commentators offer a number of reasons. Margalit and Raz argue that membership in a societal culture (what they call a 'pervasive culture') is crucial to people's well-being for two reasons. The first reason is the one I have discussed above—namely, that cultural membership provides meaningful options, in the sense that 'familiarity with a culture determines the boundaries of the imaginable'. Hence if a culture is decaying or discriminated against, 'the options and opportunities open to its members will shrink, become less attractive, and their pursuit less likely to be successful' (Margalit and Raz 1990: 449).

But why cannot the members of a decaying culture simply integrate into another culture? According to Margalit and Raz, this is difficult, not only because it is 'a very slow process indeed', but also because of the role of cultural membership in people's self-identity. Cultural membership has a 'high social profile', in the sense that it affects how others perceive and respond to us, which in turn shapes our self-identity. Moreover, national identity is particularly suited to serving as the 'primary foci of identification', because it is based on belonging, not accomplishment:

> Identification is more secure, less liable to be threatened, if it does not depend on accomplishment. Although accomplishments play their role in people's sense of their own identity, it would seem that at the most fundamental level our sense of our own identity depends on criteria of belonging rather than on those of accomplishment. Secure identification at that level is particularly important to one's well-being.

Hence cultural identity provides an 'anchor for [people's] self-identification and the safety of effortless secure belonging'. But this in turn means that people's self-respect is bound up with the esteem in which their national group is held. If a culture is not generally respected, then the dignity and self-respect of its members will also be threatened (Margalit and Raz 1990: 447–9). Similar arguments about the role of respect for national membership in supporting dignity and self-identity are given by Charles Taylor (1992*a*) and Yael Tamir (1993: 41, 71–3).

Tamir also emphasizes the extent to which cultural membership adds an 'additional meaning' to our actions, which become not only acts of individual accomplishment, but also 'part of a continuous creative effort whereby culture is made and remade'. And she argues that, where institutions are 'informed by a culture [people] find understandable and meaningful', this 'allows a certain degree of transparency that facilitates their participation in public affairs'. This in turn promotes a sense of belonging and relationships of mutual recognition and mutual responsibility (Tamir 1993: 72, 85–6). Other commentators make the related point that the mutual intelligibility which comes from shared national identity promotes relationships of solidarity and trust (Miller 1993; Barry 1991: 174–5). James Nickel emphasizes the potential harm to valuable intergenerational bonds when parents are unable to pass on their culture to their children and grandchildren (Nickel 1995). Benedict Anderson emphasizes the way national identity enables us to transcend our mortality, by linking us to something whose existence seems to extend back into time immemorial, and forward into the indefinite future (Anderson 1983).

No doubt all of these factors play a role in explaining people's bond to their own culture. I suspect that the causes of this attachment lie deep in the human condition, tied up with the way humans as cultural creatures need to make sense of their world, and that a full explanation would involve aspects of psychology, sociology, linguistics, the philosophy of mind, and even neurology (Laponce 1987).

But whatever the explanation, this bond does seem to be a fact, and, like Rawls, I see no reason to regret it. I should emphasize, again, that I am only dealing with general trends. Some people seem most at home leading a truly cosmopolitan life, moving freely between different societal cultures. Others have difficulty making sense of the cultural meanings within their own culture. But most people, most of the time, have a deep bond to their own culture.

It may seem paradoxical for liberals like Rawls to claim that the bonds to one's culture are 'normally too strong to be given up'. What has happened to the much vaunted liberal freedom of choice? But Rawls's view is in fact common within the liberal tradition, as we saw in Chapter 4. The freedom which liberals demand for individuals is not primarily the freedom to go beyond one's language and history, but rather the freedom to move around within one's societal culture, to distance oneself from particular cultural roles, to choose which features of the culture are most worth developing, and which are without value.

This may sound like a rather 'communitarian' view of the self. I do not think this is an accurate label. One prominent theme in recent communitarian writing is the rejection of the liberal view about the importance of being free to revise one's ends. Communitarians deny that we can 'stand apart' from (some of) our ends. According to Michael Sandel, a leading American communitarian, some of our ends are 'constitutive' ends, in the sense that they define our sense of personal identity (Sandel 1982: 150–65; cf. MacIntyre 1981: ch. 15; Bell 1993: 24–54). It makes no sense, on his view, to say that my ends might not be worthy of my allegiance, for they define who I am. Whereas Rawls claims that individuals 'do not regard themselves as inevitably bound to, or identical with, the pursuit of any particular complex of fundamental interests that they may have at any given moment' (1974: 641), Sandel responds that we are in fact 'identical with' at least some of our final ends. Since these ends are constitutive of people's identity, there is no reason why the state should not reinforce people's allegiance to those ends, and limit their ability to question and revise these ends.

I believe that this communitarian conception of the self is mistaken. It is not easy or enjoyable to revise one's deepest ends, but it is possible, and sometimes a regrettable necessity. New experiences or circumstances may reveal that our earlier beliefs about the good are mistaken. No end is immune from such potential revision. As Dworkin puts it, it is true that 'no one can put everything about himself in question all at once', but it 'hardly follows that for each person there is some one connection or association so fundamental that it cannot be detached for inspection while holding others in place' (Dworkin 1989: 489).

Some people may think of themselves as being incapable of questioning or revising their ends, but in fact 'our conceptions of the good may and often do change over time, usually slowly but sometimes rather suddenly', even for those people who think of themselves as having constitutive ends (Rawls 1985: 242). No matter how confident we are about our ends at a particular moment, new circumstances or experiences may arise, often in unpredictable ways, that cause us to re-evaluate them. There is no way to predict in advance when the need for such a reconsideration will arise. As I noted earlier, a liberal society does not compel people to revise their commitments—and many people will go years without having any reason to question their basic commitments—but it does recognize that the freedom of choice is not a one-shot affair, and that earlier choices sometimes need to be revisited.

Since our judgements about the good are fallible in this way, we have an interest, not only in pursuing our existing conception of the good, but also in being able to assess and potentially revise that conception. Our current ends are not always worthy of our continued allegiance, and exposure to other ways of life helps us make informed judgements about what is truly valuable.

The view I am defending is quite different, therefore, from the communitarian one, although both views claim that we have a deep bond to a particular sort of social group. The difference is partly a matter of scope. Communitarians typically talk about our attachment to subnational groups—churches, neighbourhoods, family, unions, etc.—rather than to the larger society which encompasses these subgroups. But this difference in scope reflects an even deeper divergence. Communitarians are looking for groups which are defined by a shared conception of the good. They seek to promote a 'politics of the common good', in which groups can promote a shared conception of the good, even if this limits the ability of individual members to revise their ends. They believe that members have a 'constitutive' bond to the group's values, and so no harm is done by limiting individual rights in order to promote shared values.

As most communitarians admit, this 'politics of the common good' cannot apply at the national level. As Sandel puts it, 'the nation proved too vast a scale across which to cultivate the shared self-understandings necessary to community in the . . . constitutive sense' (Sandel 1984: 93; cf. MacIntyre 1981: 221; Miller 1988–9: 60–7). The members of a nation rarely share moral values or traditional ways of life. They share a language and history, but often disagree fundamentally about the ultimate ends in life. A common national identity, therefore, is not a useful basis for communitarian politics, which can only exist at a more local level.

The liberal view I am defending insists that people can stand back and assess moral values and traditional ways of life, and should be given not only the legal right to do so, but also the social conditions which enhance this capacity (e.g. a liberal education). So I object to communitarian politics at the subnational level. To inhibit people from questioning their inherited social roles can condemn them to unsatisfying, even oppressive, lives.[16] And at the national level, the very fact which makes national identity so inappropriate for communitarian politics—namely, that it does not rest on shared values—is precisely what makes it an appropriate basis for liberal politics. The national culture provides a meaningful context of choice for people, without limiting their ability to question and revise particular values or beliefs.

Put another way, the liberal ideal is a society of free and equal individuals. But what is the relevant 'society'? For most people it seems to be their nation. The sort of freedom and equality they most value, and can make most use of, is freedom and equality within their own societal culture. And they are willing to forgo a wider freedom and equality to ensure the continued existence of their nation.

For example, few people favour a system of open borders, where people could freely cross borders and settle, work, and vote in whatever country they desired. Such a system would dramatically increase the domain within which people would be treated as free and equal citizens. Yet open borders would also make it more likely that people's own national community would be overrun by settlers from other cultures, and that they would be unable to ensure their survival as a distinct national culture. So we have a choice between, on the one hand, increased mobility and an expanded domain within which people are free and equal individuals, and, on the other hand, decreased mobility but a greater assurance that people can continue to be free and equal members of their own national culture. Most people in liberal democracies clearly favour the latter. They would rather be free and equal within their own nation, even if this means they have less freedom to work and vote elsewhere, than be free and equal citizens of the world, if this means they are less likely to be able to live and work in their own language and culture.

And most theorists in the liberal tradition have implicitly agreed with this. Few major liberal theorists have endorsed open borders, or even seriously considered it. They have generally accepted—indeed, simply taken for granted—that the sort of freedom and equality which matters most to people is freedom and equality within one's societal culture. Like Rawls, they assume that 'people are born and are expected to lead a complete life' within the same 'society and culture', and that this defines the scope within which people must be free and equal (Rawls 1993*a*: 277).[17]

In short, liberal theorists have generally, if implicitly, accepted that cultures or nations are basic units of liberal political theory. In this sense, as Yael Tamir puts it, 'most liberals are liberal nationalists' (1993: 139)—that is, liberal goals are achieved in and through a liberalized societal culture or nation.

5. Hard Cases

So far, I have suggested that liberals should care about the viability of societal cultures, because they contribute to people's autonomy, and because people are deeply connected to their own culture. I have also argued that national minorities typically have the sort of societal culture that should be protected, while immigrants typically do not, since they instead integrate into, and thereby enrich, the culture of the larger society. This leaves a number of unresolved questions: (1) how should liberal states respond to societal cultures that are illiberal? (2) if people have such a deep bond with their own language and culture, why not allow immigrants to develop their own societal cultures? and (3) have some national minorities over time ceased to possess a societal culture? I will look at each in turn.

1. How should liberals respond to illiberal cultures? Some nations and nationalist movements are deeply illiberal. Some cultures, far from enabling autonomy, simply assign particular roles and duties to people, and prevent people from questioning or revising them. Other cultures allow this autonomy to some, while denying it to others, such as women, lower castes, or visible minorities. Clearly, these sorts of cultures do not promote liberal values.

This shows that liberals cannot endorse cultural membership uncritically. Indeed, if the liberal commitment to respecting national identity flows from its role in enabling autonomy, should we not encourage or compel the members of illiberal cultures to assimilate to more liberal cultures? But again this ignores the way people are bound to their own cultures. The aim of liberals should not be to dissolve non-liberal nations, but rather to seek to liberalize them. This may not always be possible. But it is worth remembering that all existing liberal nations had illiberal pasts, and their liberalization required a prolonged process of institutional reform. To assume that any culture is inherently illiberal, and incapable of reform, is ethnocentric and ahistorical. Moreover, the liberality of a culture is a matter of degree. All cultures have illiberal strands, just as few cultures are entirely repressive of individual liberty. Indeed, it is quite misleading to talk of 'liberal' and 'illiberal' cultures, as if the world was divided into completely liberal societies on the one hand, and completely illiberal ones on the other. The task of liberal reform remains incomplete in every society, and it would be ludicrous to say that only purely liberal nations should be respected, while others should be assimilated.

So, as a general rule, liberals should not prevent illiberal nations from maintaining their societal culture, but should promote the liberalization of these cultures. The issue of how to promote liberalization, and more generally how liberal states should treat non-liberal minorities, is a large topic, which I pursue at length in Chapter 8.

2. If people have a deep bond with their own culture, as I have suggested, should we not allow immigrants to re-create their own societal cultures (and thereby effectively become a national minority)? There is nothing incoherent or impossible about this proposal. After all, many existing nations were initially formed by uprooted settlers establishing colonies in a new land. This is true of the English and French nations in Canada and the United States.

But there are important differences between colonists and immigrants. As Steinberg notes of the English colonists in America, 'it is not really correct to refer to the colonial settlers as "immigrants". They came not as migrants entering an alien society, forced to acquire a new national identity, but as a colonial vanguard that would create a new England in the image of the one they left behind.' They distinguished themselves from the non-English colonials who 'were typically regarded as aliens who were obliged to adapt to English rule in terms of both politics and culture' (Steinberg 1981: 7).[18] There was a fundamentally different set of expectations accompanying colonization and immigration—the former resulted from a deliberate policy aimed at the systematic re-creation of an entire society in a new land; the latter resulted from individual and familial choices to leave their society and join another existing society.

None the less, this just raises the question—should governments treat immigrants as if they were colonists? Why not encourage immigrants to settle together—even set aside homelands for them—and give them the resources and self-government powers necessary to re-create a societal culture based on their mother tongue? Some consideration was in fact given to allowing Pennsylvania to be a German-speaking state after the American Revolution. And even today we could imagine encouraging new immigrants from another country to settle as a 'colony', and redistributing political boundaries and powers to enable them to exercise self-government.

I do not think that such a policy would be inherently unjust, although it is difficult to imagine any country actually adopting it. But nor is it unjust that the American government (and other Western democracies) have decided not to give immigrants the legal status and resources needed to become national minorities. After all, most immigrants (as distinct from refugees) choose to leave their own culture. They have uprooted themselves, and they know when they come that their success, and that of their children, depends on integrating into the institutions of English-speaking society.

The expectation of integration is not unjust, I believe, so long as immigrants had the option to stay in their original culture. Given the connection between choice and culture which I sketched earlier, people should be able to live and work in their own culture. But like any other right, this right can be waived, and immigration is one way of waiving one's right. In deciding to uproot themselves, immigrants voluntarily relinquish some of the rights that go along with their original national membership.[19]

For example, if a group of Americans decide to emigrate to Sweden, they have no right that the Swedish government provide them with institutions of self-government or public services in their mother tongue. One could argue that a government policy which enabled American immigrants to re-create their societal culture would benefit everyone, by enriching the whole society. But the immigrants have no *right* to such policies, for in choosing to leave the United States they relinquish the national rights that go with membership in their original culture. Similarly, Swedish immigrants to America have no basis for claiming the language rights or self-government rights needed to recreate their societal culture.

Moreover, on a practical level, most existing ethnic groups are too 'dispersed, mixed, assimilated and integrated' to exercise self-government. They are not sufficiently 'compact, self-conscious [and] culture-maintaining' to have the territorial and institutional prerequisites for self-government (Glazer 1983: 227, 283; cf. Oliver 1992). And to try to re-create these prerequisites amongst already-settled immigrants would probably require coercion of half-integrated immigrants.

This does not mean that voluntary immigrants have no claims regarding the expression of their identity. On the contrary, if we reject the option of enabling immigrants to re-create their societal culture, then we must address the issue of how to ensure that the mainstream culture is hospitable to immigrants, and to the expression of their ethnic differences. Integration is a two-way process—it requires the mainstream society to adapt itself to immigrants, just as immigrants must adapt to the mainstream (Parekh 1990).

Enabling integration requires, in the first place, strong efforts at fighting prejudice and discrimination. This involves not only the rigorous enforcement of anti-discrimination laws, but also changes to the way immigrants are portrayed in school textbooks, government documents, and the media. Moreover, enabling integration may require some modification of the institutions of the dominant culture in the form of group-specific polyethnic rights, such as the right of Jews and Muslims to exemptions from Sunday closing legislation, or the right of Sikhs to exemptions from motorcycle helmet laws. Without these exemptions, certain groups would be disadvantaged (often unintentionally) in the mainstream. Immigrants can rightfully insist on maintaining some of their heritage, and dominant institutions should be adapted to accommodate those differences.

In terms of linguistic integration, the goal of ensuring that immigrants learn English need not require the abandonment of the mother tongue. Indeed, there is strong evidence that immigrants are more likely to learn English if use of their mother tongue is not discouraged. ESL (English-as-a-second-language) programmes, and public opinion generally, have historically treated the desire to retain and use one's mother tongue in private life, and to pass it on to one's children, as evidence of a failure of integration on the part of immigrants. Current policy has operated on the assumption that the ideal is to make immigrants and their children as close as possible to unilingual native-speakers of English (i.e. that learning English requires losing their mother tongue), rather than aiming to produce people who are fluently bilingual (i.e. that learning English involves gaining a language, in addition to one's mother tongue).

This is a deeply misguided policy. It is not only harmful to the immigrants and their families, cutting them off unnecessarily from their heritage. But it also deprives society of a valuable resource in an increasingly globalized economy. And, paradoxically, it has proven to be counter-productive even in terms of promoting integration. People learn English best when they view it as supplementing, rather than displacing, their mother tongue (Skutnabb-Kangas 1988).[20] Moreover, there is an undercurrent of racism in the traditional attitude towards immigrant languages. As Richard Ruiz puts it, '*Adding* a foreign language to English is associated with erudition, social and economic status and, perhaps, even patriotism . . . but *maintaining* a non-English language implies disadvantage, poverty, low achievement and disloyalty' (Ruiz 1983: 55).

So there are many ways that special efforts should be made to accommodate the cultural differences of immigrants. But all of these measures take the form of adapting the institutions and practices of the mainstream society so as to accommodate ethnic differences, not of setting up a separate societal culture based on the immigrants' mother tongue. Hence these claims are best met within the parameters of what I have been calling 'polyethnic rights', not national rights.

Moreover, there is little evidence that immigrants are seeking national rights, rather than polyethnic rights. Some commentators interpreted the 'ethnic revival' in the United States in the 1970s as a repudiation of integration into the mainstream society. But, as I noted in Chapter 4, this is dubious. Ethnic groups were demanding increased recognition and visibility within the mainstream society, not national self-government. Gans calls this 'symbolic ethnicity', to emphasize that it is almost entirely lacking in any real institutionalized corporate existence (Gans 1979). The fact is that 'the institutional cement' needed to have a distinct societal culture is almost entirely lacking in American immigrant groups (Steinberg 1981: 58; cf. Edwards 1985: 9–10; Fishman 1989: 666–8). This is not surprising, since 'ethnicity cannot long survive the erosion of the material and institutional underpinnings which was precipitated by the immigrant experience' (Steinberg 1981: 74).

The ethnic revival, in other words, involved a revision in the terms of integration, not a rejection of integration. The ethnic revival amongst German-Americans, for example, was not a revival of the idea that Pennsylvania should be a German-speaking state. The fact that such a proposal seems so ludicrous shows, I think, that the older American ethnic groups have long ago abandoned any interest in being treated as national minorities.[21] The ethnic revival aimed, in large part, to make the possession of an ethnic identity an acceptable, even normal, part of life in the mainstream society. In this it was strikingly successful, which helps explain why the 'revival' lost its political urgency (Fishman 1989: 678–80).

So far I have been talking about voluntary immigrants. The case of refugees fleeing persecution is different, since they did not choose to give up their culture. Indeed, many refugees flee their homeland precisely to be able to continue practising their language and culture, which is being oppressed by the government (e.g. the Kurds). Since they have not relinquished the rights which go with membership in their original culture, refugees arguably should, in principle, be able to re-create their societal culture in some other country, if they so desire. But which country? The sad fact is that the national rights of refugees are, in the first instance, rights against their own government. If that government is violating their national rights, there is no mechanism for deciding which other country should redress that injustice. And, unfortunately, it is likely that few countries would voluntarily accept any refugees if they were thereby committed to treating refugees as national minorities. Moreover, refugee groups, even more than immigrant groups, are typically too small and dispersed to re-form into self-governing communities.[22]

The best that refugees can realistically expect is to be treated as immigrants, with the corresponding polyethnic rights, and hope to return to their homeland as quickly as possible.[23] This means that long-term refugees suffer an injustice, since they did not voluntarily relinquish their national rights. But this injustice was committed by their home government, and it is not clear that we can realistically ask host governments to redress it.

The line between involuntary refugees and voluntary immigrants is difficult to draw, especially in a world with massive injustice in the international distribution of resources, and with different levels of respect for human rights. If a middle-class American chooses to emigrate to Sweden, that is clearly voluntary, and very few of us would think that she had a claim of justice that the Swedish government provide her with free English-language services (or vice versa for a middle-class Swede emigrating to the United States). But if a peasant from Ethiopia emigrates to the United States, her decision is voluntary in a very limited sense, even if she was not subject to persecution in her homeland, since it may have been the only way to ensure a minimally decent life for herself or her children. Indeed, her plight may have been as dire as that of some political refugees. (This is reflected in the rise of the term 'economic refugees'.)

Under these conditions, we may be more sympathetic to demands for national rights. We may think that people should not have to give up their culture in order to avoid dire poverty. Moreover, the plight of the Ethiopian peasant is at least partly our responsibility. I believe that rich countries have obligations of international justice to redistribute resources to poor countries, and had we done so, perhaps she would not have faced this awful choice. Enabling immigrants from poor countries to re-create their societal culture may be a way of compensating for our failure to provide them with a fair chance at a decent life in their own country.

Perhaps then my argument should be limited to what Rawls calls 'ideal theory'—that is, what would the claims of immigrants be in a just world? I believe that if the international distribution of resources were just, then immigrants would have no plausible claim of justice for re-creating their societal culture in their new country. But the international distribution of resources is not just, and until that injustice is rectified, perhaps immigrants from poor countries have stronger claims. On the other hand, the only long-term solution is to remedy the unjust international distribution of resources. After all, treating Ethiopian immigrants to the United States as a national minority does nothing for the far greater number of Ethiopians condemned to abject poverty in Ethiopia. As with the case of refugees, it is not clear that treating economic refugees to a new country as a national minority provides an appropriate way to redress injustices that must ultimately be solved in the original homeland.

3. Have some national minorities lost their societal culture? I have just argued that ethnic groups lack the 'institutional cement' needed to form or maintain a distinct societal culture. But haven't some national minorities also lost the societal integration and institutional life which constitute a societal culture? After all, societal cultures are not permanent and immutable. (If they were, group-specific rights would not be needed to protect them.) And given the coercive attempts to assimilate many national minorities—particularly indigenous peoples—it would not be surprising if there is very little left of some cultures. Some indigenous peoples have been decimated in size, denied the right to maintain their own institutions, and progressively demoralized.

Under these circumstances, would it not be better for the members of the national minority to integrate into the mainstream, rather than struggle in vain to preserve something that is already lost? This is a legitimate question, and it is worth noting that a few indigenous peoples have in fact chosen as a group to relinquish their national rights, and in effect to be treated as a disadvantaged ethnic or racial group.

In some circumstances this might be the most prudent course, and any system of group-differentiated rights must leave this option open. While national minorities may have the right to maintain themselves as a distinct society, they are certainly under no duty to do so.[24] However, I believe that the decision about whether to integrate must be up to the members of the minority themselves. It is not for people outside the group to decide if and when the societal culture is too thin to warrant maintaining.

For one thing, majority cultures would have a perverse incentive to destroy the societal culture of national minorities, and then cite that destruction as a justification for compelling assimilation. We should not establish a system which enables majorities to profit from their own injustices. Moreover, weakened and oppressed cultures can regain and enhance their richness, if given the appropriate conditions. There is no reason to think that indigenous groups, for example, cannot become vibrant and diverse cultures, drawing on their cultural traditions while incorporating the best of the modern world, if given the requisite preconditions. It is the potentiality of societal cultures that matters, not just their current state, and it is even more difficult for outsiders to judge the potentiality of a culture than to judge its current state.[25]

In general, then, I believe that national minorities have societal cultures, and immigrant groups do not. There is of course no necessity about this. It is possible to settle immigrant groups collectively, and to empower them, so that they become in effect national minorities, just as it is possible to tear down and disperse national minorities so that they become indistinguishable from uprooted immigrants. The history of racism, ethnocentrism, cultural imperialism, segregation, ghettoization, and discrimination against both national minorities and immigrants has created groups whose status is riven with contradictions and complexities. Moreover, as I discussed in Chapter 2, there are some ethnocultural groups, such as the African-Americans, that were never appropriately seen as immigrants or national minorities. There are many such hard cases and grey areas.[26]

By emphasizing the distinction between national minorities and ethnic groups, my aim is not to resolve all these hard cases. I do not think there is any magical formula that will cover them all. Some historic injustices may be intractable, and elude any theoretical solution. However, we can at least be clear about what the relevant interests are. What matters, from a liberal point of view, is that people have access to a societal culture which provides them with meaningful options encompassing the range of human activities. Throughout the world, many minority groups are denied this access. They are caught in a contradictory position, unable either to fully participate in the mainstream of society or to sustain their own distinct societal culture. In so far as polyethnic rights for immigrants or self-government rights for national minorities help secure access to a societal culture, then they can contribute to individual freedom. Failure to recognize these rights will create new tragic cases of groups which are denied the sort of cultural context of choice that supports individual autonomy.

6. *Individuating Cultures*

So far I have been taking for granted that there are such things as 'separate' and 'distinct' cultures, and that it makes sense to ask whether there is one or two or more of them in a particular country. But is this realistic? Some people deny that it is meaningful to talk about individuating cultures in this way. According to Jeremy Waldron, the project of individuating societal cultures presupposes that cultures are somehow isolated and impervious to external influences. Yet in reality, he notes, there is an enormous amount of interchange between them. Cultures have influenced each other so much, he says, that there is no meaningful way to say where one culture ends and another begins. Indeed, there are no such things as cultures, just innumerable cultural fragments from innumerable cultural sources, without any 'structure' connecting them or underlying them.

Waldron accepts that the meaningfulness of options depends on the fact that they have cultural meanings. But he rejects the assumption that the options available to a particular individual must come from a *particular* culture. As he puts it,

> From the fact that each option must have a cultural meaning, it does not follow that there must be one cultural framework in which each available option is assigned a meaning. Meaningful options may come to us as items or fragments from a variety of cultural sources . . . [The fact] that people need cultural materials does not show that what people need is 'a rich and secure cultural structure'. It shows the importance of access to a variety of stories and roles; but it does not . . . show the importance of something called membership in a culture. (Waldron 1992*a*: 783–4)

For example, Waldron notes the influence of the Bible, Roman mythology, and *Grimms' Fairy-Tales* on American culture, and says that these cannot plausibly be seen as part of a single 'cultural structure', since they are

> drawn from a variety of disparate cultural sources: from first-century Palestine, from the heritage of Germanic folklore, and from the mythology of the Roman Republic . . . They are familiar to us because of the immense variety of cultural materials, various in their provenance as well as their character, that are in fact available to us. But neither their familiarity nor their availability constitute them as part of a single cultural matrix. Indeed, if we were to insist that they are all part of the same matrix because they are all available to us, we would trivialize the individuation of cultures beyond any sociological interest. (1992*a*: 784–5)

Waldron raises an interesting point. On any liberal view, it is a good thing that cultures learn from each other. Liberals cannot endorse a notion of culture that sees the process of interacting with and learning from other cultures as a threat to 'purity' or 'integrity', rather than as an opportunity for enrichment.[27] Liberals want a societal culture that is rich and diverse, and much of the richness of a culture comes from the way it has appropriated the fruits of other cultures. So we do not want to build closed walls around cultures, to cut them off from 'the general movement of the world', as John Stuart Mill put it.[28]

According to Waldron, it is inconsistent to desire a richer and more diverse cultural life and yet insist on maintaining distinct cultures. This emphasis on individuating cultures thwarts the process of cultural enrichment and diversification, Waldron claims, since the only non-trivial way of individuating cultures is to define them in terms of a common ethnic source that precludes learning from other cultures. So if we want to increase the range of valuable options available to people, we would be better off abandoning the idea of separate cultures, and instead promoting a *mélange* of cultural meanings from different sources.

However, Waldron's conclusion is, I think, mistaken. It is true that the options available to the members of any modern society come from a variety of ethnic and historical sources. But what makes these options 'available', or meaningful, to us? After all, there are limits on the 'cultural materials' which people find meaningful. I have argued that options are available to us if they become part of the shared vocabulary of social life—i.e. embodied in the social practices, based on a shared language, that we are exposed to.[29] Indeed, I think Waldron's examples support this view. For surely one of the reasons why *Grimms' Fairy-Tales* are so much a part of our culture is precisely that they have been translated and widely distributed in English. Were *Grimms' Fairy-Tales* only available in the original language, as is the case with the folklore of many other world cultures, they would not be available to us. It is often possible to trace the path by which our culture incorporates the cultural materials of other nations. The works of other cultures may become available to us through translation, or through the influx of immigrants who bring certain cultural narratives with them as they integrate. That we learn in this way from other cultures, or that we borrow words from other languages, does not mean that we do not still belong to separate societal cultures, or speak different languages.

Waldron is worried that the desire of national minorities to maintain their separate cultures requires insulating them from the outside world. For example, he interprets defenders of self-government for indigenous peoples as concerned with preserving the 'purity' and 'authenticity' of their culture. No doubt this is the motivation of some minority leaders, just as it is the motivation of many majority groups who seek to protect the purity of their culture from external influence (e.g. the Iranian government seeking to avoid Western influence; the French government seeking to avoid foreign 'contamination' of their language).

But there is no inherent connection between the desire to maintain a distinct societal culture and the desire for cultural isolation. In many cases, the aim of self-government is to enable smaller nations to interact with larger nations on a more equitable basis. It should be up to each culture to decide when and how they will adopt the achievements of the larger world. It is one thing to learn from the larger world; it is another thing to be swamped by it, and self-government rights may be needed for smaller nations to control the direction and rate of change.

For example, most indigenous peoples favour economic development 'provided they can control its pace and enjoy some of its benefits' (Gurr 1993: 300). Indeed, it is often majority cultures which have insisted on the 'purity' of minority cultures. For example, some governments have argued that land claims should only be given to indigenous groups which have maintained their 'authentic culture'. The Brazilian government has tried to reinterpret Indian land rights so that they only apply to 'real Indians'—that is, those who have not adopted any of the conveniences or products of the industrialized world. The (intentional) result is that ultimately there will 'be virtually no holders of Indian rights and coveted lands would become available' (da Cunha 1992: 284).[30]

This is not how most indigenous peoples themselves understand the function of their national rights; nor is it how they understand the nature of their cultural identity, which is dynamic, not static. While indigenous peoples do not want modernization forced upon them, they demand the right to decide for themselves what aspects of the outside world they will incorporate into their cultures, and many indigenous peoples have moved toward a more urbanized and agricultural lifestyle. And they demand the right to use their traditional resources in the process.

It is natural, and desirable, for cultures to change as a result of the choices of their members. We must, therefore, distinguish the existence of a culture from its 'character' at any given moment.[31] The character of a culture can change dramatically, as the Quiet Revolution in Quebec shows. In the space of a decade, French Quebec changed from a religious and rural society to a secular and urban one. Indigenous groups are undergoing similar changes. And of course every nation in Western society has undergone the same transition, although perhaps not as quickly. The process of modernization does not change the fact that these nations still form separate societal cultures, with their own institutions, using their own languages.

It is right and proper that the character of a culture change as a result of the choices of its members. This is indeed why systems of internal restrictions are illegitimate from a liberal standpoint. People should be able to decide what is best from within their own culture, and to integrate into their culture whatever they find admirable in other cultures. This follows from the liberal belief in the fallibility and revisability of our conceptions of the good, which I discussed earlier in this chapter.

But this is different from the culture itself being threatened—that is, for the very survival of the culture as a distinct society to be in jeopardy—as a result of decisions made by people outside the culture. This can happen if the land, language rights, and political institutions of a national minority are taken away. The desire of national minorities to survive as a culturally distinct society is not necessarily a desire for cultural purity, but simply for the right to maintain one's membership in a distinct culture, and to continue developing that culture in the same (impure) way that the members of majority cultures are able to develop theirs. The desire to develop and enrich one's culture is consistent with, and indeed promoted by, interactions with other cultures, so long as this interaction is not conducted in circumstances of serious inequality in power.

So the unavoidable, and indeed desirable, fact of cultural interchange does not undermine the claim that there are distinct societal cultures.

7. *Conclusion*

In this chapter, I have tried to show that liberals should recognize the importance of people's membership in their own societal culture, because of the role it plays in enabling meaningful individual choice and in supporting self-identity. While the members of a (liberalized) nation no longer share moral values or traditional ways of life, they still have a deep attachment to their own language and culture. Indeed, it is precisely because national identity does not rest on shared values—as Tamir puts it, national identity lies 'outside the normative sphere' (Tamir 1993: 90)—that it provides a secure foundation for individual autonomy and self-identity. Cultural membership provides us with an intelligible context of choice, and a secure sense of identity and belonging, that we call upon in confronting questions about personal values and projects. And the fact that national identity does not require shared values also explains why nations are appropriate units for liberal theory—national groupings provide a domain of freedom and equality, and a source of mutual recognition and trust, which can accommodate the inevitable disagreements and dissent about concep-

tions of the good in modern society.

In so far as this is so, group-differentiated rights that protect minority cultures can be seen, not only as consistent with liberal values, but as actually promoting them. This does not mean that every measure that contributes to the stability of minority cultures is justified. In some cases, measures to protect cultural membership may be unnecessary, or come at too high a price in terms of other liberal goals. If measures to protect minority cultures are either unnecessary or too costly, then a policy of 'benign neglect' may be justified in certain circumstances. But I will argue in the next chapter that to insist on benign neglect in all circumstances is neither fair nor even possible, and that certain group-differentiated rights are required by the principles of liberal justice.

CHAPTER 6

Justice and Minority Rights

I have argued that access to a societal culture is essential for individual freedom. I have also argued that most people have a deep bond to their own culture, and that they have a legitimate interest in maintaining this bond. But what particular claims are justified by this interest? Not all interests can be satisfied in a world of conflicting interests and scarce resources. Protecting one person's cultural membership has costs for other people and other interests, and we need to determine when these trade-offs are justified.

As I noted in Chapter 1, many liberals believe that people's interest in cultural membership is adequately protected by the common rights of citizenship, and that any further measures to protect this interest are illegitimate. They argue that a system of universal individual rights already accommodates cultural differences, by allowing each person the freedom to associate with others in the pursuit of shared religious or ethnic practices. Freedom of association enables people from different backgrounds to pursue their distinctive ways of life without interference. Every individual is free to create or join various associations, and to seek new adherents for them, in the 'cultural marketplace'. Every way of life is free to attract adherents, and if some ways of life are unable to maintain or gain the voluntary adherence of people that may be unfortunate, but it is not unfair. On this view, giving political recognition or support to particular cultural practices or associations is unnecessary and unfair. It is unnecessary, because a valuable way of life will have no difficulty attracting adherents. And it is unfair, because it subsidizes some people's choices at the expense of others.

Proponents of this 'strict separation of state and ethnicity' view need not deny that people have a deep bond to their own culture (although some do). They may just argue that cultures do not need state assistance to survive. If a societal culture is worth saving, one could argue, the members of the culture will sustain it through their own choices. If the culture is decaying, it must be because some people no longer find it worthy of their allegiance. The state, on this view, should not interfere with the cultural market-place—it should neither promote nor inhibit the maintenance of any particular culture. Rather, it should respond with 'benign neglect' to ethnic and national differences.

I think this common view is not only mistaken, but actually incoherent. The idea of responding to cultural differences with 'benign neglect' makes no sense. Government decisions on languages, internal boundaries, public holidays, and state symbols unavoidably involve recognizing, accommodating, and supporting the needs and identities of particular ethnic and national groups. The state unavoidably promotes certain cultural identities, and thereby disadvantages others. Once we recognize this, we need to rethink the justice of minority rights claims. In this chapter, I will argue that some self-government rights and polyethnic rights are consistent with, and indeed required by, liberal justice. (I examine the case of group representation rights in Chapter 7.) I will consider three sorts of arguments that attempt to defend these measures within a broadly liberal framework: equality, historical agreement, and diversity. I will argue that each has some merit, although the latter two depend in part on the first. In each case, I will first consider how these arguments apply to the self-government rights of national minorities, and then examine their application to the polyethnic rights of ethnic groups.

1. *The Equality Argument*

Many defenders of group-specific rights for ethnic and national minorities insist that they are needed to ensure that all citizens are treated with genuine equality. On this view, 'the accommodation of differences is the essence of true equality',[1] and group-specific rights are needed to accommodate our differences. I think this argument is correct, within certain limits.

Proponents of 'benign neglect' will respond that individual rights already allow for the accommodation of differences, and that true equality requires equal rights for each individual regardless of race or ethnicity.[2] As I noted in Chapter 4, this assumption that liberal equality precludes group-specific rights is relatively recent, and arose in part as an (over-)generalization of the racial desegregation movement in the United States. It has some superficial plausibility. In many cases, claims for group-specific rights are simply an attempt by one group to dominate and oppress another.

But some minority rights eliminate, rather than create, inequalities. Some groups are unfairly disadvantaged in the cultural market-place, and political recognition and support rectify this disadvantage. I will start with the case of national minorities. The viability of their societal cultures may be undermined by economic and political decisions made by the majority. They could be outbid or outvoted on resources and policies that are crucial to the survival of their societal cultures. The members of majority cultures do not face this problem. Given the importance of cultural membership, this is a significant inequality which, if not addressed, becomes a serious injustice.

Group-differentiated rights—such as territorial autonomy, veto powers, guaranteed representation in central institutions, land claims, and language rights—can help rectify this disadvantage, by alleviating the vulnerability of minority cultures to majority decisions. These external protections ensure that members of the minority have the same opportunity to live and work in their own culture as members of the majority.

As I discussed in Chapter 3, these rights may impose restrictions on the members of the larger society, by making it more costly for them to move into the territory of the minority (e.g. longer residency requirements, fewer government services in their language), or by giving minority members priority in the use of certain land and resources (e.g. indigenous hunting and fishing rights). But the sacrifice required of non-members by the existence of these rights is far less than the sacrifice members would face in the absence of such rights.

Where these rights are recognized, members of the majority who choose to enter the minority's homeland may have to forgo certain benefits they are accustomed to. This is a burden. But without such rights, the members of many minority cultures face the loss of their culture, a loss which we cannot reasonably ask people to accept.

Any plausible theory of justice should recognize the fairness of these external protections for national minorities. They are clearly justified, I believe, within a liberal egalitarian theory, such as Rawls's and Dworkin's, which emphasizes the importance of rectifying unchosen inequalities. Indeed inequalities in cultural membership are just the sort which Rawls says we should be concerned about, since their effects are 'profound and pervasive and present from birth' (Rawls 1971: 96; cf. Dworkin 1981).[3]

This equality-based argument will only endorse special rights for national minorities if there actually is a disadvantage with respect to cultural membership, and if the rights actually serve to rectify the disadvantage. Hence the legitimate scope of these rights will vary with the circumstances. In North America, indigenous groups are more vulnerable to majority decisions than the Québécois or Puerto Ricans, and so their external protections will be more extensive. For example, restrictions on the sale of land which are necessary in the context of indigenous peoples are not necessary, and hence not justified, in the case of Quebec or Puerto Rico.[4]

At some point, demands for increased powers or resources will not be necessary to ensure the same opportunity to live and work in one's culture. Instead, they will simply be attempts to gain benefits denied to others, to have more resources to pursue one's way of life than others have. This was clearly the case with apartheid, where whites constituting under 20 per cent of the population controlled 87 per cent of the land mass of the country, and monopolized all the important levers of state power.

One could imagine a point where the amount of land reserved for indigenous peoples would not be necessary to provide reasonable external protections, but rather would simply provide unequal opportunities to them. Justice would then require that the holdings of indigenous peoples be subject to the same redistributive taxation as the wealth of other advantaged groups, so as to assist the less well off in society. In the real world, of course, most indigenous peoples are struggling to maintain the bare minimum of land needed to sustain the viability of their communities. But it is possible that their land holdings could exceed what justice allows.[5]

The legitimacy of certain measures may also depend on their timing. For example, many people have suggested that a new South African constitution should grant a veto power over certain important decisions to some or all of the major national groups. This sort of veto power is a familiar feature of various 'consociational democracies' in Europe, and, as I discuss in the next chapter, under certain circumstances it can promote justice. But it would probably be unjust to give privileged groups a veto power before there has been a dramatic redistribution of wealth and opportunities (Adam 1979: 295). A veto power can promote justice if it helps protect a minority from unjust policies that favour the majority; but it is an obstacle to justice if it allows a privileged group the leverage to maintain its unjust advantages.

So the ideal of 'benign neglect' is not in fact benign. It ignores the fact that the members of a national minority face a disadvantage which the members of the majority do not face. In any event, the idea that the government could be neutral with respect to ethnic and national groups is patently false. As I noted in Chapter 5, one of the most important determinants of whether a culture survives is whether its language is the language of government—i.e. the language of public schooling, courts, legislatures, welfare agencies, health services, etc. When the government decides the language of public schooling, it is providing what is probably the most important form of support needed by societal cultures, since it guarantees the passing on of the language and its associated traditions and conventions to the next generation. Refusing to provide public schooling in a minority language, by contrast, is almost inevitably condemning that language to ever-increasing marginalization.

The government therefore cannot avoid deciding which societal cultures will be supported. And if it supports the majority culture, by using the majority's language in schools and public agencies, it cannot refuse official recognition to minority languages on the ground that this violates 'the separation of state and ethnicity'. This shows that the analogy between religion and culture is mistaken. As I noted earlier, many liberals say that just as the state should not recognize, endorse, or support any particular church, so it should not recognize, endorse, or support any particular cultural group or identity (Ch. 1, s. 1). But the analogy does not work. It is quite possible for a state not to have an established church. But the state cannot help but give at least partial establishment to a culture when it decides which language is to be used in public schooling, or in the provision of state services. The state can (and should) replace religious oaths in courts with secular oaths, but it cannot replace the use of English in courts with no language.

This is a significant embarrassment for the 'benign neglect' view, and it is remarkable how rarely language rights are discussed in contemporary liberal theory.[6] As Brian Weinstein put it, political theorists have had a lot to say about 'the language of politics'—that is, the symbols, metaphors, and rhetorical devices of political discourse—but have had virtually nothing to say about 'the politics of language'—that is, the decisions about which languages to use in political, legal, and educational forums (Weinstein 1983: 7–13). Yet language rights are a fundamental cause of political conflict, even violence, throughout the world, including Canada, Belgium, Spain, Sri Lanka, the Baltics, Bulgaria, Turkey, and many other countries (Horowitz 1985: 219–24).

One could argue that decisions about the language of schooling and public services should be determined, not by officially recognizing the existence of various groups, but simply by allowing each political subunit to make its own language policy on a democratic basis. If a national minority forms a majority in the relevant unit, they can decide to have their mother tongue adopted as an official language in that unit. But this is because they are a local majority, not because the state has officially recognized them as a 'nation'.

This is sometimes said to be the American approach to language rights, since there is no constitutional definition of language rights in the United States. But in fact the American government has historically tried to make sure that such 'local' decisions are always made by political units that have an anglophone majority. As discussed in Chapter 2, decisions about state borders, or about when to admit territories as states, have been explicitly made with the aim of ensuring that there will be an anglophone majority. States in the American south-west and Hawaii were only offered statehood when the national minorities residing in those areas were outnumbered by settlers and immigrants. And some people oppose offering statehood to Puerto Rico precisely on the grounds that it will never have an anglophone majority (Rubinstein 1993; Glazer 1983: 280).

This illustrates a more general point. Leaving decisions about language to political subunits just pushes back the problem. What are the relevant political units—what level of government should make these decisions? Should each neighbourhood be able to decide on the language of public schooling and public services in that neighbourhood? Or should this decision be left to larger units, such as cities or provinces? And how do we decide on the boundaries of these subunits? If we draw municipal or provincial boundaries in one way, then a national minority will not form even a local majority. But if we draw the boundaries another way, then the national minority will form a local majority. In a multination state, decisions on boundaries and the division of powers are inevitably decisions about which national group will have the ability to use which state powers to sustain its culture.[7]

For example, as I noted in Chapter 2, the Inuit in Canada wish to divide the Northwest Territories into two, so that they will form the majority in the eastern half. This is seen as essential to the implementation of their right of self-government. Some liberals object that this proposal violates the separation of state and ethnicity by distributing public benefits and state powers so as to make it easier for a specific group to preserve its culture. But all decisions regarding boundaries and the distribution of powers in multination states have this effect. We can draw boundaries and distribute legislative powers so that a national minority has an increased ability within a particular region to protect its societal culture; or we can draw boundaries and distribute legislative powers so that the majority nation controls decisions regarding language, education, immigration, etc. on a country-wide basis.

The whole idea of 'benign neglect' is incoherent, and reflects a shallow understanding of the relationship between states and nations. In the areas of official languages, political boundaries, and the division of powers, there is no way to avoid supporting this or that societal culture, or deciding which groups will form a majority in political units that control culture-affecting decisions regarding language, education, and immigration.

So the real question is, what is a fair way to recognize languages, draw boundaries, and distribute powers? And the answer, I think, is that we should aim at ensuring that all national groups have the opportunity to maintain themselves as a distinct culture, if they so choose. This ensures that the good of cultural membership is equally protected for the members of all national groups. In a democratic society, the majority nation will always have its language and societal culture supported, and will have the legislative power to protect its interests in culture-affecting decisions. The question is whether fairness requires that the same benefits and opportunities should be given to national minorities. The answer, I think, is clearly yes.

Hence group-differentiated self-government rights compensate for unequal circumstances which put the members of minority cultures at a systemic disadvantage in the cultural market-place, regardless of their personal choices in life. This is one of many areas in which true equality requires not identical treatment, but rather differential treatment in order to accommodate differential needs.[8]

This does not mean that we should entirely reject the idea of the cultural market-place. Once the societal cultures of national groups are protected, through language rights and territorial autonomy, then the cultural market-place does have an important role to play in determining the character of the culture. Decisions about which particular aspects of one's culture are worth maintaining and developing should be left to the choices of individual members. For the state to intervene at this point to support particular options or customs within the culture, while penalizing or discouraging others, would run the risk of unfairly subsidizing some people's choices (Kymlicka 1989*b*). But that is not the aim or effect of many rights for national minorities, which are instead concerned with external protections (see Ch. 3, s. 1).

Let me now turn to polyethnic rights for ethnic groups. I believe there is an equality-based argument for these rights as well, which also invokes the impossibility of separating state from ethnicity, but in a different way. I argued in Chapter 5 that the context of choice for immigrants, unlike national minorities, primarily involves equal access to the mainstream culture(s). Having uprooted themselves from their old culture, they are expected to become members of the national societies which already exist in their new country. Hence promoting the good of cultural membership for immigrants is primarily a matter of enabling integration, by providing language training and fighting patterns of discrimination and prejudice. Generally speaking, this is more a matter of rigorously enforcing the common rights of citizenship than providing group-differentiated rights. In so far as common rights of citizenship in fact create equal access to mainstream culture, then equality with respect to cultural membership is achieved.

But even here equality does justify some group-specific rights. Consider the case of public holidays. Some people object to legislation that exempts Jews and Muslims from Sunday closing legislation, on the ground that this violates the separation of state and ethnicity. But almost any decision on public holidays will do so. In the major immigration countries, public holidays currently reflect the needs of Christians. Hence government offices are closed on Sunday, and on the major religious holidays (Easter, Christmas). This need not be seen as a deliberate decision to promote Christianity and discriminate against other faiths (although this was undoubtedly part of the original motivation). Decisions about government holidays were made when there was far less religious diversity, and people just took it for granted that the government work-week should accommodate Christian beliefs about days of rest and religious celebration.

But these decisions can be a significant disadvantage to the members of other religious faiths. And having established a work-week that favours Christians, one can hardly object to exemptions for Muslims or Jews on the ground that they violate the separation of state and ethnicity. These groups are simply asking that their religious needs be taken into consideration in the same way that the needs of Christians have always been taken into account. Public holidays are another significant embarrassment for the 'benign neglect' view, and it is interesting to note how rarely they are discussed in contemporary liberal theory.

Similar issues arise regarding government uniforms. Some people object to the idea that Sikhs or Orthodox Jews should be exempted from requirements regarding headgear in the police or military. But here again it is important to recognize how the existing rules about government uniforms have been adopted to suit Christians. For example, existing dress-codes do not prohibit the wearing of wedding rings, which are an important religious symbol for many Christians (and Jews). And it is virtually inconceivable that designers of government dress-codes would have ever considered designing a uniform that prevented people from wearing wedding rings, unless this was strictly necessary for the job. Again, this should not be seen as a deliberate attempt to promote Christianity. It simply would have been taken for granted that uniforms should not unnecessarily conflict with Christian religious beliefs. Having adopted dress-codes that meet Christian needs, one can hardly object to exemptions for Sikhs and Orthodox Jews on the ground that they violate 'benign neglect'.

One can multiply the examples. For example, many state symbols such as flags, anthems, and mottoes reflect a particular ethnic or religious background ('In God We Trust'). The demand by ethnic groups for some symbolic affirmation of the value of polyethnicity (e.g. in government declarations and documents) is simply a demand that their identity be given the same recognition as the original Anglo-Saxon settlers.

It may be possible to avoid some of these issues by redesigning public holidays, uniforms, and state symbols. It is relatively easy to replace religious oaths with secular ones, and so we should. It would be more difficult, but perhaps not impossible, to replace existing public holidays and work-weeks with more 'neutral' schedules for schools and government offices.[9]

But there is no way to have a complete 'separation of state and ethnicity'. In various ways, the ideal of 'benign neglect' is a myth. Government decisions on languages, internal boundaries, public holidays, and state symbols unavoidably involve recognizing, accommodating, and supporting the needs and identities of particular ethnic and national groups. Nor is there any reason to regret this fact. There is no reason to regret the existence of official languages and public holidays, and no one gains by creating unnecessary conflicts between government regulations and religious beliefs. The only question is how to ensure that these unavoidable forms of support for particular ethnic and national groups are provided fairly—that is, how to ensure that they do not privilege some groups and disadvantage others. In so far as existing policies support the language, culture, and identity of dominant nations and ethnic groups, there is an argument of equality for ensuring that some attempts are made to provide similar support for minority groups, through self-government and polyethnic rights.

2. *The Role of Historical Agreements*

A second argument in defence of group-differentiated rights for national minorities is that they are the result of historical agreements, such as the treaty rights of indigenous peoples, or the agreement by which two or more peoples agreed to federate.

There are a variety of such agreements in Western democracies, although their provisions have often been ignored or repudiated. For example, the American government has unilaterally abrogated certain treaties with Indian tribes, and the Canadian government proposed in 1969 to extinguish all of its Indian treaties. The language rights guaranteed to Chicanos in the American south-west under the 1848 Treaty of Guadelupe Hidalgo were rescinded by the anglophone settlers as soon as they formed a majority. The language and land rights guaranteed to the Métis under the Manitoba Act of 1870 suffered the same fate in Canada. Yet many treaties and historical agreements between national groups continue to be recognized, and some have considerable legal force. For example, the 1840 Treaty of Waitangi signed by Maori chiefs and British colonists in New Zealand, declared a 'simple nullity' in 1877, has re-emerged as a central legal and political document (Sharp 1990).

The importance of honouring historical agreements is emphasized by proponents of group-differentiated rights, but has had little success convincing opponents. Those people who think that group-differentiated rights are unfair have not been appeased by pointing to agreements that were made by previous generations in different circumstances, often undemocratically and in conditions of substantial inequality in bargaining power. Surely some historical agreements are out of date, while others are patently unfair, signed under duress or ignorance. Why should not governments do what principles of equality require now, rather than what outdated and often unprincipled agreements require?[10]

One answer is to reconsider an underlying assumption of the equality argument. The equality argument assumes that the state must treat its citizens with equal respect. But there is the prior question of determining which citizens should be governed by which states. For example, how did the American government acquire the legitimate authority to govern Puerto Rico or the Navaho? And how did the Canadian government acquire legitimate authority over the Québécois and the Métis?

As I noted in Chapter 2, United Nations declarations state that all 'peoples' are entitled to 'self-determination'—i.e. an independent state. Obviously this principle is not reflected in existing boundaries, and it would be destabilizing, and indeed impossible, to fulfil. Moreover, not all peoples want their own state. Hence it is not uncommon for two or more peoples to decide to form a federation. And if the two communities are of unequal size, it is not uncommon for the smaller culture to demand various group-differentiated rights as part of the terms of federation. Forming a federation is one way of exercising a people's right of self-determination, and the historical terms of federation reflect the group's judgement about how best to exercise that right.

For example, the group-differentiated rights accorded French Canadians in the original confederation agreement in 1867, and the group-differentiated rights accorded Indians under various treaties, reflect the terms under which these communities joined Canada. It can be argued that these agreements define the terms under which the Canadian state acquired authority over these groups. These communities could have exercised their self-determination in other ways, but chose to join Canada, because they were given certain promises. If the Canadian government reneges on these promises, then it voids (morally, if not legally) the agreement which made those communities part of Canada.[11] Because these agreements define the terms under which various groups agreed to federate with Canada, the authority of the Canadian state over these groups flows from, but is also limited by, these agreements (Chartrand 1991; 1993: 240–1).

In short, the way in which a national minority was incorporated often gives rise to certain group-differentiated rights. If incorporation occurred through a voluntary federation, certain rights might be spelled out in the terms of federation (e.g. in treaties), and there are legal and moral arguments for respecting these agreements. If incorporation was involuntary (e.g. colonization), then the national minority might have a claim of self-determination under international law which can be exercised by renegotiating the terms of federation so as to make it a more voluntary federation (Macklem 1993; Danley 1991).

This historical argument may justify the same rights as the equality argument. Many of the group-differentiated rights which are the result of historical agreements can be seen as providing the sort of protection required by the equality argument. For example, the right to local autonomy for Indian tribes/bands could be justified on the equality argument, if it helps the larger state show equal concern for the members of Indian communities. Autonomy is also justified on the historical argument, in so far as Indian peoples never gave the federal government jurisdiction over certain issues.

Indeed, it is likely that the equality and historical arguments will yield similar policies. If local autonomy is required to ensure that members of a minority are not disadvantaged, then it is likely that the minority would have demanded autonomy as part of the terms of federation (had the negotiations been fair).

The negotiations between English and French regarding the terms of federation in Canada provide a clear example of this. The Québécois realized that if they agreed to enter the Canadian state in 1867, they would become a permanent minority in the country, and so could be outvoted on decisions made at the federal level. They therefore faced the question whether they should remain outside Confederation, maintaining their status as a separate colony within the British Empire, and hoping one day to become a separate country with a francophone majority.

Québécois leaders agreed to join Canada, even though they would be a minority in the federal parliament. But in return they insisted that jurisdiction over language and education be guaranteed to the provinces, not the federal government. This was 'the non-negotiable condition in return for which they were prepared to concede the principle of representation by population' in the new parliament, a principle that 'would institutionalize their minority position' within the new country (J. Smith 1993: 75). In deciding whether to accept the terms of federation, therefore, Québécois leaders were explicitly concerned about equality—that is, how to ensure that they would not be disadvantaged in the new country. Since they had considerable bargaining power in the negotiations, they were able to ensure their equality in the agreement, through guarantees of language rights and provincial autonomy.

While the equality and historical arguments often lead to the same result, they are none the less quite distinct. On the historical argument, the question is not how should the state treat 'its' minorities, but rather what are the terms under which two or more peoples decided to become partners? The question is not how should the state act fairly in governing its minorities, but what are the limits to the state's right to govern them?

For example, the two arguments may generate different answers to the question of federal funding of self-government rights. Under the equality argument, fairness may require positive state support for the measures required to maintain the viability of the national group. If fairness requires recognizing self-government in certain areas of jurisdiction, then presumably fairness will also require providing the resources needed to make self-government meaningful. The historical argument, however, may only generate a negative right to non-interference from the federal state. If the members of the national minority never gave the federal government the authority to govern them in certain areas, the federal government is unlikely to accept responsibility for funding minority self-government (unless this is itself part of the historical agreement). Any federal obligation to support self-government might be seen more as a form of humanitarian foreign aid than as a matter of domestic egalitarian justice.[12]

Contemporary political philosophers have had very little to say about the moral status of such historical agreements. For example, while Rawls recognizes a moral duty to respect treaties between countries (Rawls 1971: 378), he does not say anything about treaties or other agreements between nations within a country. This is surprising, because such agreements played a vital role in the creation and expansion of many countries, including the United States and Canada.

Respect for such agreements is important, I believe, not only to respect the self-determination of the minority, but also to ensure that citizens have trust in the actions of government. Historical agreements signed in good faith give rise to legitimate expectations on the part of citizens, who come to rely on the agreements made by governments, and it is a serious breach of trust to renege on them.

One difficulty with historical agreements is that they are often hard to interpret. For example, the Canadian government claims Quebec's 'right to be different' was implicitly recognized in the original Confederation agreement (Government of Canada 1991*a*: p. vi). But others deny this, and insist that Confederation was a union of provinces, not a compact between two cultures. Similar disputes arise over the interpretation of some Indian treaties. Moreover, some Indian tribes did not sign treaties, or signed them under duress. It seems arbitrary and unfair that some groups signed historical agreements while others, through no fault of their own, did not.

Where historical agreements are absent or disputed, groups are likely to appeal to the equality argument. Indian tribes/bands which have clear treaty rights often rest their claim for group-differentiated status on historical agreement; groups who did not sign treaties are more likely to appeal to the equality argument. It is often quite arbitrary whether a particular group happened to sign a particular agreement. However, the equality argument can help those groups which, for whatever reason, lack historical rights.[13]

Historical agreements are much less common in the case of ethnic groups, since immigrants are rarely promised any special rights before arriving in their new country. Indeed, opponents of polyethnic rights sometimes say that ethnic groups should not expect any new group-differentiated rights, precisely because they agreed to come knowing full well that such rights did not exist. Yet there are some cases of polyethnic rights based on historical agreement. For example, the Hutterites (a Christian sect) were explicitly promised by Canadian immigration officials that they would be exempted from certain laws regarding education, land ownership, and military service if they settled in western Canada. (The Canadian government was anxious at the time to settle the newly opened up western frontier.)

This now seems like an anomalous case of an immigrant group given privileges denied to other citizens, and attempts have been made to eliminate these historical rights. On the other hand, solemn promises were given to the Hutterites, who would have emigrated elsewhere had these promises not been made. In this sense, they too can claim that the historical agreement defines the terms under which the Canadian government acquired authority over them.

In assessing group-differentiated rights claims, therefore, we need to know whether the rights being claimed are rectifying disadvantages, or recognizing historical agreements arising from the terms of federation. Both of these are legitimate grounds for group-differentiated rights, I believe, but both raise some difficult issues.

For example, how should we respond to agreements that are now unfair, due to changing conditions? The land claims recognized in various treaties may be too much, or too little, given changes in the size and lifestyle of indigenous communities. The powers given to Quebec in 1867 may no longer be appropriate in an age of telecommunications. To stick to the letter of historical agreements when they no longer meet the needs of minorities seems wrong.

Because of these changing circumstances, and because the original agreements are hard to interpret, many minority communities want to renegotiate their historical agreements. They want to make their group-differentiated rights more explicit in the constitution, and often more expansive. This is a major cause of the current constitutional crisis in Canada. For it has given those Canadians who see group-differentiated rights as unfair a chance to restrict, rather than entrench, such rights.

This suggests that, if we wish to defend group-differentiated rights, we should not rely solely on historical agreements. Since historical agreements must always be interpreted, and inevitably need to be updated and revised, we must be able to ground the historical agreements in a deeper theory of justice. The historical and equality arguments must work together.

3. The Value of Cultural Diversity

A third defence of group-differentiated rights for national minorities appeals to the value of cultural diversity. As I have discussed, liberals extol the virtue of having a diversity of lifestyles within a culture, so presumably they also endorse the additional diversity which comes from having two or more cultures in the same country. Surely intercultural diversity contributes to the richness of people's lives, as well as intracultural diversity (Schwartz 1986: ch. 1).

This argument is attractive to many people because it avoids relying solely on the interests of group members, and instead focuses on how the larger society also benefits from group-differentiated rights. As Richard Falk puts it, 'societal diversity enhances the quality of life, by enriching our experience, expanding cultural resources'. Hence protecting minority cultures 'is increasingly recognized to be an expression of overall enlightened self-interest' (Falk 1988: 23). Whereas the first two arguments appeal to the *obligations* of the majority, this third argument appeals to the *interests* of the majority, and defends rights in terms of self-interest not justice.

Cultural diversity is said to be valuable, both in the quasi-aesthetic sense that it creates a more interesting world, and because other cultures contain alternative models of social organization that may be useful in adapting to new circumstances.[14] This latter point is often made with respect to indigenous peoples, whose traditional lifestyles provide a model of a sustainable relationship to the environment. As Western attitudes towards nature are increasingly recognized to be unsustainable and self-destructive, indigenous peoples 'may provide models, inspiration, guidance in the essential work of world order redesign' (Falk 1988: 23; cf. Clay 1989: 233; O'Brien 1987: 358).

There is some truth in this argument about the value of cultural diversity. None the less, I think it is a mistake to put much weight on it as a defence of national rights. First, one of the basic reasons for valuing intracultural diversity has less application to intercultural diversity. The value of diversity within a culture is that it creates more options for each individual, and expands her range of choices. But protecting national minorities does not expand the range of choices open to members of the majority in the same way. As I explained last chapter, choosing to leave one's culture is qualitatively different from choosing to move around within one's culture. The former is a difficult and painful prospect for most people, and very few people in the mainstream choose to assimilate into a minority culture. Indeed, measures to protect national minorities may actually reduce diversity within the majority culture, compared with a situation where minorities, unable to maintain their own societal culture, are forced to integrate and add their distinctive contribution to the diversity of the mainstream culture. Having two or more cultures within a state does expand choices for each individual, but only to a limited degree, and it would be implausible to make this the primary justification for minority rights.

There are other aesthetic and educational benefits from cultural diversity, apart from the value of expanding individual choice. But it is not clear that any of these values by themselves can justify minority rights. One problem is that the benefits of diversity to the majority are spread thinly and widely, whereas the costs for particular members of the majority are sometimes quite high. Every one may benefit, in a diffuse way, from having flourishing minority cultures in Quebec and Puerto Rico. But some members of the majority culture are asked to pay a significant price so that others can gain this diffuse benefit. For example, unilingual anglophones residing in Quebec or Puerto Rico are unlikely to get government employment or publicly funded education in English—benefits which they would take for granted elsewhere. Similarly, non-Indians residing on Indian lands may be discriminated against in terms of their access to natural resources, or their right to vote in local elections. It is not clear that the diffuse benefits of diversity for society as a whole justify imposing these sorts of sacrifices on particular people. It seems to me that these sacrifices are only consistent with justice if they are needed, not to promote benefits to the members of the majority, but to prevent even greater sacrifices to the members of the national minority.

Moreover, there are many ways of promoting diversity, and it seems likely that protecting national minorities involves more cost to the majority than other possible ways. For example, a society could arguably gain more diversity at less cost by increasing immigration from a variety of countries than by protecting national minorities. The diversity argument cannot explain why we have an obligation to sustain the particular sort of diversity created by the presence of a viable, self-governing national minority.

There is one further problem with the diversity argument. Let us say that the aesthetic or educational value of diversity does justify imposing certain costs on people in the majority culture. Why then does the value of diversity not also justify imposing a duty on the members of the minority to maintain their traditional culture? If the benefits of cultural diversity to the larger society can justify restricting individual liberties or opportunities, why does it matter whether these restrictions are imposed on people inside or outside the group? I noted earlier that a liberal theory of minority rights can accept external protections, but not internal restrictions. It is difficult to see how the diversity argument can make this distinction. Because it appeals to the interests of the larger society, it cannot explain why minorities should be able to decide for themselves whether or how to maintain their culture.

So it seems to me that the diversity argument is insufficient, by itself, to justify the rights of national minorities. Protecting national minorities does provide benefits to the majority, and these are worth pointing out. But these diffuse benefits are better seen as a desirable by-product of national rights, rather than their primary justification. To date, most majority cultures have not seen it in their 'enlightened self-interest' to maintain minority cultures. No doubt this is due in part to ethnocentric prejudice, but we must recognize the powerful interests that majority nations often have in rejecting self-government rights for national minorities—e.g. increased access to the minority's land and resources, increased individual mobility, political stability, etc. It is unlikely that majorities will accept national rights solely on the basis of self-interest, without some belief that they have an obligation of justice to accept them. Conversely, it is unlikely that majorities will accept their obligations of justice towards national minorities without a belief that they gain something in the process. The diversity argument works best, therefore, when it is combined with arguments of justice.

The diversity argument is more plausible as a defence of polyethnic rights for ethnic groups. Unlike national self-government, these rights do contribute directly to diversity within the majority culture. Moreover, they do not involve the same sort of restrictions on the mobility or economic opportunities of the majority. Indeed, certain polyethnic policies can be seen as natural extensions of state policies regarding the funding of the arts, museums, educational television, etc.[15] Yet here again the problem arises that there are many ways of promoting diversity. Teaching children to be bilingual promotes diversity, but this cannot explain why we should teach immigrant languages in particular. Hence the diversity argument supplements, but cannot replace, justice arguments based on equality or historical agreement.

4. *The Analogy with States*

So far, I have been assuming that the burden of proof lies on those who wish to find room for group-differentiated rights within the liberal tradition. But we can and should question this assumption. In many ways, it is opponents of group-differentiated rights who are proposing a revision of liberal theory and practice. As I discussed in Chapter 4, certain group-differentiated rights have been a long-established part of the liberal tradition. Moreover, such rights are logically presupposed by existing liberal practice.

For example, most liberal theorists accept without question that the world is, and will remain, composed of separate states, each of which is assumed to have the right to determine who can enter its borders and acquire citizenship. I believe that this assumption can only be justified in terms of the same sorts of values which ground group-differentiated rights within each state. I believe that the orthodox liberal view about the right of states to determine who has citizenship rests on the same principles which justify group-differentiated citizenship within states, and that accepting the former leads logically to the latter.

This point is worth exploring in some depth. The existence of states, and the right of governments to control entry across state borders, raises a deep paradox for liberals. Most liberal theorists defend their theories in terms of 'equal respect for persons', and the 'equal rights of individuals'. This suggests that all 'persons' or 'individuals' have an equal right to enter a state, participate in its political life, and share in its natural resources.

In fact, however, these rights are typically reserved for *citizens*. And not everyone can become a citizen, even if they are willing to swear allegiance to liberal principles. On the contrary, there are millions of people who want to gain citizenship in various liberal democracies, but who are refused. Even the most open Western country in terms of immigration accepts only a fraction of the number of people who would come if there were genuinely open borders. Indeed, would-be immigrants are often refused entry, turned back at the border by armed border guards. These people are refused the right to enter and participate in the state because they were not born into the right group.

Citizenship, therefore, is an inherently group-differentiated notion. Unless one is willing to accept either a single world-government or completely open borders between states—and very few liberal theorists have endorsed either of these—then distributing rights and benefits on the basis of citizenship is to treat people differentially on the basis of their group membership.[16]

This creates a profound contradiction within most liberal theories. As Samuel Black notes, liberal theorists often begin by talking about the moral equality of 'persons', but end up talking about the equality of 'citizens', without explaining or even noticing the shift (Black 1991). What can justify restricting the rights of citizenship to members of a particular group, rather than all persons who desire it?

Some critics have argued that liberals cannot justify this restriction, and that the logic of liberalism requires open borders, except perhaps for temporary restrictions in the name of public order.[17] And surely that is right if we cling to the idea that liberalism should be indifferent to people's cultural membership and national identity. Open borders would dramatically increase the mobility and opportunities of individuals, and, if liberalism requires treating people solely 'as individuals' without regard for their group membership, then open borders clearly are preferable from a liberal point of view.

I believe, however, that some limits on immigration can be justified if we recognize that liberal states exist, not only to protect standard rights and opportunities of individuals, but also to protect people's cultural membership. Liberals implicitly assume that people are members of societal cultures, that these cultures provide the context for individual choice, and that one of the functions of having separate states is to recognize the fact that people belong to separate cultures. I noted examples of this in the liberal tradition in Chapter 4, and with Rawls's discussion of citizenship and the bonds of culture in Chapter 5. Once we make these assumptions explicit, however, it is clear that, in multination states, some people's cultural membership can only be recognized and protected by endorsing group-differentiated rights within the state.

Liberal theorists invariably limit citizenship to the members of a particular group, rather than all persons who desire it. The most plausible reason for this—namely, to recognize and protect our membership in distinct cultures—is also a reason for allowing group-differentiated citizenship within a state. There may be other reasons for restricting citizenship to a particular group which do not make any reference to the importance of cultural groups. It is difficult to say, since few liberals actually discuss the shift from 'equality of persons' to 'equality of citizens'. But I think it is fair to say this: in so far as liberal theorists accept the principle that citizenship can be restricted to the members of a particular group, the burden of proof lies on them to explain why they are not also committed to accepting group-differentiated rights within a state.[18] So long as liberals believe in separate states with restricted citizenship, the burden of proof lies as much with opponents of group-differentiated rights as with their defenders.

5. Conclusion

In the last two chapters, I have tried to show that liberals can and should accept a wide range of group-differentiated rights for national minorities and ethnic groups, without sacrificing their core commitments to individual freedom and social equality.

It may be useful briefly to summarize my argument. I have tried to show how freedom of choice is dependent on social practices, cultural meanings, and a shared language. Our capacity to form and revise a conception of the good is intimately tied to our membership in a societal culture, since the context of individual choice is the range of options passed down to us by our culture. Deciding how to lead our lives is, in the first instance, a matter of exploring the possibilities made available by our culture.

However, minority cultures in multination states may need protection from the economic or political decisions of the majority culture if they are to provide this context for their members. For example, they may need self-governing powers or veto rights over certain decisions regarding language and culture, and may need to limit the mobility of migrants or immigrants into their homelands.

While these group-differentiated rights for national minorities may seem discriminatory at first glance, since they allocate individual rights and political powers differentially on the basis of group membership, they are in fact consistent with liberal principles of equality. They are indeed required by the view, defended by Rawls and Dworkin, that justice requires removing or compensating for undeserved or 'morally arbitrary' disadvantages, particularly if these are 'profound and pervasive and present from birth' (Rawls 1971: 96). Were it not for these group-differentiated rights, the members of minority cultures would not have the same ability to live and work in their own language and culture that the members of majority cultures take for granted. This, I argued, can be seen as just as profound and morally arbitrary a disadvantage as the inequalities in race and class that liberals more standardly worry about.

This equality-based argument for group-differentiated rights for national minorities is further strengthened by appeals to historical agreements and the value of cultural diversity. And it is confirmed by the way that liberals implicitly invoke cultural membership to defend existing state borders and restrictions on citizenship. I have also argued that polyethnic rights for ethnic groups can be justified in terms of promoting equality and cultural diversity within the mainstream culture.

These claims are by no means uncontroversial, and there are many places where they could be challenged. One could deny that cultural meanings are dependent on a societal culture, or that individuals are closely tied to their own particular societal culture. One could also deny that minority cultures are vulnerable to the decisions of the larger society; or that this vulnerability constitutes an injustice; or that historical agreements have any moral weight; or that cultural diversity is worth promoting.

Yet I think each of these claims is plausible. Anyone who disputes them would be required to provide some alternative account of what makes meaningful choices available to people, or what justice requires in terms of language rights, public holidays, political boundaries, and the division of powers. Moreover, one would also have to offer an alternative account of the justification for restricting citizenship to the members of a particular group, rather than making it available to anyone who desires it. It is not enough to simply assert that a liberal state should respond to ethnic and national differences with benign neglect. That is an incoherent position that avoids addressing the inevitable connections between state and culture.

The idea that group-differentiated rights for national and ethnic groups can and should be accepted by liberals is hardly a radical suggestion. In fact, many multination liberal democracies already accept such an obligation, and provide public schooling and government services in the language of national minorities. Many have also adopted some form of federalism, so that national minorities will form a majority in one of the federal units (states, provinces, or cantons). And many polyethnic liberal states have adopted various forms of polyethnic policies and group-specific rights or exemptions for immigrant groups. Like Jay Sigler, I believe that providing a liberal defence of minority rights 'does not create a mandate for vast change. It merely ratifies and explains changes that have taken place in the absence of theory' (Sigler 1983: 196).

But if there are strong arguments in favour of group-differentiated rights, why have liberals so often rejected them? As I noted in Chapter 4, the explanation cannot be that liberalism is premissed on 'abstract individualism', on a conception of the individual as a solitary atom who is independent of her cultural environment. I hope that Chapters 4 and 5 have dispelled any perception that liberals ignore individuals' dependence on society and culture.

But this raises a puzzle. If individual autonomy and self-identity are tied to membership in one's societal culture, developing a theory of the rights of minority cultures would seem to be one of the very first tasks of any liberal theory. Why then have so few contemporary liberal theorists supported measures to protect cultural groups, such as group-specific language rights, land claims, or federal autonomy? I have explored some of the historical reasons in Chapter 4. Another part of the explanation, I think, is that contemporary liberal theorists implicitly assume that countries contain only one nation. They are well aware that modern states are culturally diverse—indeed, the pluralistic nature of modern liberal democracies is a pervasive theme in their writings. But they implicitly assume that this diversity is the sort that comes either from variations in people's conceptions of the good or from immigration—that is, they focus on philosophical, religious, and ethnic diversity within a single culture based on a shared language.[19] They do not recognize or discuss the existence of states that are multinational, with a diversity of societal cultures, languages, and national groups.

For example, Dworkin notes that 'in the modern world of immigration and boundary shifts', citizens do not share a racial or ethnic background, and that the communal life of the political community cannot include a single 'ethnic allegiance' (1989: 497). But, as I noted earlier, he does assume a common 'cultural structure' based on a 'shared language' (1985: 230, 233; 1989: 488). Similarly, while Rawls emphasizes the 'fact of pluralism'—particularly religious pluralism—he equates the political community with a single 'complete culture', and with a single 'people' who belong to the same 'society and culture' (1978: 70 n. 8; 1993*a*: 18, 222, 277; 1993*b*: 48).

This implicit assumption that states are uninational is rarely explained or defended. It is not as if these theorists explicitly reject the possibility that national minorities have special rights, or directly criticize the arguments of equality or history in defence of these rights. On the contrary, they simply ignore the issue entirely. There is no discussion by contemporary liberal theorists of the differences between nation-states and polyethnic or multination states, or of the arguments for modifying liberal principles in countries which are a 'federation of peoples'.

This shows, I think, that it is a mistake to subsume the issue of minority rights under one of the more familiar debates in contemporary political philosophy—e.g. the debate between 'individualists' and 'communitarians', or between 'universalists' and 'contextualists', or between 'impartialists' and 'difference theorists', or between 'rationalists' and 'postmodernists'. This is a very common tendency (see e.g. I. Young 1993*a*; Gochnauer 1991; Galenkamp 1993; Trakman 1992; Torres 1991; Addis 1991; cf. Todorov 1993: 392–9). But it stems from an over-simplified view of the issues involved in minority rights. According to many commentators, the central question in assessing minority rights is whether one accepts in principle the idea of giving political recognition to communities or group differences. Defenders of individualism and universalism are then said to be opposed in principle to such recognition, whereas defenders of community and difference are in principle supportive of them. But, as I have emphasized, all political theories must accord recognition to certain forms of group differences and support certain cultural communities. This is inevitable in any theory which confronts issues of language policy, public holidays, political boundaries, and immigration rules. This is as true of liberal individualists and socialist internationalists as of conservatives, communitarians, and postmodernists.

So the debate over minority rights is not about whether it is ever legitimate to support 'communities' or to recognize 'difference'. Rather, the debate is whether to support the particular sort of cultural difference and community exhibited by national minorities. And, as I have noted, some liberals, despite their 'individualism' and 'universalism', recognize that justice requires extending the same support to national minorities that majority nations receive. Conversely, some communitarians and particularists, despite their commitment to 'community' and 'difference', have been reluctant to accept the demands of national minorities. They view national minorities in the same way they view ethnic groups or new social movements—that is, as forms of difference and community that can and should be accommodated by group-specific rights within the larger society. They are unwilling to accept that national minorities require recognition as separate and self-governing societies alongside the mainstream society.[20]

As I noted in Chapter 4, the history of minority rights suggests that there is little or no correlation between meta-ethical debates and support for the rights of national minorities. People's views on minority rights are shaped, not only by their foundational moral or philosophical premisses, but by more concrete factors, including ethnocentric prejudice, fears about international peace and superpower relations, and concerns about the preconditions of democratic consensus and social harmony. These considerations do not correlate in any simple or consistent way with people's underlying philosophical and moral premisses.

These larger philosophical debates are not irrelevant to the policy debate over minority rights. But the connection between the two debates is mediated by many additional assumptions about the nature of ethnic and national differences, and their role in domestic and international politics. It is these additional assumptions that largely account for the actual position endorsed by particular theorists, whatever their deeper philosophical premisses.

For this reason, the demands of national minorities and ethnic groups raise a deep challenge to all Western political traditions. All of these traditions have been shaped, implicitly or explicitly, by the same historical influences which have shaped liberal thinking. The task of developing a consistent and principled theory of minority rights is not one that liberals face alone.

Even if group-differentiated rights can be defended on grounds of justice, there will still be those liberals who fear them for a variety of reasons. For example, some liberals argue that these rights are divisive, because they emphasize differences over commonalities. These critics argue that, while group-differentiated rights may be fair on equality or historical grounds, they are unworkable. To strengthen my argument, and allay these fears, I will address the issue of social unity in Chapter 9. First, however, I will briefly examine some of the issues raised by the idea of representation rights.

CHAPTER 7

Ensuring a Voice for Minorities

In the previous two chapters I have tried to provide a liberal defence for a wide range of self-government rights for national minorities, and polyethnic rights for ethnic groups. But there is no simple formula for deciding exactly which rights should be accorded to which groups. There have been unresolved issues at every step along the way: not all groups fall neatly into either the 'national minority' or 'ethnic group' category; historical agreements are often difficult to interpret; the vulnerabilities and disadvantages faced by minorities are not easy to measure or rectify; and appeals to equality, history, and diversity may lead in conflicting directions. The grey areas only increase when we move on to consider the status of illiberal minorities (Ch. 8), and the need to promote social unity (Ch. 9).

These indeterminacies are unavoidable, given the complexity of the interests, principles, and historical circumstances at stake. As a result, many important areas of conflict can only be resolved on a case-by-case basis, in the light of the particular history of a group, its status in the larger society, and the choices and circumstances of its members. In short, they must be resolved politically, by good-faith negotiations and the give and take of democratic politics. This means that we need to think about the fairness, not only of specific group-differentiated rights, but also of the decision-making procedure by which these rights are defined and interpreted.

Fairness in a decision-making procedure implies, amongst other things, that the interests and perspectives of the minority be listened to and taken into account. To achieve this, the standard political rights provided by the common rights of citizenship are obviously of critical importance. Where minorities have the right to vote and run for office, to organize politically, and to advocate their views publicly, this is often sufficient to ensure that their interests receive a fair hearing.

However, just as individual civil rights are sometimes insufficient for the fair accommodation of group differences, so individual political rights are sometimes insufficient to represent these differences fairly. As I noted in Chapter 2, various groups remain seriously under-represented in legislatures, despite the absence of any legal restrictions on the political rights of their individual members. For example, African-Americans constitute approximately 12.4 per cent of the population in the United States, but hold only 1.4 per cent of the total elected offices—that is, they have one-ninth of the offices they would have based on their demographic weight (what has been called their 'proportional electoral representation'). Hispanic-Americans constitute 8 per cent of the population, but hold only 0.8 per cent of elected offices, or one-tenth of their proportional electoral representation. In Canada, Aboriginal peoples constitute 3.5 per cent of the population, but hold only 1 per cent of seats in the federal legislature, or just over one-quarter of their proportional electoral representation.

Under-representation is not only a problem for ethnic, national, and racial minorities. For example, women in Canada constitute over 50 per cent of the population, but hold just 13 per cent of seats in the federal legislature, or one-quarter of their proportional electoral representation. (And many other Western democracies are even worse in this regard.) People with disabilities and the economically disadvantaged are also significantly under-represented. Indeed, 'middle-class status is a virtual prerequisite for candidacy for major office'.[1]

As a result, many people throughout the Western democracies see the electoral and legislative processes as 'unrepresentative', in the sense that they fail to reflect the diversity of the population. And this has led to increasing interest in the idea that a certain number of seats in the legislature should be reserved for the members of disadvantaged or marginalized groups.

In the United States, this has primarily taken the form of 'redistricting'—that is, redrawing the boundaries of electoral districts so as to create black-majority or Hispanic-majority districts. The fact that blacks form a majority in a particular district does not guarantee that a black representative will be elected, but that is the clear tendency. However, this is a very limited mechanism for overcoming under-representation, since boundary-drawing techniques do not work for groups which are territorially dispersed. Even for African-Americans, redistricting has been most useful in the south, where blacks were historically concentrated. But blacks are increasingly dispersed throughout the United States, and there is often no way to redraw boundaries so as to create black-majority districts.[2]

More wide-ranging forms of group representation have been proposed. In Canada, for example, a number of recommendations for guaranteed representation were made during the recent round of constitutional negotiations. Reforming the Canadian Senate has been a goal for decades, in part because it is still an unelected body. In recent years, proposals for reform have increasingly focused, not only on electing Senators, but also on electing Senators from under-represented groups. The National Action Committee on the Status of Women (the most powerful feminist lobby group in Canada) recommended that 50 per cent of Senate seats be reserved for women, and that proportionate representation of ethnic minorities also be guaranteed; the Francophone Association of Alberta recommended that at least one of the proposed six Senators elected from each province represent the official language minority of that province; and various government commissions have advocated Aboriginal-only districts not only in the Senate, but also in the House of Commons.[3]

These sorts of proposals are not unique to Canada, and certain forms of group representation already exist in many countries.[4] This chapter will explore the idea of 'group representation', and how it relates to various features of the existing system of representative democracy. I will argue that group representation is not inherently illiberal or undemocratic, and indeed is consistent with many features of our existing systems of representation (s. 1). Moreover, there are some circumstances where group representation is particularly appropriate (s. 2). However, there are also a number of difficulties facing proposals for group representation that remain to be properly addressed (s. 3).

Some people have argued that under-representation can be overcome without resorting to the idea of guaranteed representation. For example, political parties can be made more inclusive, by reducing the barriers which inhibit ethnic and racial minorities, women, or the poor from becoming party candidates or leaders. Options here include caps on nomination campaign expenses; public funding of nomination campaign expenses, either directly or through tax deductions for campaign contributions; establishing formal search committees within each party to help identify and nominate potential candidates from disadvantaged groups; even financial incentives to parties which nominate or elect members of disadvantaged groups, etc.[5]

Another way to reform the process is to adopt some form of proportional representation, which has been associated in some countries with greater inclusiveness of candidates. Under the system of single-member first-past-the-post elections used in most Anglo-American countries, the local constituency association for each party can only nominate one candidate. Nomination campaigns, therefore, are zero-sum—selecting a black (or a woman) means rejecting a white (or a man). Proportional representation, by contrast, allows for and encourages 'ticket-balancing'—that is, making sure that the party list includes both whites and blacks, men and women, indigenous peoples and immigrants. Moreover, proportional representation makes under-representation in the nomination process more visible and accountable. Under the single-member system, if nine out of ten local constituencies choose a white male, this seems like the unintended result of ten independent decisions, none of which was necessarily intentionally discriminatory or exclusionary. But if a party puts forward a list of ten people for election under proportional representation with only one woman or one person of colour, its decision not to field a more representative slate of candidates is clearly deliberate. For these and other reasons, it is likely that proportional representation would lead to a more representative legislature than a single-member, first-past-the-post system.[6]

Many people believe that these measures to redress the under-representation of various groups should be tried first, and only if they prove unsuccessful (or if they are working too slowly) should group representation be tried. However, in some countries these measures have been tried and found wanting, and demands for group representation are not likely to disappear (L. Young 1994). So it is important to consider what role group representation can play within liberal-democratic theory.

1. *What's New about Group Representation?*

Some people believe that group representation is a radical departure from existing conceptions of representative democracy, one which threatens to undermine cherished liberal democratic norms of individual rights and responsible citizenship. Others believe that group representation is the logical extension of existing principles and mechanisms of representation, and is consistent with the broader features of liberal-democratic political culture.

There is a certain amount of truth in both views. On the one hand, group representation is a radical departure from the system of single-member geographically defined constituencies used in many Anglo-American democracies. And it does pose a profound challenge to our traditional notion of representation, which I will discuss in the next section.

But it is also true that group representation is continuous with certain long-standing features of the electoral process. For example, group representation can be seen as an extension of the long-standing practice in many countries of drawing the boundaries of local constituencies so as to correspond with 'communities of interest'. While constituencies are supposed to be of roughly equal size, they are not intended to be random collections of equal numbers of citizens. Rather, constituency boundaries are drawn so far as possible in such a way that people within the constituency share certain interests—economic, ethnic, religious, environmental, historical, or other—which would then be represented in legislature. In both the United States and Canada, for example, district boundaries have been drawn so as to create predominantly rural ridings. Rural and agricultural interests might not otherwise be heard in an increasingly urbanized society.

The use of this practice to create black-majority ridings in the United States is relatively recent, since the Voting Rights Act of 1965. However, this quickly became the best-known, and most contentious, example of drawing boundaries to correspond with 'communities of interest'. It is particularly controversial when the revised districts have a very unusual shape. One recent case in North Carolina involved creating a snake-like district which was 160 miles long, but less than a mile wide, following an interstate highway that many blacks had settled beside.[7]

The controversial nature of these contorted boundaries is due in part to the fact that they often resemble the way white politicians in the South used to gerrymander boundaries so as to *prevent* black-majority districts. They too redrew boundaries in very odd shapes. Of course, the more recent redistricting is intended to rectify under-representation, whereas the older gerrymandering was intended to create and compound black under-representation. But the idea of 'race-conscious' districting is still suspect in many Americans' minds. And indeed the Supreme Court recently ruled in *Shaw* v. *Reno* (1993) that it will be very wary of any redistricting that involves 'segregating' races for the purposes of voting, since it fears that this will harden racial stereotypes and fan racial conflict.

However, it is important to remember that are many other, quite uncontroversial, examples of drawing boundaries to correspond with 'communities of interest', such as farmers, workers, immigrant groups, and religious sects. The practice has only become a source of major controversy when it involves racial groups. And it seems unfair that this practice be available in principle to everyone except blacks, one of the most under-represented groups in the United States. It would be paradoxical to argue that, because there is a history of racial discrimination and prejudice, the group which has suffered most from this discrimination will be given the least opportunity to benefit from redistricting.[8]

In Canada, the practice of promoting the representation of such communities of interest is widely accepted, and is required by law under the Electoral Boundaries Readjustment Act (1964) and the Representation Act (1985), and was affirmed by a recent Royal Commission on electoral reform:

> When a community of interest is dispersed across two or more constituencies, its voters' capacity to promote their collective interest is diminished accordingly. Their incentive to participate is likewise reduced because the outcome has a lesser relevance to their community of interest. When this occurs, especially if it could have been avoided, the legitimacy of the electoral system is undermined. (RCERPF 1991: 149; cf. Spitz 1984: 48–50)

In this passage, the Commission has in mind territorially concentrated communities of interest, and, as I noted earlier, boundary-drawing techniques only work for such groups. But the Commission's argument would seem to apply equally to non-territorial communities of interest. If special measures should be taken to ensure the representation of communities that are dispersed across two constituencies, why not take measures to ensure the representation of communities of interest which are dispersed across the entire country, like women, the disabled, ethnic minorities, or the poor? If the former promotes effective representation, increased participation, and electoral legitimacy, why not the latter?[9]

The commitment to representing communities of interest shows that politics in the United States and Canada has never been based on a purely individualistic conception of the franchise or of representation. On the individualistic view, all that matters is that individuals have an equal vote within equal constituencies. This is all that is required to meet the principle that each individual has an equal right to vote, and it should be a matter of indifference how these boundaries are drawn, so long as constituencies are of equal size. But this ignores the reality that people vote as members of communities of interest, and wish to be represented on this basis. As the Royal Commission put it,

> neither the franchise nor representation is merely an individualistic phenomenon; both also take expression through collective or community functions.

The individualistic perspective is based upon a partial and incomplete understanding of the electoral process and representation. In advancing the ideal of equally weighted votes, it does promote a critical constitutional right. But in ignoring the community dimension, this perspective is unrealistic at best; at worst it ignores the legitimate claims of minority groups. (RCERPF 1991: 152–3)

It can be argued that the underlying logic of these practices can be extended to defend the principle of (non-territorial) group representation.

Demands for group representation by disadvantaged groups can also be seen as an extension of the principle of special Senate representation for smaller regions. The American Senate, like the Australian Senate, gives each state an equal number of Senators regardless of its population. While the Canadian Senate currently gives larger provinces more seats, in line with the principle of representation by population, many Canadians have sought to have the American model adopted in Canada, to ensure effective representation for smaller provinces that might be neglected in the House of Commons.

If disadvantaged or marginalized regions need special Senate representation, why not disadvantaged or marginalized groups such as racial minorities, women, or the poor? The argument for special regional representation in the Senate assumes that the significant economic and cultural diversity between regions leads to different and sometimes conflicting interests; that the interests of smaller or poorer regions might not be effectively represented under a pure system of majority rule; and that majority rule is only legitimate 'in a set of governmental structures that ensure adequate sensitivity to the concerns of minorities'.[10] But each of these claims can also be made for various social groups; the diverse conditions and experiences of men and women, anglophones and Hispanics, whites and blacks, immigrants and indigenous peoples, able-bodied and the disabled, rich and poor give rise to different and sometimes conflicting interests; and the interests of smaller or poorer groups might not be represented under a system of majority rule. So why not develop representational structures that will ensure adequate sensitivity to the interests of these minorities?

There are, then, important aspects of political life in the United States and Canada which lend some support to the idea of group representation. Of course, this hardly resolves the issue. After all, the practice of drawing boundaries to represent communities of interest has been controversial, particularly for racial groups, as has the practice of giving an equal number of Senate seats to each state or province.[11] Rather than extending the logic of these practices to include the representation of non-territorial social groups, some people would prefer to cut back on these practices and cling to a more individualistic model of the electoral process that makes no accommodation for any groups at any level.

2. *Why Group Representation?*

To assess the merit of group representation, therefore, we need to step back, and look more carefully at the idea of representation. The idea that the existing political system is 'unrepresentative' is a common one, but the notion of representation underlying it is rarely explored in depth. While the middle-class white men who dominate politics in most Western democracies are not *demographically* representative of the population at large, they are the *elected* representatives of the population at large, and often have widespread electoral support from minority and disadvantaged groups. The claim that minority groups are not fully represented in the legislature, therefore, seems to presuppose that people can only be fully 'represented' by someone who shares their gender, class, occupation, ethnicity, language, etc.

This is sometimes called the idea of 'mirror representation'—that is, the legislature is said to be representative of the general public if it mirrors the ethnic, gender, or class characteristics of the public (Birch 1964: 16; Pitkin 1967: ch. 4). Or, put another way, a group of citizens is represented in a legislature if one or more of the members of the assembly are the same sort of people as the citizens. This contrasts with the more familiar idea in democratic theory which defines representation in terms of the procedure by which office-holders are elected, rather than their personal attributes. On this traditional view, a group of citizens is represented in the legislature if they participated in the election of one or more members of the assembly, even if the elected members are very different in their personal characteristics.

Why are the personal characteristics of representatives so important? There is surprisingly little written about the competing conceptions of representation which underlie recent proposals for group representation. However, there are a number of reasons why personal characteristics might be important. Some commentators argue that people must share certain experiences or characteristics in order truly to understand each other's needs and interests. On this view, a white man simply cannot know what is in the interests of a woman or a black man: 'no amount of thought or sympathy, no matter how careful or honest, can jump the barriers of experience' (A. Phillips 1994: 76).

Another argument says that even if white men can understand the interests of women and blacks, they cannot be trusted to promote those interests. For example, Christine Boyle argues that, because the interests of men differ from women in terms of income, discrimination, legal rights, and child-care, 'it seems reasonable to conclude that it is impossible for men to represent women'. The reason is not necessarily that men do not understand women's interests, but rather that 'at some point members of one group feel that someone belonging to another group has such a conflict of interest that representation is impossible, or at least unlikely' (Boyle 1983: 797–8; cf. Minow 1991: 286).

There is undoubtedly some truth to both these arguments—there are limits to the extent to which we can put ourselves in other people's shoes, even if we sincerely try to do so, and limits to the extent to which most people sincerely try to do so. None the less, taken as a general and complete theory of representation, the idea of mirror representation suffers from a number of infirmities. (I will consider later the more plausible idea that a degree of mirror representation may be justified in certain specific contexts, rather than as a general theory of representation.)

For one thing, the idea that the legislature should mirror the general population, taken to its logical conclusion, leads away from electoral politics entirely towards selection of representatives by lottery or random sampling. As Pitkin notes, 'selection by lot, or a controlled random sample, would be best calculated to produce the microcosm of the whole body of the people' (Pitkin 1967: 73, quoting Alfred DeGrazia). And indeed some theorists have proposed this (Burnham 1985), although most people, including most proponents of group representation, would see this as abandoning the democratic principle that representatives should be authorized by, and accountable to, the public. Yet, as I discuss below, it remains unclear how to resolve the conflict between mirror representation and democratic accountability.

Second, the claim that whites cannot understand the needs of blacks, or that men cannot understand the needs of women, can become an excuse for white men not to try to understand or represent the needs of others. Indeed some commentators say this has happened in New Zealand, where the Maori have guaranteed seats in the Parliament. The non-Maori have been said to have interpreted this as absolving them of any responsibility to take an interest in Maori affairs (Fleras 1985: 566; Gibbins 1991: 171; Mulgan 1989: 139–41). As Minow puts it, the assumption that people 'cannot empathize across lines of difference' can become 'a self-fulfilling prophesy' (Minow 1991: 293), particularly if the assumption is embodied in rules and institutional expectations.

Third, the claim that men cannot understand the interests of women cuts both ways. It implies that women cannot understand and therefore represent men. Of course, many men may believe this. But the unattractive implication is that people can only speak for their own group. Some proponents of group representation accept this result. According to Baines, 'if the truth be known, women [are not] particularly interested in representing men' (Baines 1992: 56). Yet most proponents of group representation do not favour 'the kind of politics in which people were elected only to speak for their own group identity or interests' (A. Phillips 1992: 85).

These objections do not prove that the members of one group can in fact understand and therefore represent the interests of the members of other groups who have significantly different experiences or characteristics. But the argument that the members of one group cannot understand the interests of other groups, if accepted, seems to undermine the possibility of group representation as well. For it surely applies within groups as well as between them. Each group has subgroups, with their own distinctive experiences and characteristics. If men cannot represent women, can white women represent women of colour? Within the category of women of colour, can Asian women represent African-Caribbean women? Can middle-class heterosexual able-bodied Asian women represent poor, disabled, or lesbian Asian women? Taken to its conclusion, the principle of mirror representation seems to undermine the very possibility of representation itself. If 'no amount of thought or sympathy, no matter how careful or honest, can jump the barriers of experience', then how can anyone represent anyone else?[12]

These difficulties suggest that the idea of mirror representation should be avoided as a general theory of representation. There undoubtedly are limits to the extent to which people are able and willing to 'jump the barriers of experience'. But the solution is not to accept those limitations. Rather we should fight against them, in order to create a political culture in which people are more able and more willing to put themselves in other people's shoes, and truly understand (and therefore become able to represent) their needs and interests. This is no easy task—it may require changes to our education system, to the media portrayal of various groups, and to the political process, to make it more a system of 'deliberative democracy'; and there still would be no guarantee that the members of one group would understand the needs of another. This is the 'challenge of empathy'.[13] But to renounce the possibility of cross-group representation is to renounce the possibility of a society in which citizens are committed to addressing each other's needs and sharing each other's fate.

In fact, very few proponents of group representation endorse the idea of mirror representation as a general theory of representation. Instead, group representation is defended on more contextual grounds, as an appropriate mechanism for representing certain groups under certain conditions. These contextual arguments for group representation fall into two major camps: systemic discrimination and self-government.

Group representation rights are often defended as a response to some systemic disadvantage or barrier in the political process which makes it impossible for the group's views and interests to be effectively represented. For example, Iris Young argues that special representation rights should be extended to 'oppressed groups' because:

> In a society where some groups are privileged while others are oppressed, insisting that as citizens persons should leave behind their particular affiliations and experiences to adopt a general point of view serves only to reinforce the privilege; for the perspective and interests of the privileged will tend to dominate this unified public, marginalizing or silencing those of other groups. (I. Young 1989: 257)

According to Young, oppressed groups are at a disadvantage in the political process, and 'the solution lies at least in part in providing institutionalized means for the explicit recognition and representation of oppressed groups' (I. Young 1989: 259. cf. I. Young 1990: 183–91; Boyle 1983: 791). These measures would include public funds for advocacy groups, guaranteed representation in political bodies, and veto rights over specific policies that affect a group directly.

The point here is not that the legislature should mirror society, but rather that the historical domination of some groups by other groups has left a trail of barriers and prejudices that makes it difficult for historically disadvantaged groups to participate effectively in the political process.

In so far as these rights are seen as a response to oppression or systemic disadvantage, they are most plausibly seen as a temporary measure on the way to a society where the need for special representation no longer exists—a form of political 'affirmative action'. Society should seek to remove the oppression and disadvantage, thereby eliminating the need for these rights. The Voting Rights Act, which endorses redistricting for blacks and Hispanics, is specifically written as a temporary measure. It must be renewed regularly, to see if this sort of affirmative gerrymandering is still required.

As with any other affirmative action programme, there are questions about whether the programme will actually work, whether there are viable alternatives that are less controversial, and whether it is possible to target those people who are truly disadvantaged, without being unfairly under-inclusive or over-inclusive. These issues are familiar from the debates over affirmative action in the economy and academy. The experience of affirmative action programmes in other spheres suggests that there are very few general answers to these sorts of questions—everything depends on the specifics of the actual programme being proposed.[14]

However, the issue of group representation is complicated in many countries, because some representation rights are defended, not on grounds of overcoming systemic discrimination, but as a corollary of the right to self-government for national minorities.

As I discussed in Chapter 2, self-government rights set limits on the authority of the federal government over a national minority. Moreover, these limits may be 'asymmetrical'. For example, Puerto Ricans, or residents of Indian reservations, may be exempt from certain pieces of federal legislation which apply to other areas of the United States. The same applies to Quebecers and Indian bands in Canada. These sorts of limits on federal authority are not seen as a temporary measure, nor as a remedy for a form of oppression that we might (and ought) someday to eliminate. On the contrary, national minorities often claim an 'inherent' right of self-government, which they see as pre-dating their incorporation into the larger state, and as enduring into the indefinite future.

The relationship between self-government and group representation is complicated, and adds a new dynamic into the more familiar debate over group representation as a remedy for discrimination. On the one hand, in so far as self-government reduces the jurisdiction of the federal government over a national minority, self-government seems to entail that the group should have *reduced* influence (at least on certain issues) at the federal level. For example, if self-government for the Québécois leads to the asymmetrical transfer of powers from Ottawa to Quebec, so that the federal government would be passing laws that would not apply to Quebec, it seems only fair that Quebecers not have a vote on such legislation (particularly if they could cast the deciding vote). For example, it would seem unfair for Quebec MPs to decide federal legislation on immigration if the legislation does not apply to Quebec. The same would apply to Aboriginal MPs elected by specially created Aboriginal districts voting on legislation from which Aboriginals would be exempt.

Many national minorities do have this sort of reduced influence at the federal level. For example, residents of Puerto Rico help select presidential candidates, but do not vote in presidential elections. And they have only one representative in Congress, a 'commissioner' who has a voice but no vote, except in committees. This reduced representation is seen by some as evidence that Puerto Rico is 'colonized'. But while the details of the existing arrangement are certainly subject to criticism, the existence of reduced representation can be seen as a corollary of Puerto Rican self-government, not just its colonial subjugation.[15]

On the other hand, the right to self-government in certain areas does seem to entail the right to representation on any bodies which can intrude on those areas. Hence it would seem to be a corollary of self-government that Quebec, for example, be guaranteed representation on any body which can interpret or modify their powers of self-government, or which can make decisions in areas of concurrent or conflicting jurisdiction (e.g. the Supreme Court). And indeed Quebec is guaranteed three of the nine seats on the Court.[16]

To over-simplify, then, self-government for a national minority seems to entail guaranteed representation on *intergovernmental* bodies, which negotiate, interpret, and modify the division of powers, but reduced representation on *federal* bodies which legislate in areas of purely federal jurisdiction from which they are exempted.[17]

It is a mistake, therefore, to argue (as various commentators and commissions in Canada have) that proposals to provide guaranteed representation of Aboriginal people in the federal legislature is 'a logical extension of aboriginal self-government' (Special Joint Committee 1992: 52). If anything, the logical consequence of self-government is reduced representation, not increased representation. The right to self-government is a right against the authority of the federal government, not a right to share in the exercise of that authority. It is for this reason that many Indians who claim self-government oppose guaranteed seats in the House of Commons. On this view, guaranteed representation in the Commons might give the central government the sense that they can rightfully govern Indian communities.[18]

Of course, Indians may also claim special representation in the federal legislature on grounds of systemic disadvantage. Claims of inherent self-government do not preclude claims based on temporary disadvantage. However, it is important to know which claim is being made, since they apply with different force to different governmental bodies, over different time-frames, and to different subgroups within Indian communities.[19] Since the claims of self-government are seen as inherent and permanent, so too are the guarantees of representation which follow from that self-government, whereas claims based on disadvantage are (in principle) temporary. Both claims reflect a desire for 'empowerment', but the sort of power being claimed is significantly different.

3. Evaluating Group Representation

I have tried to show that group representation has important continuities with existing practices of representation in liberal democracies, and, while the general idea of mirror representation is untenable, there are two contextual arguments which can justify limited forms of group representation under certain circumstances—namely, overcoming systemic disadvantage and securing self-government.[20] These arguments provide grounds for thinking that group representation can play an important if limited role within the system of representative democracy. However, any proposal for group-based representation must answer a number of difficult questions. In this final section of the chapter, I want to flag some of these questions, to indicate the sorts of issues that need to be addressed when developing or evaluating any specific proposal for group representation.

Which groups should be represented? How do we decide which groups, if any, should be entitled to group-based representation? Many critics of group representation take this to be an unanswerable question, or rather that any answer to it will be arbitrary and unprincipled. The result will be an unlimited escalation of demands for political recognition and support, and bitter resentment amongst those groups whose demands are denied. Since there is no way to stop this 'torrent of new demands on the part of previously marginalized groups', it is better to reject all claims for group representation (Galston 1991: 142; cf. Glazer 1983: 227–9).

But the arguments above suggest that there are ways of drawing principled distinctions between various groups. Groups have a claim to representation if they meet one of two criteria: (1) are the members of the group subject to systemic disadvantage in the political process? or (2) do the members of the group have a claim to self-government?

Of these two criteria, self-government is the easier to apply. As I noted in Chapter 2, self-government rights are typically demanded by national minorities. In Canada, for example, Aboriginals and the Québécois are seen as having rights of self-government. In the United States, the clearest examples of groups with recognized rights of self-government are Puerto Rico, Indian tribes, the Chamorros of Guam, and other Pacific Islanders.

The criteria of systemic disadvantage are more complicated. Many groups claim to be disadvantaged in some respect, even though they may be privileged in others, and it is not clear how one measures overall levels of disadvantage. According to Iris Young, there are five forms of oppression: exploitation, marginalization, powerlessness, cultural imperialism, and 'random violence and harassment motivated by group hatred or fear' (I. Young 1989: 261; 1990: 40). She adds that 'Once we are clear that the principle of group representation refers only to oppressed social groups, then the fear of an unworkable proliferation of group representation should dissipate' (I. Young 1990: 187).

However, her list of 'oppressed groups' in the United States would seem to include 80 per cent of the population. She says that 'in the United States today, at least the following groups are oppressed in one or more of these ways: women, blacks, Native Americans, Chicanos, Puerto Ricans and other Spanish-speaking Americans, Asian Americans, gay men, lesbians, working-class people, poor people, old people, and mentally and physically disabled people' (I. Young 1989: 261). In short, everyone but relatively well-off, relatively young, able-bodied, heterosexual white males.

Even then, it is hard to see how this criterion would avoid an 'unworkable proliferation', since each of these groups has subgroups that might claim their own rights. In the case of Britain, for example, the category of 'black' people obscures deep divisions between the Asian and Afro-Caribbean communities, each of which in turn comprises a wide variety of ethnic groups. As Phillips asks, given the almost endless capacity for fragmentation, 'What in this context then counts as "adequate" ethnic representation?' (A. Phillips 1992: 89; cf. Minow 1991: 286).

On the other hand, as Young observes, a large number of political parties and trade unions have allowed group representation for many years without entering an escalating spiral of increasing demands and resentment (I. Young 1989: 187–9; A. Phillips 1991: 65). And, as I noted earlier, we already have some experience with the issue of identifying disadvantaged groups in the context of affirmative action programmes.[21] Yet the problem is formidable—and certainly none of the proposals for group representation to date has addressed it in a satisfactory way. This is one reason why alternative reform schemes are preferable, if they are available and effective. However, the problem of identifying disadvantaged groups is not unique to issues of political representation, and it may not be avoidable in a country committed to redressing injustice.

It is important to note that not all historically disadvantaged groups are in favour of the group representation strategy. Many immigrant groups prefer to work within existing political parties to make them more inclusive, rather than trying to get guaranteed seats in legislation.[22] The option of refusing group representation must of course be available to each group. The additional visibility which comes with group representation carries risks as well as benefits, and each group should be free to evaluate these considerations in light of its own circumstances.

How many seats should a group have? If certain groups do need group representation, how many seats should they have? There are two common answers to this question that are often conflated, but which should be kept distinct, since they lead in different directions.

One view is that a group should be represented in proportion to its numbers in the population at large. For example, Canada's National Action Committee on the Status of Women (NAC) proposed that women be guaranteed 50 per cent of Senate seats, which is essentially their proportional electoral representation. The second view is that there should be a threshold number of representatives, sufficient to ensure that the group's views and interests are effectively expressed. The first view follows naturally from a commitment to the general principle of mirror representation. But, as I noted earlier, most proponents of group representation wish to avoid the principle of mirror representation. And once we drop that principle, it is not clear why proportional representation is preferable to a threshold level of representation.

For example, Anne Phillips rejects the underlying premiss of mirror representation that one has to be a member of a particular group in order to understand or represent that group's interests. But she goes on to say that 'in querying the notion that *only* the members of particular disadvantaged groups can understand or represent their interests [one] might usefully turn this question round and ask whether such understanding or representation is possible without the presence of *any* members of the disadvantaged groups?' (Phillips 1994: 89 n. 12). Phillips's argument is that, without a threshold number of seats, others will not be able to understand, and so be able to represent, the interests of a disadvantaged group.

Applying this criterion of a threshold number of seats may lead to different results from the criterion of proportional electoral representation. In the case of women, the threshold number of seats necessary to present women's views effectively is arguably less than the proportional number of seats. The president of NAC defended the guarantee of 50 per cent Senate seats for women on the ground that this would ensure women a 'place at the table' (Rebick and Day 1992)—that is, she demanded proportional representation, but defended it in terms of the need for threshold representation. But does having a place at the table require having 50 per cent of the places at the table?

In other cases, however, the threshold number of seats necessary for effective representation may be greater than the proportional number of seats. Evidence suggests that if there are only one or two members from a marginalized or disadvantaged group in a legislative assembly or committee, they are likely to be excluded, and their voices ignored (Guinier 1991*a*: 1434–7). Yet proportional representation for some disadvantaged groups, such as racial minorities or immigrant groups, will only amount to such token representation. The number of seats necessary for effective presentation of their views, therefore, may exceed the number of seats required for proportional electoral representation.

The choice between proportional and threshold representation may depend on the nature of the decision-making process—i.e. whether the legislative body has adopted consensual, consociational, super-majority, or other kinds of compromise decision-making rules, as opposed to simple majority voting rules. The more consensual the process, the more threshold representation may be sufficient.[23]

How are group representatives held accountable? What mechanisms of accountability can be put in place to ensure that the legislators who hold reserved seats in fact serve the interests of the groups they are supposed to represent? How do we ensure that their 'representatives' are in fact accountable to the group?

Here again we need to distinguish two very different answers. The Maori model in New Zealand involves setting up a separate electoral list for the Maori, so that some legislators are elected solely by Maori voters.[24] This model of group representation does not try to specify the characteristics of the candidate—indeed, it would be possible, however unlikely, that Maori voters might elect a white MP. What matters, on this model, is not who is elected, but how they are elected—that is, they are elected by, and hence accountable to, the Maori.

This is similar to the practice of drawing constituency boundaries so that they largely coincide with a 'community of interest'. It is safe to assume that these communities use their electoral strength to elect 'one of their own'. But they can, and sometimes do, elect someone who is not a member of their group. This does not undermine the value of accommodating communities of interest, because the justification for this practice is not mirror representation (which could be secured by a lottery or random sample). The justification is rather to promote the representation of the group's interests by making a legislator accountable to the community. Thus many defenders of redistricting in the USA insist that they are more interested in accountability than mirror representation:

> affirmative gerrymandering is, in my view, misconceived if it is seen as a mechanism to guarantee that blacks will be represented by blacks, Hispanics by Hispanics, and whites by whites; rather, the proper use of affirmative gerrymandering is to guarantee that important groups in the population will not be substantially impaired in their ability to elect representatives of *their choice*. (Grofman 1982: 98)

The Maori model attempts to provide the same sort of accountability to smaller or more territorially dispersed groups.

In many proposals for group representation, however, there are no separate electoral lists or gerrymandered constituencies. These proposals focus on the characteristics of the candidates, rather than the characteristics of the electorate. For example, the NAC proposal required that 50 per cent of Senators in Canada be women, but they would be chosen by the general electorate, which contains as many men as women. And while the NAC proposal would guarantee a proportional number of seats for racial minorities, these Senators would also be chosen by the general electorate, which is predominantly white.

In this model, group representation means having legislators who belong to one's group, even though they are not elected by one's group. But it is unclear in what sense this is a form of *representation*, for there are no mechanisms in this model for establishing what each group wants, or for ensuring that the 'representatives' of the group act on the basis of what the group wants. The representative is not accountable to the group, and so may simply ignore the views of that group. Indeed, given that the group's 'representatives' are chosen by the general electorate, it might be unwise for representatives to act in ways that upset the sentiments of the members of the dominant groups. As Phillips puts it, 'Accountability is always the other side of representation, and, in the absence of procedures for establishing what any group wants or thinks, we cannot usefully talk of their political representation' (Phillips 1992: 86–8).

This suggests that there is an asymmetry between the problem of exclusion and the solution of inclusion (Phillips 1995). That is, it may be reasonable to conclude that a group which falls far short of its proportional electoral representation is therefore 'under-represented', particularly if the group has been subject to historical discrimination or disadvantage. But it does not follow that reversing this exclusion through guaranteed seats ensures that the group's interests or perspectives are then 'represented'. The idea that the presence of women legislators, for example, would *by itself* ensure the representation of women's interests, even in the absence of any electoral accountability, only makes sense if one thinks that there is 'some fundamental unity between women, some essential set of experiences and interests that can be represented by any of the sex' (Phillips 1995). But this is implausible, not only in the case of women, but also in the case of ethnic, national, or racial minorities, given the heterogeneity of interests and perspectives within each of these groups.

So here again we have conflicting models, based on conflicting ideals. The Maori model guarantees that some representatives are solely accountable to Maori voters, although it does not guarantee that the representatives are themselves Maori—that is, it does not guarantee that the representative 'mirrors' the electorate. The NAC model guarantees that representatives mirror important groups in the electorate, but it does not guarantee that the representatives are accountable to the group they mirror. Of course, many proponents of guaranteed representation for disadvantaged groups believe in the need for accountability, and would like to find some way of making sure that representatives are accountable to the groups they are supposed to represent. But to date, the ideals of mirror representation and democratic accountability have not yet been adequately integrated.

4. Conclusion

Summary

Demands for group representation appeal to some of the most basic practices and principles of representative democracy, and some forms of group representation may be able to play an important if limited role within a democratic political system. However, any proposal for group representation must answer a number of difficult questions, in terms of identifying the truly disadvantaged groups and holding their 'representatives' accountable.

Even if these issues can be answered, some liberals will object to group representation on the grounds that institutionalizing group differences, and ascribing political salience to them, would have serious implications for social unity. Giving this sort of salience to groups is said to act 'like a corrosive on metal, eating away at the ties of connectedness that bind us together as a nation' (Ward 1991: 598). Indeed, the American Supreme Court's primary objection to black-majority redistricting was that it promoted 'balkanization'.[25] As I have noted, these concerns about social unity have arisen whenever any form of group-differentiated rights is proposed, and I address them in Chapter 9.

Of course, issues of representation cannot be reduced to the composition of the legislature. Representation in the legislature needs to be situated within the context of other mechanisms for representing the views or interests of a group, such as legal challenges to unfavourable legislation in the courts and interest-group advocacy. Any assessment of the need for group representation must take these alternative routes to representation into account.

But many of the difficulties which affect disadvantaged groups in the electoral process also affect their access to these alternative mechanisms of representation. Moreover, legislatures have a special symbolic role in representing the citizens of the country. Citizens who do not see themselves reflected in the legislature may become alienated from the political process and question its legitimacy. If not the only route to representation, legislative representation is a uniquely important one, and the desire to be adequately represented in it must be taken seriously.

That is a rather vague conclusion, I am afraid, and I have not tried to define or defend any specific model of group representation. Indeed, I do not think it is possible to say much more at the general level. Democracy involves a commitment to the principle of political equality, but there is no way to deduce the single best system of representation from that abstract principle (Beitz 1989; Dworkin 1987; Dahl 1989: chs. 10–14). There are many ways of achieving political equality, and the results of particular electoral mechanisms are notoriously context-specific. They depend heavily on the political culture of the country, including the way that parties are organized, and the voting patterns of citizens. Similar electoral reforms in different countries have had strikingly different results for the representation of disadvantaged groups. (Compare the impact of proportional representation with party lists in Italy and Norway.)

All I have tried to show in this chapter is that group representation is not inherently illiberal or undemocratic.[26] It is a plausible extension of our existing democratic traditions, and there may be some circumstances where it is the most appropriate way to ensure an adequate voice for minority interests and perspectives. Since it is vital that minorities have a fair hearing in the political process, proposals for group representation themselves deserve a fair hearing.

CHAPTER 8

Toleration and its Limits

So far, I have argued that liberals can and should endorse certain group-differentiated rights for ethnic groups and national minorities. But this endorsement is always a conditional and qualified one. The demands of some groups exceed what liberalism can accept. Liberal democracies can accommodate and embrace many forms of cultural diversity, but not all. This chapter will explore the limits of liberal tolerance, and how liberal states should respond when those limits are transgressed.

Liberal principles impose two fundamental limitations on minority rights. First, a liberal conception of minority rights will not justify (except under extreme circumstances) 'internal restrictions'—that is, the demand by a minority culture to restrict the basic civil or political liberties of its own members.[1] Liberals are committed to supporting the right of individuals to decide for themselves which aspects of their cultural heritage are worth passing on. Liberalism is committed to (perhaps even defined by) the view that individuals should have the freedom and capacity to question and possibly revise the traditional practices of their community, should they come to see them as no longer worthy of their allegiance.

Liberal principles are more sympathetic to demands for 'external protections', which reduce a minority's vulnerability to the decisions of the larger society. But even here there are important limits. Liberal justice cannot accept any such rights which enable one group to oppress or exploit other groups, as in apartheid. External protections are legitimate only in so far as they promote equality between groups, by rectifying disadvantages or vulnerabilities suffered by the members of a particular group.

In short, a liberal view requires *freedom within* the minority group, and *equality between* the minority and majority groups. A system of minority rights which respects these two limitations is, I believe, impeccably liberal. It is consistent with, and indeed promotes, basic liberal values.

Because of these two limitations, a liberal conception of minority rights cannot accommodate all the demands of all minority groups. For example, some cultural minorities do not want a system of minority rights that is tied to the promotion of individual freedom or personal autonomy. Some groups may in fact resist such a system because it might imply that the internal structure of their community should be reorganized according to liberal standards of democracy and individual freedom.

For example, the tribal government of the Pueblo Indians discriminates against those members of the tribe who reject the traditional religion of the group. Similarly, some minority cultures discriminate against girls in the provision of education, and deny women the right to vote or hold office. These measures do not protect the group from the decisions of the larger society. Rather, they limit the freedom of individual members within the group to revise traditional practices. As such, they are inconsistent with any system of minority rights that appeals to individual freedom or personal autonomy. Indeed, restricting religious freedom, or denying education to girls, violates one of the reasons liberals have for wanting to protect cultural membership—namely, that membership in a culture enables informed choice about how to lead one's life. These sorts of internal restrictions cannot be justified or defended within a liberal conception of minority rights.

Given these limitations and qualifications, some defenders of minority rights may think that reconciling minority rights with liberalism is a Pyrrhic victory. To find room for minority rights within liberal theory, they might say, requires qualifying these rights in such a way that they no longer correspond to the real aims of minority groups. I have defended the right of national minorities to maintain themselves as culturally distinct societies, but only if, and in so far as, they are themselves governed by liberal principles. Yet surely what some minorities desire is precisely the ability to reject liberalism, and to organize their society along traditional, non-liberal lines? Is this not part of what makes them culturally distinct? If the members of a minority lose the ability to enforce religious orthodoxy or traditional gender roles, have they not lost part of the *raison d'être* for maintaining themselves as a distinct society? Is the insistence on respect for individual rights not a new version of the old ethnocentrism, found in Mill and Marx, which sets the (liberal) majority culture as the standard to which minorities must adhere?

If a minority is seeking to oppress other groups, then most people would agree that intervention is justified in the name of self-defence against aggression. But what if the group has no interest in ruling over others or depriving them of their resources, and instead simply wants to be left alone to run its own community in accordance with its traditional non-liberal norms? In this case, it may seem wrong to impose liberal values. So long as these minorities do not want to impose their values on others, should they not be allowed to organize their society as they like, even if this involves limiting the liberty of their own members? Indeed, is it not fundamentally *intolerant* to force a peaceful national minority or religious sect—which poses no threat to anyone outside the group—to reorganize its community according to 'our' liberal principles of individual liberty?

These are difficult questions, and have given rise to important conflicts, not only between liberals and non-liberals, but also within liberalism itself. For tolerance is itself a fundamental liberal value. Yet promoting individual freedom or personal autonomy seems to entail intolerance towards illiberal groups. I suggested earlier that a theory of minority rights which precludes internal restrictions is impeccably liberal, since it is grounded firmly in the value of individual freedom. Yet others would view my theory as illiberal, precisely because its unrelenting commitment to individual autonomy is intolerant of non-liberal groups.

There is a large and growing debate amongst liberals about whether autonomy or tolerance is the fundamental value within liberal theory. This contrast is described in different ways—for example, a contrast between 'Enlightenment' and 'Reformation' liberalism (Galston 1995), or between 'comprehensive' and 'political' liberalism (Rawls 1993*a*; Moon 1993), or between 'Kantian' and *modus vivendi* liberalism (Larmore 1987). Underneath all these contrasts is a similar concern—namely, that there are many groups within the boundaries of liberal states which do not value personal autonomy, and which restrict the ability of their members to question and dissent from traditional practices. Basing liberal theory on autonomy threatens to alienate these groups and undermine their allegiance to liberal institutions, whereas a tolerance-based liberalism can provide a more secure and wider basis for the legitimacy of government.

Those liberals who emphasize toleration, and downplay autonomy, often wind up with a position regarding minority rights which is quite different from the one I have defended. For example, Chandran Kukathas is more sympathetic than I am to demands by cultural groups to impose internal restrictions on their own members, since he thinks that liberalism is not committed to the value of autonomy. Yet he is much less sympathetic to demands by minority cultures for any special external protections *vis-à-vis* the larger community. Liberal tolerance, on his view, requires that non-liberal groups be left alone, but it does not require the state to help them in any way, through public funding of schools, language rights, veto powers, or the redrawing of political boundaries (Kukathas 1992*a*; 1992*b*).

On this view, liberals should seek to accommodate illiberal groups, so long as they do not seek any support from the larger society, and do not seek to impose their values on others. It is a 'live and let live' approach, an ethic of reciprocal non-interference. In short, liberal tolerance allows for some internal restrictions, but no external protections.

I think this is mistaken, not only about the impermissibility of external protections (which I have defended in Chapter 6), but also about the legitimacy of internal restrictions. To be sure, there are important practical and moral limits on the extent to which liberal states can impose liberal values on cultural groups, particularly national minorities, which I discuss below. But there are also real conflicts between liberal principles and the demands of non-liberal groups, and we need to face these conflicts openly.

In this chapter, then, I will try to clarify the ways that liberalism can, and cannot, accommodate non-liberal groups. I will begin with the idea of tolerance, and show why the traditional liberal conception of tolerance is dependent on, rather than an alternative to, a commitment to autonomy (s. 1). I will then consider the extent to which promoting liberal principles can be seen as 'sectarian' (s. 2), before concluding with some suggestions about how liberal states should respond to non-liberal groups within their borders (s. 3).

1. *Liberalism and Tolerance*

Liberalism and toleration are closely related, both historically and conceptually. The development of religious tolerance was one of the historical roots of liberalism. Religious tolerance in the West emerged out of the interminable Wars of Religion, and the recognition by both Catholics and Protestants that a stable constitutional order cannot rest on a shared religious faith. According to Rawls, liberals have simply extended the principle of tolerance to other controversial questions about the 'meaning, value and purpose of human life' (Rawls 1987: 4; 1985: 249; 1993*a*: p. xxviii).

But if liberalism can indeed be seen as an extension of the principle of religious tolerance, it is important to recognize that religious tolerance in the West has taken a very specific form—namely, the idea of individual freedom of conscience. It is now a basic individual right to worship freely, to propagate one's religion, to change one's religion, or indeed to renounce religion altogether. To restrict an individual's exercise of these liberties is seen as a violation of a fundamental human right.

There are other forms of religious toleration which are not liberal. They are based on the idea that each religious group should be free to organize its community as it see fits, including along non-liberal lines. In the 'millet system' of the Ottoman Empire, for example, Muslims, Christians, and Jews were all recognized as self-governing units (or 'millets'), and allowed to impose restrictive religious laws on their own members.

Since the millet system has been cited as an important precedent and model for minority rights (Sigler 1983; Van Dyke 1985: 74–5; Thornberry 1991: 29), it is worth considering in more detail. The Ottoman Turks were Muslims who conquered much of the Middle East, North Africa, Greece, and Eastern Europe during the fourteenth and fifteenth centuries, thereby acquiring many Jewish and Christian subjects. For various theological and strategic reasons, the Ottomans allowed these minorities not only the freedom to practise their religion, but a more general freedom to govern themselves in purely internal matters, with their own legal codes and courts. For about five centuries, between 1456 and the collapse of the Empire in World War I, three non-Muslim minorities had official recognition as self-governing communities—the Greek Orthodox, the Armenian Orthodox, and the Jews—each of which was further subdivided into various local administrative units, usually based on ethnicity and language. Each millet was headed by the relevant church leader (the Chief Rabbi and the two Orthodox Patriarchs).

The legal traditions and practices of each religious group, particularly in matters of family status, were respected and enforced through the Empire. However, while the Christian and Jewish millets were free to run their internal affairs, their relations with the ruling Muslims were tightly regulated. For example, non-Muslims could not proselytize, and they could only build new churches under licence. There were limits on intermarriage, and non-Muslims had to pay special taxes, in lieu of military service. But within these limits, 'they were to enjoy complete self-government, obeying their own laws and customs'. Their collective freedom of worship was guaranteed, together with their possession of churches and monasteries, and they could run their own schools (see Runciman 1970: 27–35; Braude and Lewis 1982: 1–34).

This system was generally humane, tolerant of group differences, and remarkably stable. As Braude and Lewis note, 'For nearly half a millennium, the Ottomans ruled an empire as diverse as any in history. Remarkably, this polyethnic and multireligious society worked. Muslims, Christians, and Jews worshipped and studied side by side, enriching their distinct cultures' (Braude and Lewis 1982: 1).

But it was not a liberal society, for it did not recognize any principle of *individual* freedom of conscience. Since each religious community was self-governing, there was no external obstacle to basing this self-government on religious principles, including the enforcement of religious orthodoxy. Hence there was little or no scope for individual dissent within each religious community, and little or no freedom to change one's faith. While the Muslims did not try to suppress the Jews, or vice versa, they did suppress heretics within their own community. Heresy (questioning the orthodox interpretation of Muslim doctrine) and apostasy (abandoning one's religious faith) were punishable crimes within the Muslim community. Restrictions on individual freedom of conscience also existed in the Jewish and Christian communities.

The millet system was, in effect, a federation of theocracies. It was a deeply conservative and patriarchal society, antithetical to the ideals of personal liberty endorsed by liberals from Locke to Kant and Mill. The various millets differed in the extent of their enforcement of religious orthodoxy. There were many periods during the 500-year history of the millets in which liberal reformers within each community pushed for constitutional restrictions on the power of the millet's leaders. And in the second half of the nineteenth century, some of the millets adopted liberal constitutions, in effect converting a religious theocracy into a secular system of liberal-democratic self-government for the various national groups in the Empire. Liberal reformers sought to use the millets as the basis for a system of federal institutions which provided external protections for national minorities—by limiting the power of other groups over them—while still constitutionally respecting the civil and political rights of individual members.[2]

But, in general, there were significant restrictions on the freedom of individuals in the Ottoman Empire to question or reject church doctrine. The Ottomans accepted the principle of religious tolerance, where that is 'understood to indicate the willingness of a dominant religion to coexist with others' (Braude and Lewis 1982: 3), but did not accept the quite separate principle of individual freedom of conscience.[3]

The Ottoman millet system is perhaps the most developed model of non-liberal religious tolerance, but variations on that model can be found in many other times and places. And, as I noted in Chapter 3, this is the sort of system desired by some non-liberal minorities today. It is often demanded in the name of 'tolerance'. But it is not the sort of tolerance which liberals historically have endorsed. These groups do not want the state to protect each individual's right to freely express, question, and revise her religious beliefs. On the contrary, this is precisely what they object to. What they want is the power to restrict the religious freedom of their own members.[4]

So it is not enough to say that liberals believe in toleration. The question is, what sort of toleration? Historically, liberals have believed in a very specific notion of tolerance—one which involves freedom of individual conscience, not just collective worship. Liberal tolerance protects the right of individuals to dissent from their group, as well as the right of groups not to be persecuted by the state. It limits the power of illiberal groups to restrict the liberty of their own members, as well as the power of illiberal states to restrict the liberty of collective worship.

This shows, I think, that liberals have historically seen autonomy and tolerance as two sides of the same coin. What distinguishes *liberal* tolerance is precisely its commitment to autonomy—that is, the idea that individuals should be free to assess and potentially revise their existing ends (Mendus 1989: 56).

2. *Is Liberalism Sectarian?*

Is liberalism's commitment to autonomy an acceptable basis for government in a modern pluralistic society, given that some groups do not value autonomy? Should liberals try to find some alternative basis for liberal theory that can accommodate such groups—that is, find a form of tolerance that is more tolerant of illiberal groups?

Many liberals have started searching for such an alternative. In his more recent work, for example, Rawls distances himself from a commitment to autonomy, on the grounds that some people do not see their ends as potentially revisable, and to defend liberal institutions on this basis is therefore 'sectarian' (1987: 24; 1985: 246).[5] This objection is echoed by other 'political liberals' (Larmore 1987; Galston 1991; Moon 1993). They want to defend liberal institutions in a way which will appeal even to those who reject the idea that people can stand back and assess their ends.

I do not think Rawls's argument works. But this is an important issue, and worth exploring in more detail, since it helps clarify the points of conflict between liberal principles and the demands of non-liberal minorities. Rawls's proposal is not to reject the idea of autonomy entirely, but rather to restrict its scope. In particular, he wants to continue appealing to it in *political* contexts, while avoiding it in other contexts. The idea that we can form and revise our conception of the good is, he now says, strictly a 'political conception' of the person, adopted solely for the purposes of determining our public rights and responsibilities. It is not, he insists, intended as a general account of the relationship between the self and its ends applicable to all areas of life, or as an accurate portrayal of our deepest self-understandings. On the contrary, in private life it is quite possible and likely that our personal identity is bound to particular ends in such a way as to preclude rational revision. As he puts it,

> It is essential to stress that citizens in their personal affairs, or in the internal life of associations to which they belong, may regard their final ends and attachments in a way very different from the way the political conception involves. Citizens may have, and normally do have at any given time, affections, devotions, and loyalties that they believe they would not, and indeed could and should not, stand apart from and objectively evaluate from the standpoint of their purely rational good. They may regard it as simply unthinkable to view themselves apart from certain religious, philosophical and moral convictions, or from certain enduring attachments and loyalties. These convictions and attachments are part of what we may call their 'non-public identity'. (Rawls 1985: 241)

So Rawls no longer assumes that people's religious commitments are revisable or autonomously affirmed. He accepts that these ends may be so essential to our identity that we cannot stand back from them and subject them to assessment and revision. However, in political contexts, we ignore the possible existence of such 'constitutive' ends. As *citizens*, we continue to see ourselves as having a 'highest-order interest' in our capacity for autonomy, even though as *private individuals* we may not see ourselves as having or valuing that capacity. Rawls's conception of the autonomous person continues to provide the language of public justification in which people discuss their rights and responsibilities as citizens, although it may not describe their 'non-public identity' (Rawls 1980: 545).

Hence Rawls distinguishes his 'political liberalism' from the 'comprehensive liberalism' of John Stuart Mill. Mill emphasized that people should be able to assess the worth of inherited social practices in all areas of life, not just political life. People should not obey social customs just because they are customs, but only if they are worthy of allegiance. Each person must determine for himself whether these customs are 'properly applicable to his own circumstances and character' (Mill 1982: 122). This insistence on people's right to question and revise social practices was not limited to the political sphere. Indeed, Mill was mostly concerned about the way people blindly followed popular trends and social customs in their everyday personal life. Hence Mill's liberalism is based on an ideal of rational reflection that applies to human action generally, and that is intended 'to inform our thought and conduct as a whole' (Rawls 1987: 6).

Rawls worries that many people do not accept Mill's idea of autonomy as a principle governing human thought and action generally. However, he thinks that such people can none the less accept the idea of autonomy if it is restricted to political contexts, leaving them free to view their non-public identities in quite different ways. People can accept his political conception 'without being committed in other parts of their life to comprehensive moral ideals often associated with liberalism, for example, the ideals of autonomy and individuality' (Rawls 1985: 245).

Rawls's account of our non-public identity is, of course, very close to the 'communitarian' conception of the self defended by Michael Sandel (see Ch. 5, s. 4). And indeed one way to understand Rawls's 'political liberalism' is to say that, for Rawls, people are communitarians in private life, and liberals in public life. But is this a coherent position? The problem is to explain why anyone would accept the ideal of autonomy in political contexts unless they also accepted it more generally. If the members of a religious community see their religious ends as constitutive, so that they have no ability to stand back and assess these ends, why would they accept a political conception of the person which assumes that they do have that ability (and indeed a 'highest-order interest' in exercising that ability)?

Perhaps Rawls thinks that everyone can accept his political conception because those who do not generally value the capacity for autonomy can simply refrain from exercising it in private life. As I noted in Chapter 5, while a liberal society allows rational assessment and revision of one's ends, it does not compel it. Hence even if this view of autonomy conflicts with a religious minority's self-understanding, there is no cost to accepting it for political purposes.

But there is a cost to non-liberal minorities from accepting Rawls's political conception of the person—namely, it precludes any system of internal restrictions which limit the right of individuals within the group to revise their conceptions of the good. For example, it precludes a religious minority from prohibiting apostasy and proselytization, or from preventing their children learning about other ways of life. The minority may view these civil liberties as harmful. But if, for the purposes of political debate, they accept the assumption that people have a highest-order interest in exercising their capacity to form and revise a conception of the good, they have no way to express their belief in the harm of allowing proselytization and apostasy.

Consider the Canadian case of *Hofer* v. *Hofer*, which dealt with the powers of the Hutterite Church over its members. The Hutterites live in large agricultural communities, called colonies, within which there is no private property. Two lifelong members of a Hutterite colony were expelled for apostasy. They demanded their share of the colony's assets, which they had helped create with their years of labour. When the colony refused, the two ex-members sued in court. They objected to the fact that they had 'no right at any time in their lives to leave the colony without abandoning everything, even the clothes on their backs' (Janzen 1990: 67). The Hutterites defended this practice on the grounds that freedom of religion protects a congregation's ability to live in accordance with its religious doctrine, even if this limits individual freedom.

The Canadian Supreme Court accepted this Hutterite claim. But it is far from clear that the Hutterite claim can be defended within the language of Rawls's 'political liberalism'. As Justice Pigeon noted in dissent, the usual liberal notion of freedom of religion 'includes the right of each individual to change his religion at will'. Hence churches 'cannot make rules having the effect of depriving their members of this fundamental freedom'. The proper scope of religious authority is therefore 'limited to what is consistent with freedom of religion as properly understood, that is freedom for the individual not only to adopt a religion but also to abandon it at will'. Justice Pigeon thought that it was 'as nearly impossible as can be' for people in a Hutterite colony to reject its religious teachings, because of the high cost of changing their religion, and so they were effectively deprived of freedom of religion.[6]

Justice Pigeon's view, it seems to me, is most consistent with Rawls's 'political liberalism'. Pigeon is assuming, as Rawls says we should for the purposes of political argument and legal rights, that people have a basic interest in their capacity to form and revise their conception of the good. Hence, he concludes, the power of religious communities over their own members must be such that individuals can freely and effectively exercise that capacity. Were the Hutterites to accept Rawls's conception of the person, then they too would have to accept the view that freedom of religion must be interpreted in terms of an individual's capacity to form and revise her religious beliefs.[7]

The same issue arose in the case of *Wisconsin* v. *Yoder* in the United States, which dealt with the power of the Amish community over its members. The Amish, like the Hutterites in Canada, tried to make it difficult for their members to leave the group, albeit in a different way. They wanted to withdraw their children from school before the age of 16, so as to limit severely the extent to which the children learn about the outside world. And they too defended this by arguing that freedom of religion protects a group's freedom to live in accordance with its doctrine, even if this limits the individual freedom of children. The American Supreme Court accepted the Amish claim, but here again the coherence of the Amish claim depended on their explicit rejection of Rawls's 'political conception' of the person, which emphasizes the capacity to form and revise our ends.[8]

Hence Rawls's strategy of endorsing autonomy only in political contexts, rather than as a general value, does not succeed. Accepting the value of autonomy for political purposes enables its exercise in private life, an implication that will only be favoured by those who endorse autonomy as a general value.[9] Rawls has not explained why people who are communitarians in private life should be liberals in political life. Rawls may be right that 'Within different contexts we can assume diverse points of view toward our person without contradiction so long as these points of view cohere together when circumstances require' (Rawls 1980: 545). But he has not shown that these points of view do cohere. On the contrary, they clearly conflict on issues of intra-group dissent such as proselytization, apostasy, and mandatory education.

Why has Rawls not seen this conflict? Perhaps because he thinks that his political conception is the only one that can protect religious minorities from the intolerance of the majority. In a number of places he suggests that, once we recognize the inevitable plurality of religious groups in society, the only viable way to prevent persecution of minority faiths is to guarantee 'equal liberty of conscience' for individuals (e.g. Rawls 1982*b*: 25–9; 1989: 251). But this is a mistake—one can ensure tolerance *between* groups without protecting tolerance of individual dissent *within* each group. A millet-like system ensures the former without ensuring the latter. If we want to defend civil rights for individuals, therefore, we must go beyond the need for group tolerance and give some account of the value of endowing individuals with the freedom to form and revise their final ends.[10]

Rawls is mistaken, therefore, to suppose that he can avoid appealing to the general value of individual autonomy without undermining his argument for the priority of civil rights. The mere fact of *social plurality*, disconnected from any assumption of *individual autonomy*, cannot by itself defend the full range of liberal freedoms.[11] If, as communitarians argue, people's private identity really is tied to certain ends, such that they have no interest or ability to question and revise them, then a millet-like system which allows for internal restrictions within each group may be a superior response to pluralism. If individuals are incapable of revising their inherited religious commitments, or if it is not important to enable individuals to exercise that capacity, then the millet system may best protect and advance those constitutive ends.

This is hardly a novel conclusion. Defenders of internal restrictions have long argued that, once we drop the assumption that autonomy is a general value, religious and cultural groups should be allowed to protect their members' constitutive ends by restricting certain individual rights (e.g. Kukathas 1992*a*; McDonald 1991*b*; Karmis 1993; Mason 1993). Sandel himself defends the right of the Amish to withdraw their children from school, arguing that freedom of conscience should be understood as freedom to pursue one's constitutive ends, not as freedom to choose one's religion (Sandel 1990). He argues that people's religious affiliation is so profoundly constitutive of who they are that their overriding interest is in protecting and advancing that identity, and that they have no comparable interest in being able to stand back and assess that identity. Hence there is little or no value (and perhaps even positive harm) in teaching Amish children about the outside world.

There is a genuine conflict here, which we need to face honestly. If we wish to defend individual freedom of conscience, and not just group tolerance, we must reject the communitarian idea that people's ends are fixed and beyond rational revision. We must endorse the traditional liberal belief in personal autonomy.

3. *Accommodating Non-liberal Minorities*

Why is Rawls so reluctant to endorse autonomy as a general human interest? What is wrong with Mill's 'comprehensive' liberalism? The problem, Rawls says, is that not everyone accepts this ideal of autonomy, and so appealing to it in political life would be 'sectarian'. The autonomy-based defence of individual rights invokes 'ideals and values that are not generally . . . shared in a democratic society', and hence 'cannot secure sufficient agreement'. To base liberalism on a controversial value like autonomy would mean that liberalism 'becomes but another sectarian doctrine' (Rawls 1987: 6, 24; 1985: 246).

This is a legitimate point, but Rawls overstates it, and draws the wrong conclusion from it. The idea that we have an interest in being able to assess and revise our inherited conceptions of the good is very widely shared in Western democratic societies.[12] There are some insulated minorities who reject this ideal, including some indigenous groups (the Pueblo), and religious sects (the Amish and Mennonites). These groups pose a challenge for liberal democracies, since they often demand internal restrictions that conflict with individual civil rights. We cannot simply ignore this demand, or ignore the fact that they reject the idea of autonomy.

But Rawls's strategy is no solution to the questions raised by the existence of non-liberal minorities. His strategy is to continue to enforce individual rights, but to do so on the basis of a 'political' rather than a 'comprehensive' liberalism. This obviously does not satisfy the demands of non-liberal minorities. They want internal restrictions that take precedence over individual rights. Rawls's political liberalism is as hostile to that demand as Mill's comprehensive liberalism. The fact that Rawls's theory is less comprehensive does not make his theory more sympathetic to the demands of non-liberal minorities.

How then should a liberal state treat non-liberal minorities? I have argued that any theory which does not accord substantial civil rights to the members of minority cultures is seriously deficient from a liberal point of view. Some critics claim that I am therefore 'drawn down the path of interference' in many existing minority cultures—for example, that I am committed to imposing a liberal regime on the Pueblo Indians, and forcing them to respect the religious liberty of the Protestants on the reservation.[13]

But this conflates two distinct questions: (1) what sorts of minority claims are consistent with liberal principles? (2) should liberals impose their views on minorities which do not accept some or all of these liberal principles? The first is the question of *identifying* a defensible liberal theory of minority rights; the second is the question of *imposing* that liberal theory.

So far, I have focused on the first question—i.e. identifying a defensible liberal conception of minority rights. With respect to that question, I believe that the most defensible liberal theory is based on the value of autonomy, and that any form of group-differentiated rights that restricts the civil rights of group members is therefore inconsistent with liberal principles of freedom and equality. The millet system, or the Pueblo theocracy, are therefore seriously deficient from a liberal point of view.

But that does not mean that liberals can impose their principles on groups that do not share them. This is obvious enough, I think, if the illiberal group is another country. The Saudi Arabian government unjustly denies political rights to women or non-Muslims. But it does not follow that liberals outside Saudi Arabia should forcibly intervene to compel the Saudis to give everyone the vote. Similarly, the German government unjustly denies political rights to the children and grandchildren of Turkish 'guest-workers', who were born on German soil and for whom Germany is the only home they know. But it does not follow that liberals outside Germany should use force to compel Germany to change its citizenship laws.

In these cases, the initial moral judgement is clear enough. From a liberal point of view, someone's rights are being unjustly denied by their own government. But what is not clear is the proper remedy—that is, what third party (if any) has the authority to intervene in order to force the government to respect those rights?

The same question arises when the illiberal group is a self-governing national minority within a single country. For example, the Pueblo tribal council violates the rights of its members by limiting freedom of conscience, and by employing sexually discriminatory membership rules.[14] But what third party (if any) has the authority to intervene forcibly to compel the Pueblo council to respect those rights?

Liberal principles tell us that individuals have certain claims which their government must respect, such as individual freedom of conscience. But having identified those claims, we now face the very different question of imposing liberalism. If a particular government fails to respect those claims, who has the authority to step in and force compliance? (Note that by 'imposing' liberalism, I am referring to forcible intervention by a third party to compel respect for liberal rights. Non-coercive intervention by third parties is a different matter, which I discuss below.)

The attitude of liberals toward imposing liberalism has changed over the years. In the international context, liberals have become increasingly sceptical about using force to compel foreign states to obey liberal principles. Many nineteenth-century liberals, including John Stuart Mill, thought that liberal states were justified in colonizing foreign countries in order to teach them liberal principles. Contemporary liberals, however, have generally abandoned this doctrine as both imprudent and illegitimate, and sought instead to promote liberal values through education, persuasion, and financial incentives.[15]

In the case of national minorities, however, liberals have been much more willing to endorse coercive third-party intervention. For example, many American liberals assume that the American Supreme Court has the legitimate authority to overturn any decisions of the Pueblo tribal council which violate individual rights. American liberals often assume that to have a right means not only that legislators should respect one's claim when passing legislation, but also that there should be some system of judicial review to make sure that the legislature respects one's claim. Moreover, this judicial review should occur at a country-wide level. That is, in addition to the various state and tribal courts which review the laws of state and tribal governments, there should also be a Supreme Court to which all governments within the country are ultimately answerable. Many American liberals often talk as if it is part of the very meaning of 'rights' that there should be a single court in each country with the authority to review the decisions of all governments within that country, to ensure that they respect liberal rights.

This is a very particularistic understanding of rights. In some liberal countries (e.g. Britain), there is a strong tradition of respecting individual rights, but there is no constitutional bill of rights, and no basis for courts to overturn parliamentary decisions which violate individual rights. (The same was true in Canada until 1982.) In other countries, there is judicial review, but it is decentralized—that is, political subunits have their own systems of judicial review, but there is no single constitutional bill of rights, and no single court, to which all levels of government are answerable. Indeed, this was true in the United States for a considerable period of time. Until the passage of the Fourteenth Amendment, state legislatures were answerable to state courts for the way they respected state constitutions, but were not answerable to the federal Supreme Court for respecting the federal Bill of Rights.

It is easy to see why American liberals are committed to giving the Supreme Court authority over the actions of state governments. Historically, this sort of federal judicial review, backed up by federal troops, was required to overturn the racist legislation of Southern states, which state courts had upheld. Given the central role federal courts have played in the struggle against racism, American liberals have developed a deep commitment to the principle of centralized judicial review, according to which a single body should have the authority to review and overturn the actions of all levels of government within each country, on the basis of a single bill of rights.

But should the same sort of centralized judicial review which applies to state governments also apply to self-governing national minorities, such as Indian tribal governments or the Commonwealth of Puerto Rico? Like state governments, tribal governments were not historically subject to the federal Bill of Rights. But many liberals have sought to change this, and so passed the 1968 Indian Civil Rights Act, which subjects Indian tribal governments to most aspects of the federal Bill of Rights. But even here, tribal governments are only answerable to tribal courts, not (except under special circumstances) to the federal courts. The Commonwealth of Puerto Rico has also become subject in recent years to the federal Bill of Rights, and to judicial review by federal courts, although how and why this occurred is far from clear.[16]

Contemporary liberals, then, have become more reluctant to impose liberalism on foreign countries, but more willing to impose liberalism on national minorities. This, I think, is inconsistent. Many of the reasons why we should be reluctant to impose liberalism on other countries are also reasons to be sceptical of imposing liberalism on national minorities within a country. Both foreign states and national minorities form distinct political communities, with their own claims to self-government. Attempts to impose liberal principles by force are often perceived, in both cases, as a form of aggression or paternalistic colonialism. And, as a result, these attempts often backfire. The plight of many former colonies in Africa shows that liberal institutions are likely to be unstable and transient when they have arisen as a result of external imposition, rather than internal political reform. In the end, liberal institutions can only really work if liberal beliefs have been internalized by the members of the self-governing society, be it an independent country or a national minority.[17]

There are, of course, important differences between foreign states and national minorities. Yet in both cases I believe there is relatively little scope for legitimate coercive interference. Relations between majority and minority nations in a multination state should be determined by peaceful negotiation, not force (as with international relations). This means searching for some basis of agreement. The most secure basis would be agreement on fundamental principles. But if two national groups do not share basic principles, and cannot be persuaded to adopt the other's principles, they will have to rely on some other basis of accommodation, such as a *modus vivendi*.

The resulting agreement may well involve exempting the national minority from federal bills of rights and judicial review. And, as I have noted, contemporary liberal societies have in fact provided such exemptions for some national minorities. Moreover, these exemptions are often spelled out in the historical terms of federation by which a national minority entered the larger state. In cases where the national minority is illiberal, this means that the majority will be unable to prevent the violation of individual rights within the minority community. Liberals in the majority group have to learn to live with this, just as they must live with illiberal laws in other countries.

This does not mean that liberals should stand by and do nothing. A national minority which rules in an illiberal way acts unjustly. Liberals have a right, and a responsibility, to speak out against such injustice. Hence liberal reformers inside the culture should seek to promote their liberal principles, through reason or example, and liberals outside should lend their support to any efforts the group makes to liberalize their culture. Since the most enduring forms of liberalization are those that result from internal reform, the primary focus for liberals outside the group should be to provide this sort of support.

Moreover, there is an important difference between coercively imposing liberalism and offering various incentives for liberal reforms. Again, this is clear in the international context. For example, the desire of former Communist countries to enter the EC has provided leverage for Western democracies to push for liberal reforms in Eastern Europe. Membership in the EC is a powerful, but non-coercive, incentive for liberal reform. Similarly, many people thought that the negotiations over the North American Free Trade Agreement provided an opportunity to pressure the Mexican government into improving its human rights record. The Mexican desire for a continental free-trade agreement provided the United States and Canada with some leverage to push for liberal reforms within Mexico. Obviously, there are many analogous opportunities for a majority nation to encourage national minorities, in a non-coercive way, to liberalize their internal constitutions. Of course there are limits to the appropriate forms of pressure. For example, refusing to extend trade privileges is one thing, imposing a total embargo or blockade is quite another. The line between incentives and coercion is not a sharp one, and where exactly to draw it is a much-debated point in the international context (see Damrosch 1989).

Finally, liberals can push for the development and strengthening of international mechanisms for protecting human rights. Many Indian tribes have expressed a willingness to abide by international declarations of human rights, and to answer to international tribunals for complaints of rights violations within their community. Indeed, they have shown greater willingness to accept this kind of international review than many majority nations, which jealously guard their sovereignty in domestic affairs. Most Indian tribes do not oppose all forms of external review. What they object to is being subject to the constitution of their conquerors, which they had no role in drafting, and being answerable to federal courts, composed solely of non-Indian justices.

This shows, I think, that the standard assumption of American liberals that there must be one court within each country which is the ultimate defender of individual rights seems doubly mistaken, at least in the case of multination states. History has shown the value of holding governments accountable for respecting human rights. But in multination states, the appropriate forums for reviewing the actions of self-governing national minorities may skip the federal level, as it were. Many national minorities would endorse a system in which the decisions of self-governing national minorities are reviewed in the first instance by their own courts, and then by an international court. Federal courts, dominated by the majority nation, would have little or no authority to review and overturn these decisions.

These international mechanisms could arise at the regional as well as global level. For example, European countries have agreed to establish their own multilateral human rights tribunals. Perhaps the American government and Indian tribes could agree to establish a similar bilateral human rights tribunal, on which both sides are fairly represented. There are many ways to strengthen mechanisms for respecting individual rights in a consensual way, without simply imposing liberal values on national minorities.

This is not to say that federal intervention to protect liberal rights is never justified. Obviously intervention is justified in the case of gross and systematic violation of human rights, such as slavery or genocide or mass torture and expulsions, just as these are grounds for intervening in foreign countries. The exact point at which intervention in the internal affairs of a national minority is warranted is unclear, just as it is in the international context. I think a number of factors are potentially relevant here, including the severity of rights violations within the minority community, the degree of consensus within the community on the legitimacy of restricting individual rights, the ability of dissenting group members to leave the community if they so desire, and the existence of historical agreements with the national minority. For example, whether it is justified to intervene in the case of an Indian tribe that restricts freedom of conscience surely depends on whether it is governed by a tyrannical dictator who lacks popular support and prevents people leaving the community, or whether the tribal government has a broad base of support and religious dissidents are free to leave.[18]

Cases involving newly arriving immigrant groups are very different. In these cases, it is more legitimate to compel respect for liberal principles, for reasons discussed in Chapter 5. I do not think it is wrong for liberal states to insist that immigration entails accepting the legitimacy of state enforcement of liberal principles, so long as immigrants know this in advance, and none the less voluntarily choose to come.

A more complicated case involves long-standing ethnic groups or religious sects who have been allowed to maintain certain illiberal institutions for many years, even many generations. This would include the Amish and Mennonites who emigrated to the United States and Canada early in this century, as well as the Hasidic Jews in New York. For various reasons, when these immigrant groups arrived, they were given exemptions from the usual requirements regarding integration, and were allowed to maintain certain internal restrictions. We may now regret these historical exemptions, but they were granted, and we cannot entirely dismiss them, unless they are unconscionably unjust (e.g. if they guaranteed a minority the right to maintain slaves). Relying on certain tacit or explicit assurances about their right to maintain separate institutions, these groups have now built and maintained self-contained enclaves that depend on certain internal restrictions. Had those assurances not been given, these groups might well have emigrated to some other country. As I noted in Chapter 6, it is not clear how much weight, morally speaking, should be given to these sorts of historical arguments, but it seems that these groups do have a stronger claim to maintain internal restrictions than newly arriving immigrants.[19]

4. *Conclusion*

The legitimacy of imposing liberal principles on illiberal national groups depends on a number of factors. The question of how two cultures, or two countries, should resolve differences of fundamental principle is a very complicated one which would require a book of its own. My project in this book is primarily to figure out what liberalism's fundamental principles are. Most contemporary liberal theorists have argued that the citizens of a liberal society, motivated by liberal principles of justice, would not accord political significance to their cultural membership. I have argued that this is a mistake, and that liberal principles of justice are consistent with, and indeed require, certain forms of special status for national minorities. Of course, the members of some minority cultures reject liberalism. In these cases, members of the more liberal majority will have to sit down with the members of the national minority, and find a way of living together. Liberals have no automatic right to impose their views on non-liberal national minorities. But they do have the right, and indeed the responsibility, to identify what those views actually are. Relations between national groups should be determined by dialogue. But if liberal theory is to contribute anything to that dialogue, it is surely by spelling out the implications of the liberal principles of freedom and equality. That is not the first step down the path of interference. Rather, it is the first step in starting a dialogue.

It is important to put this issue in perspective. The question of how to deal with illiberal cultures does not just arise in the context of minority cultures. While there are some illiberal national minorities, there are also illiberal majority cultures and illiberal homogeneous nation-states. (Indeed, some national minorities in Africa and Eastern Europe are much more liberal than the majority cultures.) In all of these cases, liberals both within and outside the illiberal group face the question of what actions are legitimate in promoting their liberal ideals. Whatever answers are appropriate in these other cases are likely to be appropriate for minority cultures.

Moreover, it is important not to prejudge the illiberal nature of a particular minority culture.[20] The liberality of a culture is a matter of degree. As I noted in Chapter 3, all cultures have illiberal strands, just as few cultures are entirely repressive of individual liberty. To talk as if the world was divided into completely liberal societies on the one hand, and completely illiberal ones on the other, inhibits a constructive dialogue between cultures (Parekh 1994; Modood 1993).

Even when minority leaders express a hostility to liberalism, it is important to remember the political context. These leaders may simply be responding to the fact that liberals have been resisting the minority's claims for self-government, or other external protections. If we examine the way that minority cultures actually treat their members, in terms of respect for civil liberties and tolerance of dissent, they are often just as liberal as the majority culture.

For example, when some indigenous leaders say that they value community rights above individual rights, what they often mean is that they attach profound importance to their recognition as a distinct culture and society with inherent rights of self-government.[21] They want to be recognized as a distinct national community, and, in that sense, demand a 'community right', not just individual rights. They are not necessarily saying that they attach little or no weight to individual liberty within their community. Indeed, many observers have noted that indigenous cultures are often quite individualistic in their internal organization. Many indigenous cultures display a profound antipathy to the idea that one person can be another's master (e.g. de Onis 1992: 39). The claim that indigenous peoples favour collective rights over individual rights is often a claim about the importance of indigenous self-government *vis-à-vis* the larger society, not a claim about how that self-government should be exercised *vis-à-vis* community members.

I do not mean to deny the extent of illiberal practices in some cultures. This is a profound challenge to a liberal theory of minority rights. But the challenge is not unique to minority cultures. It also arises for liberals in responding to illiberal practices in majority cultures and ethnically homogeneous nation-states. Liberals need to think more deeply about how to promote the liberalization of societal cultures, and about the role of coercive and non-coercive third-party intervention in that process. Dismissing the idea of self-government for national minorities will not make that problem go away.

CHAPTER 9

The Ties that Bind

So far, I have tried to show that group-differentiated minority rights are consistent with basic liberal principles of individual freedom and social justice, and that familiar liberal objections on these grounds are unpersuasive. But lurking behind these familiar objections is another concern, about the impact of these rights on the sense of community or fraternity.

Of course, liberals have never been very comfortable with the language of 'community' or 'fraternity'. As a result, liberal fears in this area are often rephrased in other terms, particularly the language of 'citizenship'. But, whatever the terminology, the fear is that group-differentiated rights will undermine the sense of shared civic identity that holds a liberal society together. These rights will be a source of disunity that could lead to the dissolution of the country, or, less drastically, to a reduced willingness to make the mutual sacrifices and accommodations necessary for a functioning democracy. The only way to develop a shared civic identity, many liberals believe, is to have a common (undifferentiated) citizenship status.

This concern has come up repeatedly in the liberal tradition. Indeed, as I noted in Chapter 4, until very recently most liberal opposition to minority rights was quite explicitly phrased in the language of stability, rather than freedom or justice. And social unity is a valid concern. Liberal societies require a high level of mutual concern amongst their citizens, which we cannot take for granted. And there is ample evidence from around the world that differences in ethnic and national identity can, if emphasized and politicized, form a barrier to a wider solidarity.

It is not enough, therefore, to show that minority rights are consistent in principle with freedom and justice. We also need to determine whether they are consistent with the long-term requirements of a stable liberal democracy, including the requirement of a shared civic identity that can sustain the level of mutual concern, accommodation, and sacrifice that democracies require. In this chapter, I will consider the impact of group-differentiated rights on the sense of civic identity and mutual concern. I will first examine why liberal societies require a sense of solidarity (s. 1). I will then argue that both polyethnic and representation rights can be seen as supporting this sense of solidarity (s. 2). The case of national self-government rights is more complicated (s. 3). Identifying a secure basis for solidarity in multination states is difficult, since both accepting and rejecting self-government rights can be destabilizing. Indeed, the case of multination states helps illustrate why we need a new account of the 'ties that bind' (s. 4).

1. *The Importance of Citizenship*

In a society which recognizes group-differentiated rights, the members of certain groups are incorporated into the political community, not only as individuals, but also through the group, and their rights depend, in part, on their group membership. I have sometimes described these rights as forms of 'differentiated citizenship'. But can we still talk about 'citizenship' in a society where rights are distributed on the basis of group membership?

Some liberals seem to regard this idea as a contradiction in terms. For them, citizenship is by definition a matter of treating people as individuals with equal rights under the law. This is what distinguishes democratic citizenship from feudal and other pre-modern views that determined people's political status by their religious, ethnic, or class membership. Hence John Porter insists that 'the organization of society on the basis of rights or claims that derive from group membership is sharply opposed to the concept of society based on citizenship' (Porter 1987: 128). We can find similar statements in the work of John Rawls, and other recent liberal discussions of citizenship.[1]

The claim that differentiated citizenship is a contradiction in terms is overstated. If differentiated citizenship is defined as the adoption of group-specific polyethnic, representation, or self-government rights, then virtually every modern democracy recognizes some form of it. As Parekh notes, citizenship today 'is a much more differentiated and far less homogeneous concept than has been presupposed by political theorists' (Parekh 1990: 702).

However, critics of differentiated citizenship worry that, if groups are encouraged by the very terms of citizenship to turn inward and focus on their 'difference', then, as Nathan Glazer put it in the

American context, 'the hope of a larger fraternity of all Americans will have to be abandoned' (Glazer 1983: 227). Citizenship cannot perform its vital integrative function if it is group-differentiated—it ceases to be 'a device to cultivate a sense of community and a common sense of purpose' (Heater 1990: 295). Nothing will bind the various groups in society together, and prevent the spread of mutual mistrust or conflict. If citizenship is differentiated, it no longer provides a shared experience or common status. Citizenship would be yet another force for disunity, rather than a way of cultivating unity in the face of increasing social diversity. Citizenship should be a forum where people transcend their differences, and think about the common good of all citizens (see e.g. Kukathas 1993: 156; Kristeva 1993: 7; Cairns 1993; 1995).

This is a serious concern, and points to an important gap in much contemporary liberal theory. Recent political events and trends throughout the world—increasing voter apathy and long-term welfare dependency in the United States, the resurgence of nationalist movements in Eastern Europe, the stresses created by an increasingly multicultural and multiracial population in Western Europe, the backlash against the welfare state in Thatcher's England, the failure of environmental policies that rely on voluntary citizen co-operation, etc.—have made clear that the health and stability of a modern democracy depends, not only on the justice of its basic institutions, but also on the qualities and attitudes of its citizens: e.g. their sense of identity, and how they view potentially competing forms of national, regional, ethnic, or religious identities; their ability to tolerate and work together with others who are different from themselves; their desire to participate in the political process in order to promote the public good and hold political authorities accountable; their willingness to show self-restraint and exercise personal responsibility in their economic demands, and in personal choices which affect their health and the environment; and their sense of justice and commitment to a fair distribution of resources. Without citizens who possess these qualities, 'the ability of liberal societies to function successfully progressively diminishes' (Galston 1991: 220).

Many classical liberals believed that a liberal democracy could be made secure, even in the absence of an especially virtuous citizenry, by creating checks and balances. Institutional and procedural devices such as the separation of powers, a bicameral legislature, and federalism would all serve to block would-be oppressors. Even if each person pursued her own self-interest, without regard for the common good, one set of private interests would check another set of private interests. In this way, Kant thought that the problem of good government 'can be solved even for a race of devils'. However, it has become clear that procedural-institutional mechanisms to balance self-interest are not enough, and that some level of civic virtue and public-spiritedness is required. Without this, democracies become difficult to govern, even unstable.[2]

Yet there is growing fear that the public-spiritedness of citizens of liberal democracies may be in serious decline.[3] Will the rise of group-based claims further erode the sense of shared civic purpose and solidarity? In answering this question, we need to keep in mind the distinction between the three forms of differentiated citizenship. In particular, we need to distinguish polyethnic and representation rights (s. 2), from self-government rights (s. 3).

2. *Polyethnicity and Inclusion*

Let's start with group representation rights. Generally speaking, the demand for representation rights by disadvantaged groups is a demand for *inclusion*. Groups that feel excluded want to be included in the larger society, and the recognition and accommodation of their 'difference' is intended to facilitate this. Indeed, as I discussed in Chapter 7, these representation rights can be seen as an extension of long-standing and widely accepted practices within liberal democracies. It has always been recognized that a majoritarian democracy can systematically ignore the voices of minorities. In cases where minorities are regionally concentrated, democratic systems have responded by intentionally drawing the boundaries of federal units, or of individual constituencies, so as to create seats where the minority is in a majority. Proponents of special representation simply extend this logic to non-territorial groups who may equally be in need of representation (e.g. ethnic minorities, women, the disabled). The familiar practice of defining geographic constituencies in such a way as to ensure representation of 'communities of interest' is not seen as a threat to national unity—on the contrary, it is rightly seen as promoting civic participation and political legitimacy (RCERPF 1991: 149). Why then should guaranteed representation for non-territorial communities of interest be seen as a threat to unity, rather than as evidence of a desire for integration? To be sure, there are enormous practical obstacles to such a proposal (see Ch. 7, s. 3). However, the basic impulse underlying representation rights is integration, not separation.[4]

Similarly, most polyethnic demands are evidence that members of minority groups want to participate within the mainstream of society. Consider the case of Sikhs who wanted to join the Royal Canadian Mounted Police, but, because of their religious requirement to wear a turban, could not do so unless they were exempted from the usual requirements regarding ceremonial headgear. Or the case of Orthodox Jews who wanted to join the US military, but who needed an exemption from the usual regulations so they could wear their yarmulka. Such exemptions are opposed by many people, who view them as a sign of disrespect for one of our 'national symbols'. But the fact that these men wanted to be a part of the national police force or the national military is ample evidence of their desire to participate in and contribute to the larger community. The special right they were requesting could only be seen as promoting not discouraging their integration.[5]

Some demands for polyethnic rights take the form of withdrawal from the larger society, although this is more likely to be true of religious sects than of ethnic communities *per se*. The Amish and other Christian sects have been granted exemptions from the usual requirements regarding integration (e.g. military service, compulsory education of children). But these are atypical, I believe. Moreover, it is important to note that these exemptions for religious groups have a very different origin and motivation from the current policy of 'multiculturalism'.

The decision to allow certain groups to withdraw from the larger society occurred many decades ago—often at the turn of the century—in response to the demands of white Christian and Jewish groups such as the Amish, Hutterites, Quakers, and Hasidim. 'Multiculturalism' as an official government policy, by contrast, began in the late 1960s and 1970s, in the context of increasing immigration from non-white, non-Christian countries. And most of the group-differentiated policies which have arisen under the 'multiculturalism' umbrella, and which are aimed at accommodating these new ethnic/religious groups, are not about withdrawing from the larger society. The case of the Sikhs in the RCMP is a good example—the policy is intended, not to allow Sikhs to withdraw from the larger society, but precisely to modify the institutions of mainstream society so that Sikhs can integrate into them as fully as possible.

Some recent immigrant groups make demands which are similar to the demands of older Christian sects. For example, some British Muslim groups have demanded the same sort of exemption from a liberal education granted to the Amish. But again these are atypical.

Moreover, such demands have not been accepted in Canada, the USA or Australia, since they are not the sort of demands that the new policy of polyethnicity was intended to meet. The philosophy underlying polyethnicity is an integrationist one, which is what most new immigrant groups want. It is a mistake, therefore, to describe polyethnic rights as promoting 'ghettoization' or 'balkanization'.

Some people fear that polyethnic rights impede the integration of immigrants by creating a confusing half-way house between their old nation and citizenship in the new one, reminding immigrants 'of their different origins rather than their shared symbols, society and future' (Citizen's Forum 1991: 128). But these worries seem empirically unfounded. The experience to date suggests that first- and second-generation immigrants who remain proud of their heritage are also among the most patriotic citizens of their new countries (Whitaker 1992: 255). Moreover, their strong affiliation with their new country seems to be based in large part on its willingness not just to tolerate, but to welcome, cultural difference.

Indeed, there is strikingly little evidence that immigrants pose any sort of threat to the unity or stability of a country. This fear was understandable 150 years ago, when the United States, Canada, and Australia began accepting waves of non-English immigrants. As I noted in Chapter 4 (s. 4), the idea of building a country through polyethnic immigration was quite unique in history, and many people thought it untenable. But that was 150 years ago, and there is no longer any reason for such fears to persist. It has become clear that the overwhelming majority of immigrants want to integrate, and have in fact integrated, even during the periods of large-scale influxes. Moreover, they care deeply about the unity of their new country (Harles 1993). To be sure, they want the mainstream institutions in their society to be reformed, so as to accommodate their cultural differences, and to recognize the value of their cultural heritage. But the desire for such polyethnic rights is a desire for inclusion which is consistent with participation in, and commitment to, the mainstream institutions that underlie social unity.[6]

Indeed, those ethnic groups which seek polyethnic rights are often particularly concerned with clarifying the basis of national unity. As Tariq Modood notes,

> the greatest psychological and political need for clarity about a common framework and national symbols comes from the minorities. For clarity about what makes us willingly bound into a single country relieves the pressure on minorities, especially new minorities whose presence within the country is not fully accepted, to have to conform in all areas of social life, or

in arbitrarily chosen areas, in order to rebut the charge of disloyalty. (Modood 1994: 64; 1993*a*)

Why have so many commentators failed to see the integrative impulse of polyethnic rights? In part it is prejudice against new immigrants, most of whom are non-white and non-Christian. As I have noted, there seems to be a double standard at work in many criticisms of polyethnic rights. While the special rights granted to white Jewish and Christian groups to withdraw from the larger society have at times been controversial, few people see these as serious threats to social unity or stability, and they have been part of our political culture for decades. But when accommodations were made for non-white, non-Christian groups, people started complaining about the 'tribalization' of society, and the loss of a common identity—even though these newer polyethnic rights are in fact primarily intended to promote integration! It is difficult to avoid the conclusion that much of the backlash against 'multiculturalism' arises from a racist or xenophobic fear of these new immigrant groups.

Moreover, it is likely that worries about the volatile relations between entrenched and long-standing national or racial groups get displaced onto newer immigrants. For example, in the Canadian case, 'the diversity associated with multiculturalism is easier to "blame" for disunity' than confronting the self-government demands of the Québécois or Aboriginals (Abu-Laban and Stasiulus 1992: 378). Similarly, I think that fears about the relations between whites and blacks in the United States are often displaced onto the 'ethnic revival'. In each case, the modest demands of immigrants provide an easier target than the demands of larger and more settled minorities, even though the former in fact pose little threat to the unity or stability of the country.

Finally, liberal assumptions about the relationship between citizenship and integration, particularly in the British context, have largely been shaped by the experience of the working class. The working class provided a relatively clear and successful example where common citizenship rights helped integrate a previously excluded group into a common national culture. Many liberals (and socialists) have assumed that this model could apply to other historically excluded groups, ignoring their very different circumstances.

Consider the work of T. H. Marshall, one of the most influential post-war theorists of citizenship. He believed that the working classes in England were cut off from the 'common culture', and were denied access to a 'common civilization' which should be seen as 'a common possession and heritage' (Marshall 1965: 101–2). England was deeply divided along class lines, with little interaction between members of different classes, and that, combined with the lack of material resources, made it difficult for workers to take part in the broader cultural life of the country. They had their own subcultures, of course, which were often highly developed, but they were deprived of access to the national culture.

Marshall was deeply concerned with this cultural aspect of the exclusion of the working class. Indeed, he was more concerned with cultural exclusion than with material inequality *per se*. However, because the cultural exclusion of the working class derived from their socio-economic standing, the most effective way to promote national integration was through the provision of material benefits, via the welfare state. Hence Marshall's focus was on expanding citizenship by the inclusion of universal 'social rights' to education, health care, and social security programmes. And there is ample evidence that these social rights have indeed served to promote the integration of the working class in various countries into the national culture.

Based on this example of the English working class, Marshall developed a theory about the integrative function of citizenship rights. He believed that the equal rights of citizenship would help promote national integration for previously excluded groups. These rights would generate a 'direct sense of community membership based on loyalty to a civilisation which is a common possession'.[7]

However, it has become clear that the integration of the working class cannot be generalized in this way. There are many forms of cultural exclusion, and they interact with common citizenship in different ways (Barbalet 1988: 93). In particular, Marshall's theory of integration does not necessarily work for culturally distinct immigrants, or for various other groups which have historically been excluded from full participation in the national culture—such as blacks, women, religious minorities, gays, and lesbians. Some members of these groups still feel excluded from the 'common culture', despite possessing the common rights of citizenship.

In each of these cases, groups have been excluded from full participation not because of their socio-economic status, but because of their socio-cultural identity—their 'difference'. Of course, members of these groups are often materially deprived as well. But that is not the only cause of their cultural exclusion, and so providing material benefits will not necessarily ensure their integration into a common culture, or develop a sense of shared loyalty to a common civilization.

Like the working class (but unlike national minorities), these groups are demanding inclusion into the dominant national culture.

But unlike the working class, group-differentiated rights are needed if they are to feel accepted by the community, and experience the 'direct sense of community membership based on loyalty to a civilisation which is a common possession' which Marshall saw as the basis of citizenship. The common rights of citizenship, originally defined by and for white, able-bodied, Christian men, cannot accommodate the special needs of these groups.[8] Instead, a fully integrative citizenship must take these differences into account.

3. *Self-Government and Separatism*

While polyethnic and representation rights can promote social integration and political unity, self-government rights pose a more serious challenge to the integrative function of citizenship. Both representation rights for disadvantaged groups and polyethnic rights for immigrant groups take the larger political community for granted, and seek greater inclusion in it. Demands for self-government, however, reflect a desire to weaken the bonds with the larger political community, and indeed question its very authority and permanence.

It is worth exploring this point in some depth. When disadvantaged groups demand special representation, they generally take the authority of the larger political community for granted. They assume, as John Rawls puts it, that citizens are members of 'one co-operative scheme in perpetuity', but that temporary special rights for oppressed groups are needed to achieve full membership in that co-operative scheme. Most polyethnic rights similarly take the authority of the larger polity for granted. They assume that immigrants will work within the economic and political institutions of the larger society, but that these institutions must be adapted to reflect the increasing cultural diversity of the population they serve.

In the case of self-government rights, the larger political community has a more conditional existence. National minorities claim that they are distinct 'peoples', with inherent rights of self-government. While they are currently part of a larger country, this is not a renunciation of their original right of self-government. Rather it is a matter of transferring *some aspects* of their powers of self-government to the larger polity, on the condition that other powers remain in their own hands.

This condition is often spelled out in treaties or other terms of federation, for national minorities want their self-governing powers protected securely and permanently. In this sense, the authority of the larger political community is derivative. In countries that are formed from the federation of two or more nations, the authority of the central government is limited to the powers which each constituent nation agreed to transfer to it. And these national groups see themselves as having the right to take back these powers, and withdraw from the federation, if they feel threatened by the larger community.

In other words, the basic claim underlying self-government rights is not simply that some groups are disadvantaged within the political community (representation rights), or that the political community is culturally diverse (polyethnic rights). Instead, the claim is that there is more than one political community, and that the authority of the larger state cannot be assumed to take precedence over the authority of the constituent national communities. If democracy is the rule of 'the people', national minorities claim that there is more than one people, each with the right to rule themselves.

Self-government rights, therefore, are the most complete case of differentiated citizenship, since they divide the people into separate 'peoples', each with its own historic rights, territories, and powers of self-government; and each, therefore with its own political community. They may view their own political community as primary, and the value and authority of the larger federation as derivative.[9]

It seems unlikely that according self-government rights to a national minority can serve an integrative function.[10] If citizenship is membership in a political community, then, in creating overlapping political communities, self-government rights necessarily give rise to a sort of dual citizenship, and to potential conflicts about which community citizens identify with most deeply. Moreover, there seems to be no natural stopping point to the demands for increasing self-government. If limited autonomy is granted, this may simply fuel the ambitions of nationalist leaders who will be satisfied with nothing short of their own nation-state.

Democratic multination states which recognize self-government rights are, it appears, inherently unstable for this reason. At best they seem to be a *modus vivendi* between separate communities, with no intrinsic bond that would lead the members of one national group to make sacrifices for the other. Yet, as I noted earlier, liberal justice requires this sense of common purpose and mutual solidarity within the country.

It might seem tempting, therefore, to ignore the demands of national minorities, avoid any reference to such groups in the constitution, and insist that citizenship is a common identity shared by all individuals, without regard to group membership. This is often described as the American strategy for dealing with cultural pluralism.

But in fact the Americans have only applied this strategy in the context of integrating voluntary immigrants and involuntary slaves, who arrived in America as individuals or families. Generally speaking, a quite different strategy has been applied in the context of incorporating historically self-governing groups whose homeland has become part of the larger community, such as the American Indians, Alaskan Eskimos, Puerto Ricans, and native Hawaiians. Most of these national minorities are accorded some level of self-government within the American federation. And where the common citizenship strategy was applied to national minorities it has often been a spectacular failure. For example, the policy of pressuring American Indian tribes to relinquish their distinct political status, known as the 'termination policy', had disastrous consequences, and was withdrawn in the 1950s.

Indeed, there are very few democratic multination states that follow the strict 'common citizenship' strategy. This is not surprising, because refusing demands for self-government rights will simply aggravate alienation among national minorities, and increase the desire for secession. As we saw in Chapter 6, what is called 'common citizenship' in a multination state in fact involves supporting the culture of the majority nation—for example, its language becomes the official language of the schools, courts, and legislatures; its holidays become public holidays. Moreover, a regime of common citizenship means that the minority has no way to limit its vulnerability to the economic and political decisions of the majority, since the boundaries and powers of internal political units are defined to suit the administrative convenience of the majority, not the self-government claims of the minority.

It is not surprising, then, that national minorities have resisted attempts to impose common citizenship on them. Rawls suggests that common citizenship promotes the political virtues of 'reasonableness and a sense of fairness, a spirit of compromise and a readiness to meet others halfway' (Rawls 1987: 21). But attempts to impose common citizenship in multination states may in fact threaten these virtues.

In the Ottoman Empire, for example, compromise between groups was traditionally ensured by the system of self-government for each 'millet', thereby limiting mutual interference (see Ch. 8, s. 1). In the mid-eighteenth century, however, the Ottomans stripped the millets of most of their self-governing power, and tried to promote a common citizenship status that cut across religious and ethnic boundaries, so that everyone's political rights and identity were based on a common relationship to the Ottoman state, rather than membership in a particular millet. As Karpat notes, the result was disastrous, for once the self-governing status of the millets ended,

> the relative position of the religious and ethnic groups in the Ottoman Empire toward each other began to be decided on the basis of their numerical strength. Hence they were transformed into minorities and majorities. It was obvious that sooner or later the views of the majority would prevail and its cultural characteristics and aspirations would become the features of the government itself. (Karpat 1982: 163)

A similar process occurred when indigenous peoples in North America were accorded citizenship (often against their will), and so became a numerical minority within the larger body of citizens, rather than a separate, self-governing people. Rawls suggests that a strong sense of common citizenship is needed to deal with the danger that majorities will treat minorities unfairly. But common citizenship in a multination state helps create that danger in the first place, by transforming self-governing groups into numerical majorities and minorities.

Given this dynamic, imposing common citizenship on minorities which view themselves as distinct nations or peoples is likely to increase conflict in a multination state. Should the state then try to modify that national consciousness, so as to reduce or remove the minority's desire to form a distinct national society? This option is endorsed by David Miller, who says we should not 'regard cultural identities as given, or at least as created externally to the political system', but rather should have 'a stronger sense of the malleability of such identities, that is, the extent to which they can be created or modified consciously'. Since 'subcultures threaten to undermine the overarching sense of identity' needed for a generous welfare state, the state should promote 'a common identity as citizens that is stronger than their separate identities as members of ethnic or other sectional groups' (Miller 1989: 237, 279, 286–7).

But recent history suggests that *to some extent* national identities must be taken as givens. The character of a national identity can change dramatically, as the Quiet Revolution in Quebec shows. Equally dramatic changes have occurred recently amongst indigenous communities. But the identity itself—the sense of being a distinct national culture—is much more stable. Governments in Canada and the United States have, at times, used all the tools at their disposal to destroy the sense of separate identity amongst their national minorities, from residential schools for Indian children and the prohibition of tribal customs to the banning of French- or Spanish-language schools. But despite centuries of legal discrimination, social prejudice, or plain indifference, these national minorities have maintained their sense of having a national identity. Similarly, efforts by European governments to suppress the language and national identity of the Kurds, Basques, or other national minorities have had little or no success. And Communist governments failed in their efforts to eradicate national loyalties. Despite a complete monopoly over education and the media, Communist regimes were unable to get Croats, Slovaks and Ukrainians to think of themselves primarily as 'Yugoslavs', 'Czechoslovaks', or 'Soviets'. Attempts to promote 'pan-movements' that would supersede national identities—e.g. attempts to create pan-Slavic or pan-Arabic states—have proven similarly futile (Fishman 1989: 147).

It is no longer possible (if it ever was) to eliminate the sense of distinct identity which underlies these groups' desire to form their own national societies. If anything, attempts to subordinate these separate identities to a common identity have backfired, since they are perceived by minorities as threats to their very existence, and so have resulted in even greater indifference or resentment (Whitaker 1992: 152–3; Taylor 1992*a*: 64).

Much has been made in the recent literature of the social construction of national identity, and of the 'invention of tradition' (Hobsbawm 1990). And of course much of the mythology accompanying national identities is just that—a myth. But it is important not to confuse the heroes, history, or present-day characteristics of a national identity with the underlying national identity itself. The former is much more malleable than the latter. Indeed, as I noted in Chapter 5, it seems that few if any national groups in the last 100 years have voluntarily assimilated, despite often significant economic incentives and legal pressures to do so. As Anthony Smith puts it, 'whenever and however a national identity is forged, once established, it becomes immensely difficult, if not impossible (short of total genocide) to eradicate' (A. Smith 1993: 131; cf. Connor 1972: 350–1).

Since claims to self-government are here to stay, we have no choice but to try to accommodate them. Rejecting these demands in the name of common citizenship will simply promote alienation and secessionist movements. Indeed, recent surveys of ethnonationalist conflict around the world show clearly that self-government arrangements diminish the likelihood of violent conflict, while refusing or rescinding self-government rights is likely to escalate the level of conflict (Gurr 1993; Hannum 1990; Horowitz 1985).

Yet, as I noted earlier, accepting self-government demands is likely to lead to a desire for ever-increasing autonomy, even independence. Providing local autonomy reduces the likelihood of violent conflict, yet the resulting arrangements are rarely examples of harmonious co-operation between national groups. They often become 'mere treaties of cooperation', in which quarrelsome groups 'agree to cooperate only on a limited set of issues, if they can cooperate at all' (Ordeshook 1993: 223). The sense of solidarity needed to promote the public good and to tackle urgent issues of justice is lacking. This seems increasingly true, for example, in Belgium and Canada.

We seem caught in a Gordian knot. Given this dynamic, some commentators conclude that the only solution to the problem of multination states is secession. According to Miller, where national identities have 'already become so strong that what we have is really two separate nationalities living side by side', then 'the best solution is ultimately likely to be the secession of one community' (Miller 1989: 288). Similarly, Walzer argues that 'If the community is so radically divided that a single citizenship is impossible, then its territory too must be divided' (Walzer 1983*a*: 62).

We are now back at John Stuart Mill's argument that a stable liberal democracy must be a nation-state, with a single national culture (see Ch. 4, s. 1). If national minorities are unwilling to assimilate, they must secede and establish their own state.

Perhaps we should be more willing to consider secession. We tend to assume that secession is a moral and political catastrophe, but I suspect that few people today condemn the secession of Norway from Sweden in 1905. In the Norwegian case, the process of secession was (relatively) peaceful, and the result was two healthy liberal democracies where there used to be one. There is every reason to think that any future secession of Quebec from the rest of Canada would be similar. It is difficult to see why liberals should automatically oppose such peaceful, liberal secessions.[11] After all, liberalism is fundamentally concerned, not with the fate of states, but with the freedom and well-being of individuals, and secession need not harm individual rights.

However, secession is not always possible or desirable. Some national minorities, particularly indigenous peoples, would have trouble forming viable independent states. In other cases, competing claims over land and resources would make peaceful secession virtually impossible. In general, there are more nations in the world than possible states, and since we cannot simply wish national consciousness away, we need to find some way to keep multination states together.

4. *The Basis of Social Unity in a Multination State*

What then are the possible sources of unity in a multination state which affirms, rather than denies, its national differences? I do not have a clear answer to this question. Indeed, I doubt that there are any obvious or easy answers available.

There are important examples of stable multination states, such as Switzerland, which show that there is no necessary reason why the members of a national minority cannot have both a strong national consciousness and a strong sense of patriotism and commitment to the larger polity (Sigler 1983: 188–92). As I noted in Chapter 2, this sense of patriotism is so strong that the Swiss are, in some ways, a single 'people', as well as being a federation of peoples.

But there are all too many examples of countries where the institutionalization of national identities and rights has not prevented civil strife (e.g. Lebanon; Yugoslavia). Moreover, some multination states whose long-term stability used to be taken for granted now seem rather more precarious (e.g. Belgium).

What then are the conditions which help stabilize multination states? There are few discussions of this issue. To date, defenders of national self-government have been more concerned to argue that assimilation is not a viable source of unity than to explain what should take its place.

One suggestion is that social unity depends on 'shared values'. Obviously the citizens of any modern democracy do not share specific conceptions of the good life, but they may share certain political values. For example, one government commission in Canada developed a list of seven such values which Canadians shared: (1) a belief in equality and fairness; (2) a belief in consultation and dialogue; (3) the importance of accommodation and tolerance; (4) support for diversity; (5) compassion and generosity; (6) attachment to the natural environment; (7) a commitment to freedom, peace, and non-violent change (Citizen's Forum 1991: 34–44). The hope is that focusing on these shared values will provide grounds for social unity in Canada.

This idea is also found, in a more philosophical form, in many recent liberal theorists. Rawls, for example, claims that the source of unity in modern societies is a shared conception of justice. According to Rawls, 'although a well-ordered society is divided and pluralistic . . . public agreement on questions of political and social justice supports ties of civic friendship and secures the bonds of association' (Rawls 1980: 540).

It is true that there often are shared political values within multination states, including a shared conception of liberal justice. However, it is not clear that these values, by themselves, provide a reason for two or more national groups to stay together in one country. For example, there may be (and probably is) a remarkable convergence of values between the citizens of Norway and Sweden, but is this any reason for them to reunite? I do not think so. The fact that they share the same values does not, by itself, explain whether it is better to have one state or two in that part of the world.

Similarly, as I discussed in Chapter 5, there has been a pronounced convergence in values between English- and French-speaking Canadians over the last thirty years (Dion 1992: 99; 1991: 301; Taylor 1991: 54). If the shared values approach were correct, we should have witnessed a decline in support for Quebec secession over this period, yet nationalist sentiment has in fact grown consistently. Here again, the fact that anglophones and francophones in Canada share the same principles of justice is not a strong reason to remain together, since the Québécois rightly assume that their own national state could respect the same principles. The same is true of the Flemish in Belgium.

Indeed, this reflects a very general trend. There has been a convergence of political values throughout the Western world, amongst both majority nations and national minorities. In terms of their political values, the Danes, Germans, French, and British have probably never been as similar as they are now. But this has not had any appreciable impact on the desire of these majority nations to retain their national independence. Why then should it diminish the desire of national minorities for self-government?

This suggests that shared values are not sufficient for social unity. The fact that two national groups share the same values or principles of justice does not necessarily give them any strong reason to join (or remain) together, rather than remaining (or splitting into) two separate countries. What more, or what else, is required for social unity? The missing ingredient seems to be the idea of a *shared identity*. A shared conception of justice throughout a political community does not necessarily generate a shared identity, let alone a shared civic identity that will supersede rival national identities.[12] People decide who they want to share a country with by asking who they identify with, who they feel solidarity with. What holds Americans together, despite their lack of common values, is the fact that they share an identity as Americans. Conversely, what keeps Swedes and Norwegians apart, despite the presence of shared values, is the lack of a shared identity.

Where does this shared identity come from? In nation-states, the answer is simple. Shared identity derives from commonality of history, language, and maybe religion. But these are precisely the things which are not shared in a multination state. If we look to strongly patriotic but culturally diverse countries like the United States or Switzerland, the basis for a shared identity often seems to be pride in certain historical achievements (e.g. the founding of the American Republic). This shared pride is one of the bases of the strong sense of American political identity, constantly reinforced in their citizenship literature and school curriculum.

But in many multination countries history is a source of resentment and division between national groups, not a source of shared pride. The people and events which spark pride amongst the majority nation often generate a sense of betrayal amongst the national minority.[13] Moreover, the reliance on history often requires a very selective, even manipulative, retelling of that history. Ernst Renan once claimed that national identity involves forgetting the past as much as remembering it. To build a sense of common identity in a multination state probably requires an even more selective memory of the past.[14]

Shared values and an inspiring history no doubt help sustain solidarity in a multination state, but it is doubtful that either is sufficient by itself. How then can one construct a common identity in a country which contains two or more communities which view themselves as self-governing nations? The great variance in historical, cultural, and political situations in multination states suggests that any generalized answer to this question will probably be overstated.[15]

What is clear, I think, is that if there is a viable way to promote a sense of solidarity and common purpose in a multination state, it will involve accommodating, rather than subordinating, national identities. People from different national groups will only share an allegiance to the larger polity if they see it as the context within which their national identity is nurtured, rather than subordinated.[16]

This is difficult enough in a country which simply contains two nations (e.g. Belgium). It gets much more complicated in countries which are not only multinational but also polyethnic, containing many national and indigenous groups, often of vastly unequal size, as well as immigrants from every part of the world. In this context, we need what Charles Taylor calls a theory of 'deep diversity', since we must accommodate not only a diversity of cultural groups, but also a diversity of ways in which the members of these groups belong to the larger polity (Taylor 1991: 75). For example, the member of an immigrant group in the United States may see her citizenship status as centred on the universal individual rights guaranteed by the constitution. Her ethnic identity, while important in various ways, may not affect her sense of citizenship, or what it is to be an American (or Canadian or Australian). The United States, for her, may be a country of equal citizens who are tolerant of each other's cultural differences.

But this model of belonging will not accommodate national minorities like the Puerto Ricans or Navaho. They belong to the United States through belonging to a national group that has federated itself to the larger country. According to a recent poll, 91 per cent of the residents of Puerto Rico think of themselves as Puerto Ricans first, and Americans second (Rubinstein 1993: 88). They do see themselves as Americans, but only because this does not require abandoning their prior identity as a distinct Spanish-speaking people with their own separate political community. The United States, for them, is a federation of peoples—English, Spanish, Indian—each with the right to govern themselves.

Similarly, the immigrant model of belonging will not accommodate the francophones and indigenous peoples in Canada, for whom 'the way of being a Canadian (for those who still want to be) is via their belonging to a constituent element of Canada', such as the Québécois or the Cree (Taylor 1991: 75). For these groups, Canada is a federation of national groups which respect each other's right to be a distinct societal culture within Canada.

In countries that are both polyethnic and multinational, cultural groups are not only diverse, but they have diverse images of the country as a whole. People not only belong to separate political communities, but also belong in different ways. This means that the members of a polyethnic and multination state must not only respect diversity, but also respect a diversity of approaches to diversity. As Taylor puts it, an immigrant might see herself 'as a bearer of individual rights in a multicultural mosaic', but she must nevertheless accept that a Puerto Rican, Navaho, or Québécois 'might belong in a very different way . . . through being members of their national communities'. And reciprocally, the Puerto Ricans, Navaho, and Québécois 'would accept the perfect legitimacy of the "mosaic" identity'. This sort of 'deep diversity' is 'the only formula' on which a united polyethnic, multination state can be built (Taylor 1991: 76).[17]

What would hold such a multination state together? Taylor admits that this is an open question, but suggests that citizens might 'find it exciting and an object of pride' to work together to build a society founded on deep diversity, and so be willing to make sacrifices to keep it together (Taylor 1991: 76). This seems to beg the question. Why would citizens find this exciting rather than wearying, given the endless negotiations and complications it entails?

But Taylor is pointing in the right direction. A society founded on 'deep diversity' is unlikely to stay together unless people value deep diversity itself, and want to live in a country with diverse forms of cultural and political membership. Even this is not always sufficient. For example, a sovereign Quebec would still be a very culturally diverse country, with immigrants from around the world, as well as a historically settled anglophone community, and various indigenous peoples, including the Cree, Mohawk, and Inuit. Secession rarely if ever creates homogeneous nation-states, it simply rearranges the pattern and size of groups. For citizens to want to keep a multination state together, therefore, they must value, not just 'deep diversity' in general, but also the particular ethnic groups and national cultures with whom they currently share the country.[18]

The problem, of course, is that this sort of allegiance is the product of mutual solidarity, not a possible basis for it. If citizens already have a fairly strong sense of identity towards the other ethnic and national groups in the country, they will find the prospect of sustaining their deep diversity inspiring and exciting. But a vague commitment to the value of cultural diversity, by itself, may not generate a strong sense of identification with the existing country, or the particular groups that cohabit it.

As I noted earlier, some multination states do have this strong sense of mutual identification. This is obviously true of the Swiss. Canadians also have a reasonably strong sense of solidarity. For example, while over half of Quebecers attach priority, in their self-identify, to their status as Quebec citizens, compared with just under 30 per cent who attach priority to Canadian citizenship, still 70 per cent of Quebecers say they would be willing to make personal sacrifices that would benefit only Canadians outside Quebec (*L'Actualité* 1992). This provides a level of goodwill that is not present in other multination states. And focusing on shared values, mythical history, or the excitement of deep diversity might help sustain that level of solidarity. But it is not clear how other multination states could try to create such a level of solidarity where it did not already exist. If two or more national groups simply do not want to live together, it may be impossible to create solidarity from scratch (Miller 1993: 16 n. 14).

5. *Conclusion*

Some critics see the liberal commitment to common citizenship as evidence of an excessively legalistic understanding of citizenship which neglects the broader social and cultural aspects of membership. In fact, however, most liberal theorists have recognized that citizenship is not just a legal status, defined by a set of rights and responsibilities, but also an identity, an expression of one's membership in a political community. And it is precisely in the name of a strengthened civic identity that many liberals have clung to the principle of common citizenship.

That is, underlying much liberal opposition to the demands of ethnic and national minorities is a very practical concern for the stability of liberal states. Liberal democracies require citizens to have a fairly high level of self-restraint and mutual solidarity, and it is a fair question whether the politicization of ethnic and national differences is compatible with these requirements.

Yet I believe that fears in this area are often overstated. The demands of immigrants and disadvantaged groups for polyethnic rights and representation rights are primarily demands for inclusion, for full membership in the larger society. To view this as a threat to stability or solidarity is implausible, and often reflects an underlying ignorance or intolerance of these groups.

Self-government rights, however, do pose a threat to social unity. The sense of being a distinct nation within a larger country is potentially destabilizing. On the other hand, the denial of self-government rights is also destabilizing, since it encourages resentment and even secession. Concerns about social unity will arise however we respond to self-government claims.

A fundamental challenge facing liberal theorists, therefore, is to identify the sources of unity in a democratic multination state. The nineteenth-century English theorist A. V. Dicey once said that a stable multination federation requires 'a very peculiar state of sentiment' among its citizens, since 'they must desire union, and must not desire unity'. Henri Bourassa made a similar point when he said that the 'special development' of the French-Canadian nation 'must come about in conjunction with the development of a more general patriotism that unifies us, without fusing us' (Cook 1969: 149). Liberal theory has not yet succeeded in clarifying the nature of this 'peculiar sentiment'.

CHAPTER 10

Conclusion

The late twentieth century has been described as 'the age of migration'. Massive numbers of people are moving across borders, making virtually every country more polyethnic in composition. This has also been described as 'the age of nationalism', as more and more national groups throughout the world mobilize and assert their identity. As a result, the settled rules of political life in many countries are being challenged by a new 'politics of cultural difference'. Indeed, with the end of the Cold War, the demands of ethnic and national groups have taken over centre stage in political life, both domestically and internationally.[1]

Many people see this new 'politics of difference' as a threat to liberal democracy. I have presented a more optimistic view in this book. I have tried to show that many (but not all) of the demands of ethnic and national groups are consistent with liberal principles of individual freedom and social justice. I would not say that these issues can be 'resolved' in any final sense. The issues are too complicated for that. But they can be 'managed', peacefully and fairly, assuming there is some level of goodwill.[2]

Of course, in many parts of the world, groups are motivated by hatred and intolerance, not justice, and have no interest in treating others with goodwill. Under these circumstances, the potential for ethnic and national groups to abuse their rights and powers is very high. Yugoslavia and Rwanda are only the most recent reminders of the injustices which have been committed in the name of ethnic and national differences, from racial segregation and religious pogroms to ethnic cleansing and genocide.

Given these potential abuses, many people feel a strong temptation to push the issue of minority rights off to the side. Why, they ask, can we not simply 'treat people as individuals', without regard for their ethnic or national identity? Why can we not focus on the things we share as humans, rather than what distinguishes us? I suspect that most of us have had that reaction at some point when dealing with the new and complicated 'politics of difference'.

However, that response is misguided. The problem is not that it is too 'individualistic'. In many parts of the world, a healthy dose of individualism would provide a welcome respite from group-based conflict. The problem, rather, is that the response is simply incoherent. As I have tried to show throughout this book, political life has an inescapably national dimension, whether it is in the drawing of boundaries and distributing of powers, or in decisions about the language of schooling, courts, and bureaucracies, or in the choice of public holidays. Moreover, these inescapable aspects of political life give a profound advantage to the members of majority nations.

We need to be aware of this, and the way it can alienate and disadvantage others, and take steps to prevent any resulting injustices. These steps might include polyethnic and representation rights to accommodate ethnic and other disadvantaged groups within each national group, and self-government rights to enable autonomy for national minorities alongside the majority nation. Without such measures, talk of 'treating people as individuals' is itself just a cover for ethnic and national injustice.

It is equally important to stress the limits on such rights. In particular, I have argued that they must respect two constraints: minority rights should not allow one group to dominate other groups; and they should not enable a group to oppress its own members. In other words, liberals should seek to ensure that there is equality *between* groups, and freedom and equality *within* groups. Within these limits, minority rights can play a valuable role within a broader theory of liberal justice. Indeed, they must play a role if liberalism is not to be condemned to irrelevance in many parts of the world.

In the traditional birthplace(s) of liberal theory—Britain, France, and the United States—minority rights have been ignored, or treated as mere curiosities or anomalies. This is particularly true of the claims of indigenous peoples. But it has become increasingly clear that minority rights are central to the future of the liberal tradition throughout the world. In many countries of the world—including the emerging democracies in Eastern Europe, Africa, and Asia—the status of national minorities and indigenous peoples is perhaps the most pressing issue.

People in these countries are looking to the works of Western liberals for guidance regarding the principles of liberal constitutionalism in a multination state. But the liberal tradition offers only confused and contradictory advice on this question. Liberal thinking on minority rights has too often been guilty of ethnocentric assumptions, or of over-generalizing particular cases, or of conflating contingent political strategy with enduring moral principle. This is reflected in the wide range of policies liberal states have historically adopted regarding ethnic and national groups, ranging from coercive assimilation to coercive segregation, from conquest and colonization to federalism and self-government.

The result has often been grave injustices against the ethnic and national minorities in many Western democracies. But the failure to develop a consistent and principled approach to minority rights may have even greater costs in the newly emerging democracies. At present, the fate of ethnic and national groups around the world is in the hand of xenophobic nationalists, religious extremists, and military dictators. If liberalism is to have any chance of taking hold in these countries, it must explicitly address the needs and aspirations of ethnic and national minorities.

NOTES

CHAPTER 1

1. For these estimates (and their imprecision), see Laczko 1994; Gurr 1993; Nielsson 1985. Iceland and the Koreas are commonly cited as two examples of countries which are more or less culturally homogeneous.
2. For surveys of minority rights claims worldwide, see Sigler 1983; Gurr 1993; Van Dyke 1977; Capotorti 1979; Hannum 1990.
3. On the assumption of cultural homogeneity in Western political thought, see McRae 1979; Van Dyke 1977; Walzer 1982: 1–3; McNeill 1986: 23. On the reality of cultural heterogeneity throughout history, and its causes, see McNeill 1986. On the ever-increasing scale of this diversity, see Castles and Miller 1993: 8.
4. For liberal endorsements of this position, see Glazer 1975: 220; 1978: 98; 1983: 124; Gordon 1975: 105; Porter 1975: 295; van den Berghe 1981*b*: 347; Ajzenstat 1984: 251–2; Rorty 1991: 209; Kukathas 1991: 22; Edwards 1985; Brotz 1980: 44.
5. For this debate, see Rosenfeld 1991; Sowell 1990.
6. For a variety of examples, see Barsh and Henderson 1980: 241–8; 1982: 69–70; Clinton 1990; Gordon 1975; 1978; 1981; Glazer 1975: 220; Van Dyke 1982: 28-30; Svensson 1979: 430–3; Adam 1979; Deganaar 1987; Knopff 1982: 29–39; Laforest 1991; Ajzenstat 1988: ch. 8; F. Morton 1985: 73–83; Schwartz 1986: ch. 1; Brotz 1980: 44–5; Asch 1984: 75–88, 100–4; Weaver 1985: 141–2; For more references and discussion, see Kymlicka 1989*a*: ch. 7; 1991.
7. For a summary of these developments, see Lerner 1991; Thornberry 1991; Bloed 1994; Hannum 1993.

CHAPTER 2

1. For a survey of the rights of national minorities in the United States, see O'Brien 1987. For the invisibility of these groups in American constitutional and political history, see Ball 1989; Resnik 1989; Aleinikoff 1994. For the issue of secession by American Indian tribes, see Jensen 1993. The abrogation of language rights for the Chicanos parallels the fate of the Métis in Canada, whose national rights were recognized when Manitoba entered Confederation, then taken away when English settlers became the majority in the province. Compare Glazer 1983: 277 with Weinstein 1986: 46–7; Chartrand 1991; 1993: 241.
2. That these groups see themselves as nations is evident from the names

they have chosen for their associations and institutions. For example, the provincial legislature in Quebec is called the 'National Assembly'; the major organization of Status Indians is known as the 'Assembly of First Nations'. It is important to note that Aboriginal peoples are not a single nation. The term 'Aboriginal' covers three categories of Aboriginals (Indian, Inuit, and Métis), and the term Indian itself is a legal fiction, behind which there are numerous distinct Aboriginal nations with their own histories and separate community identities. Aboriginals in Canada can be divided into eleven linguistic groups, descended from a number of historically and culturally distinct societies. It has been estimated that there are thirty-five to fifty distinct 'peoples' in the Aboriginal population. It is also potentially misleading to describe the French Canadians as a single nation. The French-speaking majority in the province of Quebec views itself as a nation—the 'Québécois'. But there are francophones outside Quebec, and the French nation in Canada was not always identified so closely with the province of Quebec. For the change in self-identity from *canadien* to *la nation canadienne-française* to *franco-québécois* to *québécois*, see McRoberts 1988; Crête and Zylberberg 1991: 424. On the use of the language of nationhood by Aboriginals and the Québécois more generally, see Cairns 1993: 188; Chartrand 1995; Long 1992; Jenson 1993.

3. Porter 1987: 154; cf. Reitz and Breton 1994; Palmer 1976. In so far as immigrant groups seem more cohesive in Canada, this is probably due to the fact that they contain a higher proportion of recent migrants than US ethnic groups, which in turn is due to Canada's higher immigration rate. In 1981, 16.1% of Canadian residents were foreign-born, compared to 6.2% of Americans (Laczko 1994: 28–9). However, the process of integration for settled immigrants and their children is similar in both countries. The term 'melting-pot' is also somewhat misleading. It referred primarily to the biological fusing of various (white) ethnic groups through intermarriage, more than the fusing of their cultural practices. According to Theodore Roosevelt, the 'representatives of many old-world races are being fused together into a new type', but 'the crucible into which all the new types are melted into one was shaped from 1776 to 1789, and our nationality was definitely fixed in all its essentials by the men of Washington's day' (quoted in Gordon 1964: 122). This was particularly true of language, as I discuss later in this chapter.
4. Johnson 1973: 119. See also Tollefson 1989: chs. 3–4 and Carlson 1975. For a comprehensive review of the history of language rights in the United States, see Kloss 1977.
5. M. Combs and L. Lynch, quoted in de la Garza and Trujillo 1991: 215. John Ogbu also discusses the importance of distinguishing Hispanic immigrants from non-immigrant Chicanos, in terms of their attitudes towards integration and success in the mainstream (Ogbu 1988). Hispanic immigrant groups have expressed an interest in bilingual

education, but they view Spanish-language education as supplementing, not displacing, the learning of English. This is unlike Spanish-language education in Puerto Rico, in which Spanish is the dominant language, and indeed many Puerto Ricans do not learn any English.

6. For one attempt to build such a unified platform, see Chavez 1991, who encourages all Hispanic groups (with the possible exception of the Puerto Ricans) to adopt the immigrant model of integration.
7. This has led to a growing debate in Europe about the nature of citizenship and its relationship with nationality (understood as membership in the national culture). On England, see Parekh 1990; 1991; Modood 1992; on France, see Colas *et al.* 1991; Leca 1992. On Europe generally, see Lenoble and Dewandre 1992; Brubaker 1989. On the status of guest-workers, see Layton-Henry 1990.
8. As René Lévesque, former premier of Quebec, put it, multiculturalism 'is a "Red Herring". The notion was devised to obscure "the Quebec business", to give an impression that we are all ethnics and do not have to worry about special status for Quebec' (quoted in Wilson 1993: 656 n. 33). Similar concerns have been raised by the Maori in New Zealand—i.e. that the rhetoric of 'multiculturalism' is a way of denying their national claims, by lumping them in with the polyethnic claims of non-British immigrants (Sharp 1990: 228; Mulgan 1989: 8–9).

   I should note that many writers use the term 'ethnic group' to refer, not to immigrant groups, but to national minorities which have not mobilized politically. On this usage, ethnic groups are pre-political national groups (e.g. Nielsson 1985). Obviously, I am using 'ethnic' and 'national' in a different way, to refer to a group's mode of incorporation into a larger society, not its level of political mobilization. On my usage, there can be quiescent national minorities, and highly mobilized immigrant groups. For the terminological issues, see Connor 1978.
9. These various senses of culture are reflected in the different meanings attached to the term 'multiculturalism' in different countries. In Canada, it typically refers to the right of immigrants to express their ethnic identity without fear of prejudice or discrimination; in Europe, it often refers to the sharing of powers between national communities; in the USA, it is often used to include the demands of marginalized social groups.
10. Part of the motivation for this approach is that many illiberal accounts of the value of national and ethnic differences end up rationalizing oppression within the minority group in the name of respect for traditions, or protecting the 'authenticity' or 'integrity' of cultures (Yuval-Davis 1993). One way to defend against this danger is to insist that gays or women form their own cultures, and that the integrity of their cultures also deserves respect. (On gays as a subculture, see Fitzgerald 1986: 25–119; Murray 1979.) I will take a more direct line of attack, however, by severing the defence of cultural rights from any illiberal hallowing of 'tradition' and 'authenticity', and instead connecting it to a liberal theory

of justice that is committed to individual autonomy and social equality (see Chs. 3–5). A related concern is that defining multiculturalism in terms of ethnic and national differences may lead to a neglect of disadvantaged groups, whose demands get obscured beneath the fashionable concern for multiculturalism. This is a legitimate concern, but it is worth noting that the danger runs in both directions. That is, some advocates of a 'politics of difference', whose focus is primarily on disadvantaged groups, obscure the distinctive demands of national groups. I think this is true, for example, of Iris Young's influential work on the 'politics of difference'. While she ostensibly includes the demands of American Indians and New Zealand Maori in her account of group-differentiated citizenship, she in fact misinterprets their demands by treating them as a marginalized group, rather than as self-governing nations (I. Young 1990: 175–83; 1993*a*). The best way to ensure that neither sort of group is made invisible is to keep them clearly distinguished.

11. On this, see O'Brien 1987: 276–80; Claude 1955: 75; Lerner 1991: 16. Actually, American delegates to the UN have alternated between emphasizing and ignoring the difference between immigrant groups and national minorities when opposing the international protection of minority rights. Sometimes they emphasize that ethnic pluralism in the United States is distinctive, because it is immigration-based. At other times, however, they have argued that their model of ethnic integration should be applied to all countries, even those with national minorities. See Sohn 1981: 272, 279; McKean 1983: 70–1, 142–3.
12. Turpel 1989–90: 33. The term 'nations' was applied to Indians in early British policy and American law, but this was not accompanied by a genuine recognition of their sovereignty. For the historical status of indigenous peoples under international law, see Barsh 1983; Lerner 1991: ch. 5; Thornberry 1991: part iv.
13. The case of Indians is complicated, since government policy in both the United States and Canada has at times defined Indians in terms of 'blood', even though this is not the way Indian communities define themselves (Barsh and Henderson 1980: 241–8; Chartrand 1995; Resnik 1989: 715; cf. Mulgan 1989: 14).
14. For that reason, it would be more accurate to talk of anglophone and francophone Canada, rather than English Canada and French Canada, since the latter terms wrongly suggest that these groups are defined by ethnic descent, rather than integration into a cultural community. I should note that the original self-conception of French Canada did define membership in terms of descent. And a substantial minority in Quebec cling to a modified version of that view. In a 1985 study, about 40% of respondents believed that the longer one's ancestors had been in Quebec, the more 'Québécois' one was, and 20% held that immigrants could not call themselves Québécois. This suggests that the development of Québécois identity from descent to participation in a francophone

society is incomplete (Crête and Zylberberg 1991: 425–30; cf. Lamoureux 1991: 59). However, all the major parties in Quebec, including the nationalist Parti Québécois, explicitly reject this descent-based view of national membership.

15. For examples of this common misunderstanding of the contrast between civic and ethnic nationalism, see Habermas 1992; Ignatieff 1993; Pfaff 1993: ch. 7; Walzer 1992*d*. I discuss this in Kymlicka 1995*a*. One reason for this misunderstanding stems from a misreading of American history. At the time of the Revolution, the overwhelming majority of Americans shared the same language, literature, and religion as the English, the nation they had just rebelled against. In order to develop a sense of distinctive nationhood, Americans emphasized certain political principles—liberty, equality, democracy—principles which had justified their rebellion. Some people conclude from this that American nationalism is ideological *rather than* cultural (Gleason 1982: 59; Pfaff 1993: 162). But that is a mistake. The Americans, as much as the English, conceived of national membership in terms of participation in a common culture. The emphasis on political principles affected the nature of that common culture, of course, and so gave American national identity a distinctively ideological character not found in England or other English-settler societies. Ideology shaped, but did not replace, the cultural component of national identity. The idea of a purely non-cultural definition of civic nationalism is implausible, and often leads to self-contradiction. See e.g. Habermas's conception of 'constitutional patriotism', which seems to imply both that citizenship should be independent of particular ethnocultural or historical characteristics like language, and that a common language is indispensable to democracy (see Habermas 1992: 6–7, 16–17; 1993: 144–8; and the discussion in Bader 1995).
16. Blacks in some Central and South American countries have a similar history of slavery, of course, though not the same post-slavery history of segregation. A loosely related case involves the indentured Indian and Chinese workers ('coolie labourers') brought by British settlers into various African and Asian colonies. They were not expected (or allowed) to integrate into the colonial society, nor were they welcomed by the indigenous majority. As a result, they had a very precarious status, which often worsened under decolonization (e.g. in Fiji—see Carens 1992).
17. On black nationalism, see Pinkney 1976; Stone 1976; Glazer 1983: 277–8. For examples of the liberal assumption that public policy can 'help [African-Americans] understand and adopt the immigrant minorities' model', and so become 'the same kind of group that the European ethnic groups have become', see Ogbu 1988: 164–5; Glazer 1983: 184; Walzer 1982: 27. (The quotes are from Ogbu and Glazer respectively.) For the recognition that successful integration will have to involve some unique elements of historical compensation, affirmative action, and (non-

territorial) separate institutions, see Brown-Scott 1994. On the divided identity of African-Americans, see Gutmann 1993: 185–7.

18. According to Gurr, minority groups involved in ethnic conflict fall into two main categories: 'regionally concentrated groups that have lost their autonomy to expansionist states but still preserve some of their cultural and linguistic distinctiveness and want to protect or reestablish some degree of politically separate existence' (i.e., national minorities); and groups who 'have a defined socioeconomic or political status within a larger society—based on some combination of their ethnicity, immigrant origin, economic roles, or religion—and are concerned about protecting or preserving that status' (i.e. ethnic groups)—see Gurr 1993: 15.
19. On the importance of individual rights to the protection of groups, see Buchanan 1989; Walzer 1990; Macdonald 1989: 122–3; Tomasi 1991; Kymlicka 1990: chs. 4–6.
20. Some indigenous peoples have argued before the UN that they too have a right to self-determination under the UN Charter (see *Mikmaq Tribal Society* v *Canada* (1984) UN Doc. E/CN.4/Sub.2/204; Grand Council of the Crees 1992). For discussions of the salt-water thesis, and the right of self-determination under international law, see Pomerance 1982; Thornberry 1991: 13–21, 214–18; Crawford 1988; Makinson 1988.
21. On English Canadian opposition to nationalist demands for decentralization, see Stark 1992. A certain amount of *de facto* asymmetry in powers has been a long-standing aspect of Canadian federalism. However, many Canadians are unwilling to recognize this asymmetry formally in the constitution (see Gagnon and Garcea 1988; Taylor 1991; Cairns 1991). This is one reason why the 1992 Charlottetown Accord was defeated in the national referendum. Some people have claimed that a federal system cannot survive if it accords special status, but this is refuted by the experience of many countries. For a survey of various forms of asymmetrical federalism, see Elazar 1987: 54–7.
22. In Germany, federalism was imposed by the Allies after World War II to help prevent the rise of nationalist or authoritarian movements. For helpful discussions of the relationship between federalism and cultural diversity, see Howse and Knop 1993; Minow 1990*b*; Majone 1990; Gagnon 1993; Long 1991; Duchacek 1977; Elkins 1992; Norman 1994.
23. Hence Nathan Glazer is quite wrong when he says that the division of the United States into federal units preceded its ethnic diversity (Glazer 1983 276–7). This is true of the original thirteen colonies, but decisions about the admission and boundaries of new states were made after the incorporation of national minorities, and these decisions were deliberately made so as to avoid creating states dominated by national minorities.
24. For a comparative review of these developments, see Fleras and Elliot 1992. A proposal to entrench Aboriginal self-government constitutionally as a third order of government in Canada was included in the 1992

Charlottetown Accord. This would have covered both the 'ethnic self-government' exercised by band councils on Indian reserves, and the 'public self-government' exercised by the Inuit majority within the new territory of Nunavut (see Asch 1984: ch. 7). For the relation of Indian self-government to federalism, see Resnik 1989; Cassidy and Bish 1989; Long 1991.

25. Gurr 1993: viii; cf. Nietschmann 1987.
26. For a discussion of these rights in the British context, see Parekh 1990: 705; 1991: 197–204; Modood 1992; Poulter 1987. In Canada, see E. Kallen 1987: 325–31. In the USA, see Minow 1990*b*; Sandel 1990. For the Muslim girls in France, see Galeotti 1993. It is sometimes said that these measures are purely 'symbolic'. But measures relating to employment are very material, affecting people's 'life chances' not just their 'lifestyles'.
27. For statistics on the (under-)representation of blacks and Hispanics in the United States, see C. Davidson 1992: 46. For statistics on the representation of various social groups in Canada, see RCERPF 1991: 93–6 and 192.
28. While self-government may entail guaranteed representation on intergovernmental bodies which negotiate, interpret, and modify the division of powers, it may also entail *reduced* representation on federal bodies which legislate in areas of purely federal jurisdiction, in so far as the self-governing group is not governed by the decisions of these federal bodies. I discuss the relationship between self-government and representation in Ch. 7.

CHAPTER 3

1. Obviously, groups are free to require such actions as terms of membership in private, voluntary associations. A Catholic organization can insist that its members attend church. The problem arises when a group seeks to use governmental power to restrict the liberty of members. Liberals insist that whoever exercises political power within a community must respect the civil and political rights of its members, and any attempt to impose internal restrictions which violate this condition is illegitimate.
2. Analogues of external protections can be claimed by non-ethnic groups. Many group-specific rights for women, gays and lesbians, or people with disabilities can be seen as providing forms of external protection, since they reduce the extent to which these groups are vulnerable to or disadvantaged by majority decisions. Moreover, as I discuss in Ch. 6, s. 4, there is a sense in which the state itself constitutes an external protection against the larger world. In this Chapter, however, I am focusing only on claims by ethnic and national groups to protection from the decisions of

other larger groups within the same state, and these (unlike internal restrictions) can only arise in a pluralist country.

3. They do involve limiting the liberty of non-members, by restricting their ability to make economic or political decisions regarding the minority community and its resources. But, as I discuss in Ch. 6, this can be seen as promoting fairness between the members of the minority and majority communities. It is an issue of justice between groups, not the priority of groups over individuals.
4. However, NWAC was willing to accept this exemption from Charter review if and when a future Aboriginal constitution is adopted which effectively protects sexual equality. And indeed various Aboriginal groups in Canada have been drafting a charter of rights and responsibilities that would regulate Aboriginal governments (Turpel 1989/90: 42–4). For disputes over the legal protection of sexual equality on Indian reserves in the USA and Canada, see Christofferson 1991; Resnik 1989; Moss 1990; Turpel 1993; Cairns 1994.
5. e.g. guaranteed representation for Indians could be seen as violating the equality rights guaranteed by the 14th Amendment of the American Constitution (or s. 15 of the Canadian Charter), as could restrictions on the mobility rights of non-Indians into Indian reserves. For reasons discussed in Ch. 5, I think it is a mistake to interpret equality rights as precluding such policies, but some non-Indians are challenging Indian self-government rights and land rights on this basis (Tsosie 1994: 496).
6. As Carens puts it, 'people are supposed to experience the realisation of principles of justice through various concrete institutions, but they may actually experience a lot of the institution and very little of the principle' (Carens 1994: 39). This is a nice way of capturing how many Aboriginals in Canada perceive the Canadian Charter and the Supreme Court. They experience the rituals and procedures of the judicial system, but not very much of the underlying principles of justice and human rights. For discussions of the application of constitutional rights to Indian governments, see Turpel 1989–90; Boldt 1993: 147–56; Boldt and Long 1984; Ball 1989: 2308–9; Resnik 1989: 725–42; Tsosie 1994; and the debate between Robert Laurence and Robert Williams in *Arizona Law Review*, 30/3 (1988).
7. For a discussion of this case, see Weston 1981; Svensson 1979. Some Maori leaders in New Zealand insist that their members have a similar duty to maintain traditional practices (Sharp 1990: 249). For a (qualified) defence of the claim that group members have such 'duties of loyalty', so that imposing internal restrictions is sometimes justified, see Nickel 1994: 95–7.
8. e.g., while the practices of suttee and female infanticide are still defended in parts of India, no Hindu immigrant organization in a Western democracy has sought the freedom to continue them. These are extreme cases, but they reflect a general trend. Internal restrictions which

are deeply rooted in the immigrant's homeland often become undesired—even unthinkable—in the new country. For cases of oppressive practices which do arise (e.g. female circumcision), see Poulter 1987.

9. On the Amish, see *Wisconsin* v. *Yoder* 406 US 210. For the Canadian cases, see Janzen 1990: chs. 5–7.
10. In a *talaq* divorce, a Muslim husband unilaterally repudiates his wife simply by repeating 'I divorce you' three times. A Muslim wife has no similar right to divorce her husband unilaterally. Legislation has been passed in Britain stating that such declarations have no legal force (Poulter 1987: 601).
11. These internal restrictions are often rationalized on the grounds that the influence of the larger society (e.g. television) is making it more difficult for members to maintain their traditional way of life; some members are 'pressured' by the seductive attractions of the larger society. It is undoubtedly true that internal dissent is often the result of exposure to external influences. But there is still a fundamental distinction between internal restrictions and external protections. External protections are intended to ensure that people are able to maintain their way of life *if they so choose*, and are not prevented from doing so by the decisions of people outside the community. Internal restrictions are intended to force people to maintain their traditional way of life, even if they would not voluntarily choose to do so because they find some other way of life more attractive. In both cases, one could say that the aim is to limit 'external influences'. But the sort of 'influence' involved, and the nature of the 'limit', is fundamentally different. In the first case, the influence of the larger society makes it impossible for people who would prefer to maintain their traditional way of life to do so. Limiting that influence through external protections helps ensure that members are able to act on their informed preferences about the good life. In the second case, the influence of the larger society provides alternatives that some members may prefer to their traditional way of life, even though they are quite able to maintain the latter if they so desire. Limiting that influence through internal restrictions involves reducing people's ability to act on their informed preferences about the good life. External protections give people the right to maintain their way of life if they so choose; internal restrictions impose a duty on people to maintain their way of life, even if they would not voluntarily choose to do so. As I discuss in Ch. 5, s. 3, a liberal theory will view interaction with and learning from other cultures as a good, not something to be resisted.
12. On this issue, see Parekh 1990 and my debate with Tariq Modood (Kymlicka 1993*b*; Modood 1993).
13. This has created the paradoxical situation that indigenous people who have rights over vast areas of land and natural resources are unable to borrow the money necessary to develop their resources. For a discussion of 'collective land rights', and their impact on the liberty of group mem-

bers, see Buchanan 1993. Provisions regarding the selling of land on the Åland Islands (a Swedish-speaking area of Finland) provide another case where property regimes intended to provide external protections have some (minor) impact on the individual liberty of group members (Minority Rights Group 1991: 12–15).

14. For some of the unavoidable impacts of Aboriginal self-government on norms of Canadian citizenship, see Gibbins 1986: 369–72. Another example of the way that internal restrictions and external protections are combined is the language laws in Quebec. This example is complex, since the laws distinguish between various kinds of language use (government services, education, workplace, and commercial signs), and various groups (resident anglophones, anglophones who move to Quebec from other provinces, francophones, and immigrants). The primary justification for these laws is to ensure equal opportunity for francophones against the economic and political pressure of the anglophone majority in Canada (and North America). As such, they have been quite successful, particularly in enabling francophones to use French in the workplace. However, some aspects of these laws involve internal restrictions. For example, the law not only guarantees that commercial signs are available in French, it also restricts the availability of signs in English, thereby preventing francophones from voluntarily choosing to use English. This is partly an internal restriction, since it is partly designed to protect the stability of Québécois society from the choices of its own members. It is also partly an over-restrictive external protection, since it unnecessarily restricts the freedom of anglophones to use their own language (see Yalden 1989; Mendes 1991; Campbell 1994).
15. The first case was *Sparrow* v. *Regina* [1990] 3 CNLR SCC; the second was *Thomas* v. *Norris* [1992] 3 CNLR BCSC. For a discussion of *Thomas*, and how it falls outside the acceptable bounds for protecting group differences, see Eisenberg 1994; Isaac 1992; L. Green 1994. I should note that some Aboriginals have objected to the *Thomas* decision on the grounds that the Supreme Court had no legitimate jurisdiction in a case that involved the internal affairs of a self-governing Indian band. I address this question of jurisdiction in Ch. 8.
16. See also the recent *Mabo* decision in Australia, which finally recognized traditional Aborigine ownership of land (*Mabo* v. *Queensland (no. 2)* (1992) 175 CLR 1). The High Court noted that Aboriginal title may be held by individuals, subgroups, or the collectivity as a whole, depending on the circumstances.
17. Granting special rights or powers to a province or territory dominated by a particular community may be easier than granting rights or powers to the community itself, since it takes advantage of the pre-existing structures of federalism, rather than establishing entirely new political structures outside the federal division of powers. There is, however, a danger in giving special rights to a provincial government, since it may create the

impression that the government primarily or exclusively serves the interests of the dominant group. It is one thing to say that the Québécois constitute a distinct cultural community entitled to special rights or powers, and that the provincial government of Quebec is the most appropriate body to exercise those rights. But there is a danger that this may lead to the very different idea of 'Québec au Québécois', as if non-francophone Quebecers were not equally citizens of the province (Howse and Knop 1993). To avoid this, it might be preferable if special rights were always exercised directly by the members of the community, rather than indirectly through a provincial government. However, this is not always possible, nor desirable, since it might generate constant conflict about who is or is not a member of the community. The question of who should exercise special rights—whether it should be the individual members of a community, or the community as a whole, or a province or territory—often depends on practical considerations about the efficacy and flexibility of different institutions. See Asch 1984: ch. 7.

18. It may well matter for individual Indians, particularly those who are subject to discrimination within the band.

19. The same problem arises with other popular terms used to describe these policies: e.g. some people refer to the various forms of group-differentiated rights as 'community rights' or 'group rights'. However, these terms also imply a false contrast with individual rights. Moreover, 'community rights' gives a misleading sense of the homogeneity of the cultural group. Ethnic and national groups are not 'communities' if that means a group of people united by a common set of beliefs or values, or even a sense of solidarity. As I discuss later, ethnic and national groups can be deeply divided in terms of their political, religious, or lifestyle commitments, and the term 'community' can serve to obscure these divisions (see I. Young 1990: ch. 8).

    The term 'minority rights' is somewhat better, since it does not imply an artificial contrast between individual and group-specific rights. However, it is potentially misleading in another way, since it has historically been used to refer to any constitutional restrictions on the scope of majority rule, including restrictions protecting the common rights of citizenship. Hence guarantees of freedom of conscience have often been seen as a 'minority right', since they have protected religious minorities from persecution by the majority. Moreover, all these terms suffer from the fact that many of the claims made by ethnic and national groups do not in fact take the form of *rights*, in the strict legal sense of that term. They may instead take the form of legislative powers or legal immunities. To avoid ambiguity, I should perhaps talk about 'the claims of the members of ethnic and national groups for group-differentiated rights, powers, status or immunities, beyond the common rights of citizenship'. To save space, however, I will use 'group-differentiated rights' or 'minority rights' as the best available shorthand.

20. See the discussion of the 'striking parallel between the communitarian attack of philosophical liberalism and the notion of collective rights' in Galenkamp 1993: 20–5. For representatives of the 'individualist' camp, see Narveson 1991; Hartney 1991. For the 'communitarian' camp, see McDonald 1991*a*; Garet 1983; Van Dyke 1982; Johnston 1989.

CHAPTER 4

1. For examples and references, see Kymlicka 1989*a*: ch. 10; 1991.
2. In Mazzini's case, the link between individual liberty and national identity seems mediated by an idiosyncratic view of Christian eschatology, which partly explains why his account of liberal nationalism has disappeared from view.
3. Shaw, quoted in Zimmern 1918: 63.
4. Mill seemed to think of all non-European societies that 'if they are ever to be farther improved, it must be by foreigners' (Mill 1972: 140). As Parekh shows, this assumption, which was invoked to defend British colonialism, has had a profoundly distorting impact on liberal thought. In order to defend colonialism, Mill was led to create an exaggerated, almost Manichaean, division between European and non-European societies. The led not only to a caricatured misunderstanding of non-European societies, but also to various fixations within liberalism itself. Having defined liberalism as 'the opposite, the antithesis' of the allegedly tradition-bound and stagnant non-European ways of life, liberals became 'obsessively anti-tradition', and started to fetishize economic growth and the domination of nature, since these features provided the clearest distinction from non-European societies (Parekh 1994). For similar trends in nineteenth-century liberal thought in France, see Todorov 1993: ch. 3; Said 1993.
5. At first glance, the ideal of benign neglect seems present in Zimmern. He distinguishes 'political Nationalism', which he sees as illiberal, from a 'social' or 'purely non-political' nationalism, which he endorses (Zimmern 1918: 71, 97). Moreover, he draws an explicit analogy between the separation of church and state and his ideal of non-political nationalism (50). But this analogy turns out to be misleading, and his model of 'non-political' nationalism does not involve any strict separation of state and nationality. On the contrary, his models of national tolerance are Belgium and Switzerland, whose systems of regional autonomy and language rights protect national minorities (96). Moreover, he endorses the establishment of a Jewish homeland in Palestine, in order that Jews can have 'an intimate national atmosphere' (98). So he endorses the idea that political boundaries, powers, and language rights should be designed to protect national groups. What he means by non-political nationalism, therefore, is simply the view that national self-government does not

require a nation-state. Rather we should seek 'supernational States or Commonwealths' which 'cherish a large number of national individualities' (99).

6. Durham also said, 'I found a struggle, not of principles, but of races'. This is misleading, in so far as it suggests that conflicts between national groups do not raise issues of principle. Durham's proposal for coercive assimilation suggests that he did not recognize the moral issues involved. For Mill's endorsement of Durham's report, see Mill 1972: 410. For a sympathetic view of Lord Durham's thought, see Ajzenstat 1984; 1988.
7. It is interesting to compare the liberal and Marxist traditions here. Like liberalism, Marxism was initially articulated in ethnically and racially homogeneous societies (i.e. Germany and England). Like liberals in the overseas colonies, Marxists in other countries were therefore faced with questions about the role of ethnic and racial minorities which their inherited theory did not address. And like colonial liberals, Marxists developed a wide range of views about how to adapt their theory to incorporate these issues. So there is a striking parallel between the liberal and Marxist traditions in this respect. Sadly, while there are many books on the history of Marxist attempts to accommodate race and nationality (most recently, Nimni 1994), there are few if any books which do the same for the liberal tradition.
8. For an interesting discussion of this change, see Barker 1948. The first edition of his book, written in 1927, was influenced by the 'after-swell' of World War I, which focused on national self-government. By the fourth edition of the book, written in 1948, the idea of national rights was already overshadowed by conflicts between rival empires built on economic ideology. He correctly predicted that this overshadowing of national identity by economic ideology would be temporary: 'When we remember how much of the life of a nation "rides underseas" (or, in the more modern phrase, how much it can act by "underground movement"), we cannot but augur survival. Confessions and empires have challenged nations before (in the Thirty Years War, or in the partitions of Poland); but the nations have weathered the storm' (Barker 1948: p. xvii).
9. American liberals are now being forced to consider the relevance of their principles to multination states, as governments and organizations in Eastern Europe seek their advice on democratization and constitution-making. Hopefully, this will lead to more sustained reflection by American theorists on the claims of national minorities, although some recent American discussions of Eastern Europe are disappointing in this regard (e.g. Siegan 1992; Ackerman 1992; for a partial exception see Ordeshook 1993: cf. Walker 1994).
10. e.g. refusal to recognize the national claims of indigenous peoples is often justified on the grounds that national minorities are a threat to national security (de Onis 1992: 55; da Cunha 1992: 282; Ahmed 1993; Maybury-Lewis 1984: 222–7; Nietschmann 1987).

11. *Statement of the Government of Canada on Indian Policy*, tabled on 25 June 1969 by Jean Chrétien, Minister of Indian Affairs and Northern Development. Reprinted in Bowles *et al.* 1972: 202–4.
12. *Regina* v. *Drybones* [1970] SCR 282 (the 'situations in *Brown* v. *Board of Education* and the instant cases are, of course, very different, but the basic philosophic concept is the same').
13. On the post-*Brown* tendency to treat indigenous peoples and other national minorities as 'racial minorities', see Barsh and Henderson 1980: 241–8; Van Dyke 1985: 194; O'Brien 1987: 323, 356; Chartrand 1995; Berger 1984: 94.
14. Many earlier American liberals strongly supported the old (Millian) model which emphasized shared cultural allegiance as the basis of political allegiance (Glazer 1983: 99). For an important exception to this earlier American liberal support for Anglo-conformity, see Bourne 1964; H. Kallen 1924: 145–7. See also the discussion of Kallen's views in Walzer 1982; Gleason 1982.
15. Glazer himself objects to polyethnic rights, even where they are not seen as matters of national rights or collective autonomy, because he thinks that the risks of coercion and divisiveness are too great to provide even modest support for polyethnicity (1983: 124).
16. In any event, the fact that Indians might choose to become an ethnic group like all the others does not show that they do not have the right to choose otherwise (people can choose not to exercise their legitimate rights). Walzer's claim recalls Thurgood Marshall's absurd comment that Indians want colour-blind laws but 'they just have not had the judgment or the wherewithal to bring lawsuits' (Friedman 1969: 50). He made this comment when serving as a lawyer for the NAACP during the *Brown* desegregation case. Once Marshall became a Supreme Court justice, his views changed, and he became a defender of Indian self-government. See Tsosie 1994.
17. In some of his more recent work, Walzer accepts that Indians and other 'incorporated nations' in the United States should have certain national rights (Walzer 1992*c*: 167). Yet in other places he continues to insist that the United States does not, and should not, recognize any national groups (Walzer 1992*d*: 101; 1992*b*: 9). His waffling on this issue may stem from his underlying theory of 'shared meanings', which presupposes that there is a single 'community of character' within each state, and from his manifest desire to believe that the United States is such a community of character. For discussions of this underlying theory, and its effect on Walzer's description of the American political community, see Rosenblum 1984: 585–9; Galston 1989: 120–2; Kymlicka 1989*a*: ch. 11.
18. There is something deeply ethnocentric about this argument, or at least about the way Glazer and Walzer present it. Glazer and Walzer say there is a 'national consensus' or 'shared understanding' in favour of

assimilation, but they clearly mean by this a consensus amongst European and Asian ethnic groups, since they admit that other groups do want national rights. Glazer says that this consensus has produced a 'fraternity of all Americans', even though he admits that it has excluded blacks, Indians, Hispanics, and Puerto Ricans. He says that national rights should be rejected in order to avoid mutual resentment. But what he really hopes to avoid is (unjustified) resentment amongst European and Asian ethnic groups, since he admits that national minorities are already (and legitimately) resentful at the denial of their national rights. Voluntary immigrant groups have illegitimately adopted the language of national rights, and in order to fight this divisive tendency, Glazer denies Indians and other national minorities the legitimate use of that language. It is difficult to avoid the conclusion that American Indians and other national minorities are pawns being sacrificed to preserve Glazer's real concern—the fraternity of immigrant groups in America. The beliefs of ethnic groups are taken by Glazer to be definitive of the 'national consensus', of 'our shared understandings', of what 'all Americans' feel. As a result, the claims of Indians are evaluated, not in terms of their intrinsic merits, but in terms of their potential effect on the 'fraternity' of immigrant groups. Glazer's commitment to benign neglect is defended through the explicit subordination of the interests of national minorities to the fraternity of ethnic groups. Much the same applies to Walzer's talk about the 'shared understanding' of national identity in America. I criticize these claims in more depth in Kymlicka 1991.

19. Both Walzer and Glazer are well-known critics of affirmative action (see Glazer 1975; Walzer 1983*a*: ch. 5), and this may explain their tendency to magnify its anti-integrationist or 'corporatist' elements. Viewing demands for affirmative action by American immigrant groups as an expression of latent nationalism is deeply implausible. Indeed, Walzer seems to recognize this. He notes that a comprehensive quota system within mainstream institutions reduces ethnic corporatism, since it reproduces within every group the same educational and employment patterns, whereas 'historically specific cultures necessarily produce historically specific patterns of interest and work' (Walzer 1982: 23–4). Walzer writes as if this is a puzzle about the ethnic revival, as if ethnic groups have not figured out what they really want. But ethnic groups were quite clear that in seeking affirmative action they were seeking inclusion, not self-government.
20. In an earlier work, Glazer suggested that benign neglect was a defining feature of liberal justice (Glazer 1975: 220). But in later work he accepts that a state which recognizes national rights may be just as 'responsive to human rights and to civil rights' as one which ignores them (Glazer 1978: 98).
21. The quotations in this and the following paragraph come from Engels,

'The Danish-Prussian Alliance', quoted in Cummings 1980: 46; and Nimni 1989: 313.

22. Generally speaking, support for Indian claims in Brazil diminishes the closer one gets to the region involved. The greatest level of support comes from people outside the country, who have pressured the federal government to recognize certain Indian claims. However, the federal government is unable actually to enforce these policies, because of the widespread opposition at the local and regional level.
23. This parallels the problem with collectivist defences of 'collective' rights (see Ch. 3). Valuing decentralization in and of itself does not explain the *group-differentiated* nature of self-government rights. Moreover, there are many aspects of economic, social, and environmental policy that can only be effectively dealt with at a federal or international level. Too much decentralization of power may result, not in the empowering of cultural minorities, but simply in leaving everyone powerless in the face of global economic and political trends. Here again, the needs of national minorities cannot be reduced to a general and undifferentiated decentralization of power.
24. As Ian Cummings puts it, Engels conceived of nationalism 'not as a sociological concept so much as a more directly political one', which led him 'to judge it in terms of liberalism or conservatism, to be supported or fought to the extent to which it corresponded with the requirements of the political movement with which he was associated' (Cummings 1980: 44). Other socialists, like Lenin and Luxemburg, recognized that coercive forms of assimilation were unacceptable, and that oppressed national groups developed a powerful sense of grievance that needed to be accommodated. But they assumed that temporary measures to support oppressed national minorities would quench any lingering sense of nationalism, and that national minorities would then move voluntarily towards assimilation. This is like Walzer's assumption that national minorities in the United States will stop seeking national rights once they are treated fairly by the mainstream society. For an important exception to this instrumental or compensatory view of cultural membership within the socialist tradition, see the work of Otto Bauer, discussed in Munck 1985; Nimni 1994: chs 5–7.
25. And of course nationalist movements which threatened Communist power, either domestically or internationally, were ruthlessly suppressed. For a comprehensive review of Marxist policy towards national groups, see Connor 1984. A similar incoherence can be seen amongst the Canadian left. The left-wing New Democratic Party was the first national political party to affirm 'special status' for Quebec in 1965, yet it continues to pass resolutions on federal economic and social policy that are perceived (in Quebec at least) as inconsistent with that commitment (D. Morton 1986: 60–1). Similarly, while the NDP now endorses an inherent right to Aboriginal self-government, in 1969 it endorsed the

Liberal proposal to eliminate the special status of Indians. And while the NDP now endorses the multiculturalism policy, many earlier leaders, such as J. S. Woodsworth, were critics of 'hyphenated-Canadians', and opposed the tendency of immigrants from one country to settle together, since this slowed down the process of assimilation (Woodsworth 1972). It would be difficult to identify a coherent account of the value of cultural membership underlying these shifts.

26. In his most recent work, Miller amends his view somewhat. He suggests that multination states are possible, so long as national minorities do not have a radically different identity from the majority nation. In some cases, it is possible to interpret the national identities of each constituent group in a way that makes them consistent with an overarching common identity. What really matters is not that people share a national identity, but that they can share a 'public culture' (Miller 1993). However, in some places, he still implies that differences in language give rise to radically incompatible national identities that cannot be reconciled in a common public culture.
27. See the references in Kymlicka 1989*a*: 255. This explanation is echoed in recent communitarian claims that liberalism depends on a notion of the self which is unencumbered by social attachments, whose freedom is exercised precisely by abstracting itself from its cultural situation—see MacIntyre 1981: ch. 15; Sandel 1982: 150–65; Bell 1993: 24–54; Taylor 1985.
28. Notice that none of the three factors which have shaped post-war liberal views involves a denial that human freedom and identity are tied to membership in a culture.

CHAPTER 5

1. For an interesting exploration of the idea of a 'society', and its requirements for a certain level of institutional completeness and intergenerational continuity, see Copp 1992.
2. e.g. American studies indicate 'an almost complete breakdown in the transmission of non-English languages between the second and third generations' (Steinberg 1981: 45). One reason why languages which do not achieve the status of a public language are unlikely to survive is that people lack the opportunity or incentive to use and develop them in cognitively stimulating ways (Skutnabb-Kangas 1988).
3. As Clarke notes, language is sometime a 'technical accomplishment', and sometimes the 'main support for a distinct cultural identity' (Clarke 1934: 20). Over time, the immigrant language shifts from the latter to the former. As the immigrants slowly lose their mother tongue, so at the same time, and as a consequence, the dominant language is (in a different sense) taken away from its original ethnic speakers. That is, as immi-

grants become members of the larger anglophone culture, the descendants of the original Anglo-Saxon settlers cease to have any exclusive or privileged say over the development and use of the English language. This helps explain why North American English has diverged from English in Britain, where Anglo-Saxons continue to be the overwhelming majority of the speakers of the language (Johnson 1973: 117).

4. In earlier times, cultures did not have to form societal culture to survive, since there were fewer society-wide institutions shaping people's options. (The language of public schools was not an issue when there were no public schools.) Indeed, the very idea of a 'societal culture' is a modern one. In medieval times, the idea that the various economic classes or castes would share a common culture was unheard of. Thus Todorov is historically correct when he says that 'Culture is not necessarily national (it is even only exceptionally so). It is first of all the property of a region, or of an even smaller geographical entity; it may also belong to a given layer of a population, excluding other groups from the same country; finally, it may also include a group of countries' (Todorov 1993: 387). However, as Todorov himself notes, there is a powerful tendency in the modern world for culture to become national in scope.
5. The following argument is presented in much more detail in Kymlicka 1989*a*: ch. 2–4; 1990: ch. 6.
6. Liberals often make an exception where individuals are particularly vulnerable to weakness of will (e.g. paternalistic legislation against addictive drugs). The connection between rational revisability, the endorsement constraint, and the liberal prohibition on state paternalism is quite complicated. For Rawls's discussion of perfectionism, see Rawls 1988: 260, 265. For Dworkin's account, see 1989: 486–7; 1990. For general discussions see Kymlicka 1989*b*; Waldron 1989; Moore 1993: ch. 6; Caney 1991; Mason 1990; McDonald 1992: 116–21; Hurka 1994.
7. Allen Buchanan calls this the 'rational revisability' model of individual choice (Buchanan 1975). The claim that we have a basic interest in being able rationally to assess and revise our current ends is often phrased in terms of the value of 'autonomy'. This label may be misleading, since there are many other conceptions of autonomy. For example, on one account of autonomy, the exercise of choice is intrinsically valuable, because it reflects our rational nature (this view is ascribed to Kant). Another account of autonomy argues that nonconformist individuality is intrinsically valuable (this view is often ascribed to Mill). I am making the more modest claim that choice enables us to assess and learn what is good in life. It presupposes that we have an essential interest in identifying and revising those of our current beliefs about value which are mistaken. When I use the term autonomy, therefore, it is in this (relatively modest) sense of 'rational revisability'. I discuss these different conceptions of autonomy in Kymlicka 1989*a*: ch. 4; 1990: ch. 6.
8. I discuss this in greater length in Kymlicka 1989*a*: ch. 8; 1995*b*. Of

course, the models we learn about in our culture are often closely related to the models in other cultures. For example, models derived from the Bible will be part of the structure of many cultures with a Christian influence. And there are international bodies, like the Catholic Church, which actively seek to ensure this commonality amongst models in different cultures. So in saying that we learn about conceptions of the good life through our culture, I do not mean to imply that the goods are therefore culture-specific, although some are.

9. In explaining his notion of the decay of a cultural structure, Dworkin says that 'We are all beneficiaries or victims of what is done to the language we share. A language can diminish; some are richer and better than others' (1985: 229). This is misleading if he means that some languages are *inherently* richer than others. All human languages have an equal capacity for evolution and adaptation to meet the needs of their speakers (Edwards 1985: 19; Skutnabb-Kangas 1988: 12). However, the range of options available in one's language can clearly decay.
10. I should note that Dworkin made his brief comments about 'cultural structures' in the context of an argument regarding public funding of the arts, and they were not intended to provide a comprehensive description or theory about the nature of cultures. However, since he is one of the few liberal theorists to address explicitly the question of the relationship between freedom and culture, I have tried to draw out the implications of his view. See also his claim that people 'need a common culture and particularly a common language even to have personalities, and culture and language are social phenomena. We can only have the thoughts, and ambitions, and convictions that are possible within the vocabulary that language and culture provide, so we are all, in a patent and deep way, the creatures of the community as a whole' (Dworkin 1989: 488; cf. Dworkin 1985: 228, and the discussion in Kymlicka 1995*b*).
11. In Rawls's terminology, we can say that access to such a culture is a 'primary good'—i.e. a good which people need, regardless of their particular chosen way of life, since it provides the context within which they make those particular choices. I explore how this argument relates to Rawls's account of 'primary goods' in more depth in Kymlicka 1989*a*: ch. 7. For related arguments about the dependence of freedom on culture, see Taylor 1985; Tamir 1993: chs. 1–2; Hargalit and Raz 1990.
12. I am trying to respond here to the cogent questions raised by Binder 1993: 253–5; Buchanan 1991: 54–5; Waldron 1992*a*; Tomasi 1995; Nickel 1995; Lenihan 1991; Margalit and Halbertal 1994, amongst others.
13. For a discussion of these costs, and the extent to which they vary between children and adults, see Nickel 1995.
14. It is worth remembering that, while many immigrants flourish in their new country, there is a selection factor at work. That is, those people who choose to uproot themselves are likely to be the people who have the weakest psychological bond to the old culture, and the strongest

desire and determination to succeed elsewhere. We cannot assume a priori that they represent the norm in terms of cultural adaptability. As John Edwards notes, the ability to communicate does not only involve pragmatic language skills, but also the 'inexpressible' knowledge of historical and cultural associations tied up with the language, and this may be difficult or impossible for immigrants to acquire fully: 'the symbolic value of language, the historical and cultural associations which it accumulates, and the "natural semantics of remembering" all add to the basic message a rich underpinning of shared connotations . . . the ability to read between the lines, as it were, depends upon a cultural continuity in which the language is embedded, and which is not open to all. Only those who grow up within the community can, perhaps, participate fully in this expanded communicative interaction' (Edwards 1985: 17).

15. The only significant difference, Dion notes, concerns openness to immigration, a difference that is understandable in the light of francophone fears as a minority.
16. The danger of oppression reflects the fact that many traditional roles and practices were defined historically on the basis of sexist, racist, classist, and homophobic assumptions. Some social roles are so compromised by their unjust origins that they should be rejected entirely, not just gradually reformed (D. Phillips 1993). In some places, Sandel qualifies his idea of constitutive ends in a way that suggests that people can, after all, stand back and assess even their most deeply held ends. But once these qualifications are added in, it is no longer clear how Sandel's conception of the person differs from the liberal one he claims to be criticizing (see Kymlicka 1989*a*: chs. 2–4; 1990: ch. 5). In his more recent work, Rawls has attempted to accommodate the communitarian view, and defend liberalism without insisting on the rational revisability of our ends. I do not think his new defence works, and I explain why in Ch. 8.
17. Of course, once that national existence is not threatened, then people will favour increased mobility, since being able to move and work in other cultures is a valuable option for some people under some circumstances. For liberal defenders of open borders—all of whom see themselves as criticizing the orthodox liberal view—see Ackerman 1980: 89–95; Carens 1987; Hudson 1986; King 1983; Bader 1995.
18. As Higham puts it, 'the English in all the colonies before the Revolution conceived of themselves as founders, settlers or planters—the formative population of those colonial societies—not as immigrants. Theirs was the polity, the language, the pattern of work and settlements, and many of the mental habits to which the immigrants would have to adjust' (Higham 1976: 6). There is surprisingly little written on the 'theory of colonization', and how it differs from individual emigration. For one exception, see Mills 1974, esp. pp. 50, 117–20.
19. Of course, the children of immigrants do not consent, and it is not clear that parents should be able to waive their children's rights. For this

reason, it is important that governments should strive to make the children of immigrants feel 'at home' in the mainstream culture, to feel that it is 'their' culture. Adult immigrants may be willing to accept a marginalized existence in their new country, neither integrated into the mainstream culture nor able to re-create their old culture. But this is not acceptable for children. It is they who would suffer most from the marginalization, since the parents at least had the benefit of being raised as full participants in a societal culture in their homeland, and can draw on this to add meaning to the practices they seek to maintain, in a diminished and fragmented way, in the new land. Children have the right to be raised as full participants in a societal culture which provides them with a diverse range of options, and parents cannot waive this right. For this reason, if we do not enable immigrants to re-create their old culture, then we must strenuously work to ensure that the children integrate into the mainstream.

20. In so far as immigrant children are disadvantaged by the lack of bilingual education, this becomes an issue of basic fairness, since liberal theories of justice consider it a serious injustice to disadvantage people on the basis of unchosen factors like ethnicity, race, or class.
21. By contrast, the fact that Puerto Ricans continue to demand that Spanish be the official language of Puerto Rico shows that national minorities have not abandoned their national rights. See also the discussion of Hispanic groups in Ch. 2.
22. I should emphasize that I am talking here about the relatively small number of refugees who have resettled in Western countries. I am not talking about the very large refugee groups which have arisen in Asia or Africa when people flee into a neighbouring country to avoid war or famine. These groups may number in the hundreds of thousands or millions (e.g. in Pakistan, or Zaïre). But in the West, refugee groups tend to be small and dispersed.
23. Canada does make certain special allowances, beyond the usual polyethnic rights, for some refugees—e.g. the Doukhobours. The Doukhobours immigrated to Canada, not voluntarily as individuals, but *en masse* in order to preserve their culture, since they were being persecuted in Russia. Other groups, such as the Hutterites, came voluntarily, but only because of explicit promises from Canadian immigration officials that they would be able to settle as a group and maintain their own social institutions, such as schools. In neither of these cases can the group be said to have chosen to relinquish the claims that go with membership in their cultural community. The special arrangements regarding taxation, education, and military service for these groups reflect the fact that some groups fall in-between the category of national minority and voluntary immigrant, with an intermediate status that involves more than polyethnic rights but less than self-government. On the rights of these groups, see Janzen 1990.

24. Réaume 1991. This is one reason why I reject the claim that minority rights can be defended in terms of the intrinsic value of cultural diversity. This claim would not really defend the *right* to maintain one's culture—it would instead impose a *duty* to maintain one's culture (see Ch. 6, s. 3). The option for integration seems most relevant in the case of the outlying members of a national minority, who have, for whatever reason, dispersed from the major territorial concentration of the group (e.g. American Indians who have left the reservation for the city; French Canadians who live in western Canada).
25. Immigrant groups may also have this potentiality, given the appropriate conditions. But, if my earlier arguments were correct, immigrants have no claim of justice to those conditions, whereas national minorities do. Also, as I discuss in the next chapter, the value of cultural membership is not the only basis for national minorities to demand group-specific rights. In particular, national minorities may have historical rights that do not depend on the maintenance of a distinct societal culture.
26. Some of these groups have given rise to nationalist movements, even though they do not fit the usual pattern of 'national' groups. Pre-existing societal cultures which have been incorporated into a larger state are the most common groups which see themselves as distinct 'nations', and which have developed 'nationalist' movements. But in some cases, an existing nation has undergone such a deep division, perhaps along racial or religious lines, that it has developed into two or more groups, each of which comes to see itself as a distinct nation or people, even though they continue to share a common language. If racial and religious differences and discrimination within a given societal culture become so entrenched that a common life comes to be seen as impossible, a sense of separate nationhood may develop within a subgroup of the larger society. And, over time, this subgroup may develop its own distinct 'pervasive' or 'societal' cultures (e.g. religious differences in the Punjab or Northern Ireland; racial differences in South Africa). Groups who share the same language, and who once shared many of the same institutions, may none the less come to feel incapable of sharing a common culture.

    Such racial and religious differences account for most of the familiar cases of nationalist movements which are not based on language. But notice that such movements, from a liberal point of view, are either the cause or result of an injustice. To exclude people from participating in a public culture and institutions on the basis of race or religion is unjust. While the excluded group may go on to develop its own pervasive culture in response, this separate culture would not have developed were it not for the original injustice. Therefore, nationalist movements based on religion or race are evidence of an injustice, a failure to live up to liberal principles. Nationalist movements based on language, however, need not be grounded in injustice, and would persist even in an ideally just world. From a liberal point of view, language-based nationalism is maximally consistent with freedom and equality, since (unlike religious-based nationalism) it does not presuppose any shared conception of the good; and (unlike racially based nationalism) is not inherently exclusionary or discriminatory.

27. e.g. the idea that governments should preserve the 'purity' of a language by preventing the adoption of foreign words is often illiberal. Many countries have adopted this aim, and established linguistic academies to try to enforce it (Edwards 1985: 27–34). This is a misguided policy, not only because it is futile to regulate word-choice in that way, but also because much of the pleasure and interest of a language comes from its diverse origins. However, this misguided attempt to preserve the purity of a language from foreign contamination is very different from the struggle to maintain the ability to use one's own (impure) language in public and private life, and not to be forced to use someone else's language. The people in France, Germany, and Spain who have been most concerned about preserving the purity of their language have no reason to worry about their ability to speak their own language. Conversely, many of the Puerto Ricans and Québécois who are concerned about maintaining their language rights have no interest in policing the adoption of foreign words.
28. As I noted earlier, Mill thought that the only or best way to ensure that smaller nations participate in the wider world is for them to assimilate to larger nations. The alternative for the members of small nations, he thought, is to 'sulk on his own rocks . . . revolving in his own little mental orbit, without participation or interest in the general movement of the world' (Mill 1972: 363–4). But isolation and assimilation are not the only options. One can enable smaller nations to participate in the larger world, but from a situation of equal power, where they can exercise some control over the rate and direction of cultural change.
29. While the members of a culture share the same language, it does not follow that all people who share the same language belong to the same culture. Not all anglophones in the world belong to the same culture. A culture, as I am defining it, involves a shared history as well as a common language, and their embodiment in particular societal practices and institutions. Hence English-speaking immigrants from Singapore, for example, must learn the 'shared vocabulary of tradition and convention' which is used in American life. A common language, then, is necessary for a shared culture, but not sufficient. Of course, the idea of a 'shared language' is itself slippery. For example, how do we distinguish different languages from different regional dialects of the same language? These judgements are somewhat arbitrary, and affected by political considerations. (Linguists like to say that a language is a dialect with an army.)
30. A similar problem arises with 'ecocentric' arguments for preserving indigenous rights—i.e. the argument that Indian lands should be protected from external development because this is the best way to preserve

the natural environment. This argument, which is popular amongst some First World environmentalists, has the result of limiting Indian claims to groups whose cultural practices and ethnic identity remain frozen in time. As da Cunha notes, many environmentalist discussions of Brazil have seen indigenous peoples as 'part of the natural scenery'. There has been a 'naturalization' of indigenous groups, who are not seen as 'agents with their own specific projects' (da Cunha 1992: 286–7; cf. Kymlicka 1995*c*). Hence environmentalists feel betrayed when indigenous peoples attempt to improve their standard of living by commercially exploiting their natural resources (e.g. by selling logging or mineral leases).

31. I explore this distinction in more depth in Kymlicka 1989*a*: ch. 8.

CHAPTER 6

1. This phrase is from the judgement of the Canadian Supreme Court in explaining its interpretation of the equality guarantees under the Canadian Charter of Rights (*Andrews* v. *Law Society of British Columbia* 1 SCR 143; 56 DLR (4th) 1). See also Government of Canada 1991b: 10.
2. For examples of this view, see Knopff 1979; F. Morton 1985; Kukathas 1992*a*; Hindess 1993; Maré 1992: 107–10; Rawls 1975: 88, 93, and the references cited in Ch. 1 n. 4.
3. I explored this relationship between national rights and liberal egalitarian justice in Kymlicka 1989*a*: ch. 9. For what it is worth, I continue to endorse the argument in that chapter, but I should have been clearer about its scope. I would now describe the argument in that chapter as an equality-based defence of certain external protections for national minorities. I did not use those terms at the time, in part because I did not have a very clear conception of the variety of rights, groups, and moral justifications that are involved in the debate.
4. I am here disagreeing with Tamir, who argues that the larger a national minority is, the more rights it should have (1993: 75). On my view, if a national group is large enough, it may have little need for group-differentiated rights, since it can ensure its survival and development through the usual operation of the economic market-place and democratic decision-making. (This might be true, for example, if a binational state contained two nations of roughly equal size and wealth.)
5. On the role of indigenous land claims in a liberal egalitarian framework, see Kymlicka 1995*c*; Penz 1992; 1993; Russell 1993; Tully 1994. It is important to note that the equality argument for land claims is not based on notions of compensatory justice. The compensatory argument says that because indigenous peoples were the legal owners of their traditional lands, and because their lands were taken away illegally, they should be compensated for this historical wrong. Since the debate over

land claims is often couched in the language of compensatory justice, I should say a word about this. I take it as given that indigenous peoples have suffered terrible wrongs in being dispossessed of their lands, and that they should be compensated for this in some way. Moreover, I believe that indigenous peoples continue to have certain property rights under the common law (in former British colonies), wherever these have not been explicitly extinguished by legislation. (That is to say, the *terra nullius* doctrine is wrong in terms both of morality and the common law.) But it is a mistake, I think, to put too much weight on historical property rights. For one thing, these claims do not, by themselves, explain why indigenous peoples have rights of self-government. Many groups have been wrongfully dispossessed of property and other economic opportunities, including women, blacks, and Japanese immigrants in the United States and Canada during World War II. Each of these groups may be entitled to certain forms of compensatory justice, but this does not by itself explain or justify granting powers of self-government (rather than compensatory programmes to promote integration and equal opportunity within the mainstream). Suffering historical injustice is neither necessary nor sufficient for claiming self-government rights (see Ch. 2, s. 2).

Moreover, the idea of compensating for historical wrongs, taken to its logical conclusion, implies that all the land which was wrongly taken from indigenous peoples in the Americas or Australia or New Zealand should be returned to them. This would create massive unfairness, given that the original European settlers and later immigrants have now produced hundreds of millions of descendants, and this land is the only home they know. Changing circumstances often make it impossible and undesirable to compensate for certain historical wrongs. As Jeremy Waldron puts it, certain historical wrongs are 'superseded' (Waldron 1992*b*). Also, the land held by some indigenous groups at the time of contact was itself the result of the conquest or coercion of other indigenous groups (Mulgan 1989: 30–1; Crowe 1974: 65–81). The compensatory argument would presumably require rectifying these pre-contract injustices as well. (For other difficulties with compensatory claims, see Brilmayer 1992.)

The equality argument does not try to turn back the historical clock, nor to restore groups to the situation they would have been in the absence of any historical injustice. (These compensatory aims actually fit more comfortably with Nozick's libertarian theory of entitlement than with a liberal egalitarian theory of distributive justice—see Lyons 1981.) The aim of the equality argument is to provide the sort of land base needed to sustain the viability of self-governing minority communities, and hence to prevent unfair disadvantages with respect to cultural membership now and in the future. In short, the equality argument situates land claims within a theory of distributive justice, rather than compensatory justice.

Waldron assumes that indigenous land claims are all based on claims for compensatory justice (Waldron 1992*b*). In fact, however, most indigenous groups focus, not on reclaiming all of what they had before European settlement, but on what they need now to sustain themselves as distinct societies (see the declaration of the World Council of Indigenous Peoples, quoted in Nettheim 1988: 115; Sharp 1990: 150–3). Historical factors are, of course, relevant in other ways. The 'historical agreement' argument I discuss below is very much history-based.

6. The only attempt I know of to reconcile official languages with 'benign neglect' is by Rainer Knopff. He argues that language has two functions: it can function as the vehicle for the transmission of a particular culture, but it can also function as 'a culturally neutral, or utilitarian, means of communication which allows those of different cultures to participate in the same political community' (Knopff 1979: 67). By placing the emphasis on the utilitarian function, governments 'can enact official languages without at the same time legislating official cultures . . . in enacting "official languages", one does not necessarily imply that the cultures which these languages transmit and represent thereby become "official cultures" ' (Knopff 1979: 67). Culture, Knopff argues, 'remains a purely private affair' in Canada, for while English and French have official backing as the 'utilitarian' languages, all languages compete on equal terms for 'cultural' allegiance. It is the 'task of the individual members of a culture to show the excellence of their product on the cultural marketplace, as it were. If they succeed, the language of that culture will become attractive to others . . . if [a] culture, and hence, language, cannot show itself to be worthy of choice in the light of standards of the good, then it deserves to disappear' (Knopff 1979: 70). This view of language as a 'culturally neutral medium' has been thoroughly discredited in the literature. In any event, it is simply not true that teaching in the English language in public schools is totally divorced from the teaching of the history and customs of the anglophone society.

7. Some commentators say that governments should draw boundaries and distribute powers so as to protect the viability of national minorities, but that they should not state in law that they are doing this. This enables the state to continue claiming that it treats all ethnic and national differences with 'benign neglect'. For example, van den Berghe argues that deliberately designing or revising federal units to protect minority cultures is consistent with 'benign neglect', so long as it does not involve the explicit legal recognition of groups. He thinks it is one thing to define the powers and boundaries of a political subunit so as to ensure the protection of a minority culture (what he calls 'indirect consociationalism'), but quite another for the constitution or statute law to cite the existence of that minority as the reason for those arrangements (what he calls 'group rights') (van den Berghe 1981*a*: 348). But surely this is hypocritical. If the agreed purpose of indirect consociationalism is to protect minority

cultures, then anyone who values honesty and transparency in government (as liberals claim to do) should want that justification to be clear to everyone. Van den Berghe's solution violates the 'publicity condition' which Rawls imposes on liberal theories of justice (Rawls 1971: 133). None the less, this attitude seems to be widely shared. While most Canadians accept that the powers and boundaries of Quebec were fixed to accommodate the needs of the francophone minority in Canada, many objected to the government's proposal to state in the constitution that Quebec formed a 'distinct society' as the homeland of the French Canadian nation, because they saw this as violating the principle that the constitution should not recognize particular ethnic or national groups. Quebecers, however, are no longer willing to have their special status hidden away. They view it as a matter of basic respect that their separate identity be recognized and affirmed at the level of constitutional principle (Taylor 1991: 64).

8. This is similar to the debate over affirmative action for women or people with disabilities. Like self-government rights, affirmative action programmes asymmetrically distribute rights or opportunities on the basis of group membership. Proponents argue that they are required for genuine equality. Critics respond that the economic market-place (like the cultural market-place) already respects equality, by treating job applicants without regard for their group membership. However, an equality-based argument for group-specific affirmative action can be made if the actual operation of the economic market-place works to the disadvantage of certain groups. As with self-government rights, the equality argument for affirmative action seeks to show how the structure of common individual rights is intended to treat all people equally, but in fact works to the disadvantage of the members of a particular collectivity. Many group-specific claims can be seen in this way—that is, as compensating for the disadvantages and vulnerabilities of certain groups within the structure of common individual rights.

   Of course, as I discussed in Ch. 1, affirmative action for women or people with disabilities differs in many ways from self-government rights for national minorities, since they are compensating for very different kinds of injustices. The former is intended to help disadvantaged groups integrate into society, by breaking down unjust barriers to full integration. The latter is intended to help cultural communities maintain their distinctiveness, by protecting against external decisions. This means that the former are (in theory) temporary, whereas the latter are permanent, barring dramatic shifts in population.

9. Imagine that schools and government offices (and presumably private businesses as well) were open seven days a week all year round, including Christmas and Easter, and that each student and employee was allowed to choose two days off per week, two weeks' vacation per year, plus, say, five additional holidays per year. This would maximize each

individual's ability to adapt their schedule to their religious beliefs. But I do not know whether this is realistic or even desirable, given the extent to which social life is built around common weekends and holidays. As an atheist, I have no commitment to resting on the sabbath or celebrating religious holidays. But I do like the fact that most of my friends and family, regardless of their religion, language, and ethnicity, do not work on the weekends or on certain public holidays. Maintaining friendships and other voluntary associations would be much more difficult if society (including schools and other government institutions) were not organized in this way. Perhaps a better solution would be to have one major holiday from each of the largest religious groups in the country. We could have one Christian holiday (say, Christmas), but replace Easter and Thanksgiving with a Muslim and Jewish holiday. This would maintain the value of common holidays, and would also encourage people of each faith to learn something about the beliefs of other faiths.

10. e.g. the Canadian government justified its proposal to eliminate the treaty rights of Indians on the grounds that 'we can only be just in our time' (Trudeau 1969: 295). Trudeau was paraphrasing John F. Kennedy's famous quote about justice for blacks in the United States.
11. Chartrand argues that this is the current situation with respect to the Métis in Canada, who agreed to join Canada on the basis of promises made to them under the Manitoba Act 1870, which have since been broken (Chartrand 1993: 241).
12. It is interesting to note that some Aboriginal groups in Canada insist that their demands for federal funding of self-government are based solely on historical compensation for the wrongful taking of land, not on appeals to distributive justice between citizens (Lyon 1984: 13–14).
13. For a subtle discussion of the complex interaction between the equality and treaty arguments in the New Zealand context, see Sharp 1990: 135–6; Mulgan 1989: ch. 4. As Sharp notes, there is a tendency to read principles of equality back into the historical treaties.
14. These arguments parallel common arguments for the protection of endangered plant and animal species, which are seen both as enriching the world aesthetically, and as providing potential sources of valuable genetic material or other substances that might be of human benefit.
15. Many liberals defend state funding of the arts or museums on the ground that the state has a responsibility to ensure an adequate range of options for future generations, which the cultural market-place may fail to protect (Dworkin 1985: ch.. 11; Raz 1986: 162; Black 1992; Kymlicka 1989*b*: 893–5). If we accept that active measures are justified to preserve the richness and diversity of our cultural resources, then programmes such as the funding of ethnic festivals or immigrant language classes can be seen as falling under this heading. Indeed, as I noted in Chapter 2, some people defend this funding simply as a way of ensuring that ethnic groups are not discriminated against in state funding of art and culture.

(I should note that other liberals view any such state funding as illegitimate (e.g. Rawls 1971: 331–2; Waldron 1989).)

16. Hence the popular contrast between 'consociational' and 'universal' modes of incorporating individuals into the state is misleading (e.g. Asch 1990). There is a distinction between models of citizenship that incorporate citizens on a uniform basis or through membership in some group. But uniform citizenship is not *universal* citizenship. No country allows for universal citizenship.
17. See the references in Ch. 5 n. 17.
18. One theorist who has attempted to square the circle is Michael Walzer. He argues that restricting citizenship in a state to the members of a particular group is justified in the name of protecting a distinct culture (what he calls a 'community of character'). He recognizes that this same argument can be given for group-differentiated rights *within* a state, but rejects such rights because they violate our 'shared understandings' (Walzer 1983*a*: ch. 2). I have argued elsewhere that Walzer's argument is unsuccessful (Kymlicka 1989*a*: ch. 11). See also Ch. 4 above. I should emphasize again that my defence of the legitimacy of partially closed borders is not intended to defend the right of national groups to maintain more than their fair share of resources. On the contrary, I would argue that a country forfeits its right to restrict immigration if it has failed to live up to its obligations to share its wealth with the poorer countries of the world. See Bader 1995; Ackerman 1980: 256–7.
19. On the tendency of liberals to treat diversity as a matter of variations in individual values and beliefs, see A. Phillips 1993; Galeotti 1993: 590. For an example of this 'overly cerebral' conception of diversity, see Rawls 1993*a*: pp. xxvii–xxix, where he treats modern conflicts of race, ethnicity, and gender as if they were analogous to conflict over religious belief during the Reformation—i.e. as conflicts over individuals' beliefs about 'the meaning, value and purposes of human life'.
20. This is true of Young's postmodernist account of minority rights. According to her view of 'relational difference', cultural groups must 'understand themselves as participating in the same society', and as 'part of a single polity', whose common decision-making procedures are seen as 'legitimately binding' on all people equally. Cultural difference within a state should be accommodated by group-differentiated rights within a single society—e.g. by group representation within the mainstream polity—rather than by establishing two or more separate and self-governing societies within a state (I. Young 1993*a*: 135). Like many liberals, she fears the impact of national rights on other political movements or on domestic peace.

CHAPTER 7

1. Raymond Wolfinger, quoted in RCERPF 1991: i. 102. For statistics on the (under-)representation of blacks and Hispanics in the United States, see C. Davidson 1992: 46. For statistics on the representation of social groups in Canada, see RCERPF 1991: 93–6 and 192.
2. Obviously, this depends on the scale of the election. It is easier to create black-majority wards in a local election than to create a black-majority congressional district in federal elections.
3. I discuss these proposals in more depth in Kymlicka 1993*a*.
4. Group representation is a basic feature of the consociational democracies, such as the Netherlands and Belgium (see Lijphart 1984; 1991). There are also cases of group representation for indigenous peoples in various Western democracies (e.g. New Zealand and Scandinavia). And there many other cases of group representation around the world (Malaysia, India, Lebanon).
5. These options are discussed in RCERPF 1991: 93–121, and in Megyery 1991*a*; 1991*b*. Of course, some members of disadvantaged groups face barriers, not only in seeking nomination or election, but simply in voting. Options for improving voter registration include the use of non-official languages on ballots, employing enumerators who speak non-official languages, permanent voter lists, increased voter education and use of alternative media for publicizing the election, and so on.
6. For an excellent discussion of the impact of PR on women's representation, from which the points in this paragraph are drawn, see L. Young 1994.
7. One critic remarked that 'if you drove down the interstate with both car doors open, you'd kill most of the people in the district', quoted in *Shaw* v. *Reno* 113 S. Ct. 2816 (1993), 2821. The redistricting plan was challenged in the courts, and the Supreme Court ruled that, prima facie, it was an unconstitutional denial of the equal protection clause. I discuss this judgement later in the chapter.
8. This may indeed be the result of the Supreme Court's judgement in *Shaw* v. *Reno*, as Justice Blackmun noted in dissent. The impact of this judgement on redistricting is unclear. The Court repeatedly emphasized the odd shape of the North Carolina black-majority district, and the judgement may only apply to such cases. Yet the main reason why the Court focused on the shape was that it provided clear evidence that the intent was to create a black-majority district (a fact which no one denied). It seems then that even redistricting that involves regularly shaped black-majority districts may now be suspect, if there is evidence that the redistricting is intentionally 'race-conscious'. (And there almost always is such evidence, since the practice is a very open one under the Voting Rights Act.)

9. Baines argues that the principle of ensuring representation for 'communities of interest' should extend to women (Baines 1992: 56). The Commission considered whether to extend the principle of group representation to non-territorial communities of interest, but rejected it (RCERPF 1991: 172). I discuss the Commission's reasoning in Kymlicka 1993*a*: 84–5.
10. Canada West Foundation 1981: 9. It is important to distinguish this argument for improved representation of regions, based on sensitivity to minority interests, from the separate argument that the Senators should represent the provinces because the upper house in a federal system represents the interests of the provincial governments. This argument has been considered and rejected in both the United States and Canada. Senators are not the delegates of the state or provincial government, chosen to defend the rights and powers of state/provincial governments, but rather serve as the people's representatives in the federal government. On the distinction between these two arguments, see Special Joint Committee 1992: 41–2. The idea that certain groups may be ignored in majority decision-making, and so need special representation, is the historical basis for the second legislative chamber which exists in many countries (e.g. the Senate in Canada and the United States, the House of Lords in Britain). Historically, these second chambers have often been used to ensure representation of a *privileged* minority. For example, the British House of Lords guarantees representation to the aristocracy and to the Church of England, while the Canadian Senate was originally established to protect men of property. Second chambers are also used to guarantee disproportionate representation to smaller regions. As Jane Jenson notes, there are numerous 'routes to representation' in Western democracies, and many of these routes have been group-based, whether that group be regional, religious, class, etc. (Jenson 1995). Contemporary proponents of group representation are simply asking that this strategy be used to protect those who really need it—i.e. disadvantaged, rather than privileged, minorities.
11. In fact, the US Supreme Court, having insisted that institutions which weigh votes differently are prohibited under the Constitution (*Lucas* v. *44th Attorney General of Colorado* 377 US 713 [1964]), was faced with the fact that the American Senate itself violates this principle. The Court admitted this, and implied that the Senate would be struck down as unconstitutional were it not itself part of the constitution.
12. A. Phillips 1992: 85–9. See also Jones 1993. In the American context, this issue has arisen regarding the capacity of middle-class blacks to represent the 'truly disadvantaged' blacks in the inner city. On this, see Reed 1988; Guinier 1991*b*.
13. The term 'challenge of empathy' comes from Minow's discussion of the debate between 'difference critics', who are sceptical of the possibility of cross-group representation, and 'empathy advocates', who insist that

people can empathize across lines of difference (Minow 1991: 284–9). On the idea of a 'deliberative democracy', and its role in helping the members of a socially diverse society to understand each other, see Cohen 1989. But see also I. Young 1993*b*; 1995, who argues that existing notions of 'deliberative democracy' are themselves culturally biased, and favour those modes of discourse and argumentation which characterize the dominant culture. On the potential role of group representation in promoting a more deliberative democracy, see Abrams 1988; Sunstein 1991; A. Phillips 1995: ch.. 4.

14. See Rosenfeld 1991; but cf. Sowell 1990, who argues that affirmative action programmes are rarely if ever beneficial, and moreover tend to generate spiralling demands and grievances. The VRA differs from affirmative action programmes in focusing, not on the composition of office-holders, but on the composition of electors. A majority-black district may elect a white or Hispanic representative. I return to this point later in the chapter.
15. As this example shows, it is difficult to know how best to remove the potential unfairness which arises when a national minority is less subject to federal authority. Puerto Rico has very limited federal representation, even though it is still very much subject to congressional authority in some areas. It would seem preferable to reduce its influence in a more issue-specific way—e.g. by allowing its congressional representative to have a full vote except on legislation from which Puerto Rico is exempt. Unfortunately, many pieces of legislation would deal with areas of jurisdiction that it is partly exempt from, and partly subject to. There is no way to divide up the business of government into watertight bundles of 'self-government' powers and 'federal' powers. This has been a serious stumbling-block in developing a workable model of asymmetrical federalism in Canada. No one is sure how best to redefine the role of Quebec MPs.
16. This representation may take the form of a permanent seat on the Supreme Court, or a seat only on those issues which directly affect it. This is the model used by the International Court of Justice, which allows each country which is party to a particular dispute to nominate one member to the Court when that case is being heard.
17. Part of the over-simplification is that while Indian self-government in the United States and Canada involves transferring powers from the federal government to Indian tribes/bands, which then become exempt from federal legislation, there is also a distinctive trust relationship between Indian peoples and the federal government which gives the federal government *more* authority over Indians than it has over other citizens. In Canada, for example, s. 91 (4) of the BNA Act gives the federal government exclusive power in matters relating to Indians and Indian lands. As a result, the federal government provides certain services to Aboriginals that other Canadians receive from provincial governments.

This is an argument in favour of increased Aboriginal representation in Parliament which helps to counterbalance the tendency of Aboriginal self-government to reduce the necessity of Aboriginal representation in Parliament (see RCERPF 1991: 181–2). This shows the extent to which arguments for group representation are very contextual, rather than flowing from any general theory of mirror representation.

In fact, the distinction between 'federal' and 'intergovernmental' is muddy in a number of places. Federal governments will unavoidably legislate in areas that impinge on self-government, just as intergovernmental bodies often make decisions that affect purely federal jurisdiction, including issues of direct concern to disadvantaged groups. In so far as this is so, we may wish to ensure that self-governing groups have some representation on an issue-specific basis at the federal level, and that disadvantaged groups have some representation on an issue-specific basis on intergovernmental bodies. A comprehensive theory of group representation, recognizing both self-government and disadvantage as grounds for representation, may need to be both institution-specific and issue-specific.

18. In fact, the original granting of the vote to Indians in 1960 was largely the result of international pressure, not any demand from Indians themselves, who saw it as a threat to their status as self-governing nations (Cairns 1995).
19. Claims based on disadvantage would apply equally to off-reserve urban Indians, who may have no meaningful self-government powers, whereas claims based on self-government would apply most clearly to Indians on reserves (Gibbins 1991: 181–2). Gibbins argues that off-reserve Aboriginals in Canada should be represented in the House of Commons through Aboriginal Electoral Districts, whereas Aboriginals on self-governing reserves should be primarily represented in Ottawa by having delegates of their tribal governments sit on intergovernmental bodies. Similarly, francophones outside Quebec may have a claim based on disadvantage to special representation in the Senate (as the Francophone Association of Alberta proposed), whereas francophones within Quebec have a claim based on self-government to special representation on the Supreme Court.
20. A third argument which has been raised for the group representation of women is that women have a distinctive moral perspective—an 'ethic of care'—which is more co-operative and altruistic than the usual male-dominated politics of self-interest. Improved representation for women would, therefore, raise the moral tenor of political life. I will not discuss this argument, since I am primarily interested in debates about group representation for ethnic and national groups. For a critique of this argument, see Dietz 1992.
21. e.g. Canadian civil service employment equity programmes identify four categories of disadvantaged people: women, Aboriginals, visible minori-

ties, and people with disabilities. The Canadian Supreme Court has begun the task of developing criteria for identifying historically disadvantaged groups in interpreting the equality guarantees in the Charter, which specifically endorse affirmative action remedies for disadvantaged groups. Indeed, both Baines and Boyle argue that guaranteed representation for women is not only consistent with the Charter, but indeed required by it. They argue that a combination of s. 3 (right to vote), s. 15 (1) (equal benefit of the law), and s. 15 (2) (affirmative action remedies) generates a legal entitlement to electoral mechanisms which ensure that women are equally represented (Boyle 1983: 791; Baines 1992: 56).

22. However, the Canadian Ethnocultural Council has 'long advocated that a tradition, written or unwritten, be established to ensure some minority presence' on the Supreme Court (Canadian Ethnocultural Council 1989: 342). On strategies for increasing the representation of ethnocultural and visible minority groups, see the essays collected in Megyery 1991*a*.
23. See Spitz 1984: 50; Lijphart 1984: 23–30; Guinier 1991*a*. A related question is whether group representatives (however many there are) should have special powers (such as a veto) in areas directly affecting their group. This seems most plausible, and indeed almost essential, for group representation based on claims of self-government. Since the justification of group representation in this case is to protect powers of self-government from federal intrusion, a veto in areas of concurrent or conflicting jurisdiction seems a logical mechanism. Whether group representation based on systemic disadvantage leads to special veto powers (e.g. veto powers for women legislators over decisions regarding reproductive rights, as Iris Young suggests) is more complicated, and would depend on the nature of the disadvantage.
24. For a discussion of the Maori model, see Fleras 1991; McLeay 1991. For a proposal to guarantee Aboriginal seats in Canada, based on the Maori model, see RCERPF 1991: 170–85.
25. The Court's judgement in *Shaw* v. *Reno* was based on the 14th Amendment, dealing with the equal protection of the law. But (as the dissenting judges emphasized) the Court made no attempt to show that whites were unfairly disadvantaged by the redistricting. (Whites would still have more than their proportional electoral representation, despite the creation of the black-majority district.) It seems clear that the real objection was not unfairness, but 'balkanization'.
26. I am taking for granted that the legitimacy of any particular form of democratic procedure depends, at least in part, on its consequences for the fair protection of people's interests. I am therefore rejecting any purely 'intrinsic' or 'proceduralist' theory of democracy which says that we can judge the legitimacy of democratic procedures independently of their actual outcomes for people's well-being. See the discussion of 'best-results' versus 'proceduralist' theories of democracy (or 'instrumental'

versus 'intrinsic' theories) in Beitz 1989. See also Dworkin's discussion of 'dependent' versus 'detached' theories in Dworkin 1988.

CHAPTER 8

1. Some restrictions on individual freedom within the minority community may be justified, on a temporary basis, where they are required to protect the society from literal disintegration. Proponents of gender or religious discrimination in minority cultures often claim that these restrictions are necessary to protect the society from disintegration. But these claims are rarely backed up with any evidence. These sorts of claims are very similar to the claims of conservatives within the larger society, who argue that the majority culture will disintegrate unless it continues discriminating against non-traditional practices (e.g. Lord Devlin's claim that discrimination against homosexuals was essential to save English society from disintegration). In this area, as in every other, citizens have the right, and the responsibility, to assess claims in the light of the usual canons of evidence. Just as there was no evidence to support Devlin's claim that legalization of homosexuality threatened English society with disintegration, so there is often no evidence to support the claims of homophobic, patriarchal, or theocratic leaders in minority cultures. As the United Nations Human Rights Committee noted, there is often simply no reason to think that the survival of Indian tribes, for example, requires violating the human rights of its members (see *Lovelace* v. *Canada* UN Doc. A/36/40 (1981) 166; cf. Thornberry 1991: 207–11). Of course, there may be cases where societal cultures would literally disintegrate without limiting certain basic rights on a temporary basis. If so, these burdens should be equally distributed amongst all the members, wherever possible, and should in any event be consistent with the principle of respect for the equality and dignity of persons. It would be unacceptable, to take an extreme example, for a minority community to sustain itself by practising slavery. Any internal restrictions which a group imposes on its own members should not allow the powerful members of the group to exploit the weaker members. I discuss this in Kymlicka 1989*a*: ch. 9.
2. For a discussion of the attempts to reform the millets, inspired by Western liberalism, see Davison 1982: 332; Braude and Lewis 1982: 18–23, 28–31; Karpat 1982: 159–63.
3. This system of toleration is, in one sense, the opposite of that in the West, since it unites, rather than separates, church and state. It is interesting to note that the two systems had similar historical origins. The Ottoman restrictions on the building and location of non-Muslim churches were similar to the system of 'licensed coexistence' established under the Edict of Nantes (1598). Under that Edict, which ended the Wars of Religion

Protestants in France could only build new churches in certain locations, and only with a state licence. In the West, however, state-licensed coexistence between Protestants and Catholics gradually evolved into a system of individual freedom of conscience. This never occurred in the Ottoman Empire.

4. Interestingly, Rawls never considers this model of tolerance. He talks about 'the principle of tolerance' as if there were just one, which he equates with the idea of freedom of conscience (e.g. Rawls 1987: 18, 23; 1989: 251; 1982*b*: 25–6; 1985: 225). Yet the millet model is arguably the more natural form of religious tolerance. The historical record suggests that 'in practice, religions have usually felt most violently intolerant not of other religions but of dissenters within their own ranks' (Elton 1984: p. xiii).
5. By Rawls's 'recent' writings, I mean his post-1985 articles, in which he emphasizes the distinction between 'political' and 'metaphysical' or 'comprehensive' conceptions of liberalism.
6. *Hofer* v. *Hofer et al.* (1970) 13 DLR (3d) 1, cited in Janzen 1990: 65–7.
7. Rawls does emphasize that the point of protecting civil rights is not to *maximize* the development and exercise of the capacity to form and revise a conception of the good. As he rightly notes, it would be 'absurd' to try to maximize 'the number of deliberate affirmations of a conception of the good'. Rather, 'these liberties and their priority are to guarantee equally for all citizens the social conditions essential for the adequate development and the full and informed exercise of these powers' (1982*b*: 47–9). It seems clear, however, that the Hutterites do not provide the social conditions essential for the 'full and informed' exercise of autonomy.
8. *Wisconsin* v. *Yoder* 406 US 205. Rawls argues that his political liberalism is more sympathetic to the demands of the Amish than Mill's comprehensive liberalism. Whereas comprehensive liberalism 'may lead to requirements designed to foster the values of autonomy and individuality as ideas to govern much if not all of life', political liberalism 'has a different aim and requires far less', since it is only concerned with promoting a liberal ideal of *citizenship* ('the state's concern with [children's] education lies in their role as future citizens'). As a result, Rawls says, political liberalism 'honors, as far as it can, the claims of those who wish to withdraw from the modern world in accordance with the injunctions of their religion, provided only that they acknowledge the principles of the political conception of justice and appreciate its political ideals of person and society' (Rawls 1988: 267–8). However, this is misleading. For one thing, the distinction between political and comprehensive liberalism is unstable, since accepting the value of autonomy for political purposes has unavoidable implications for private life (see n. 9). Moreover, many religious communities would object to political liberalism on its own terms, as a theory of citizenship. They view Rawls's ideal

of citizenship as conflicting with their religious ideals of person and society. While Rawls would want educators to prepare children for the rights and duties of citizenship, religious sects see 'a different purpose of education . . . to prepare their children for life in their communities'. They are concerned not with preparing people for exercising political rights, but with 'the need for obedience. They argue that education should reorient the individual's self-regard and nurture a desire to abide by the will of the community.' Hence these groups have sought exemption from precisely the sort of education that Rawls's 'political liberalism' insists upon. See Janzen 1990: 143, 97.

9. Indeed, the connection between the political and the private is not only causal, but conceptual. Rawls accepts that exercising autonomy in the political sphere may causally promote its exercise in private life. But he insists that this is a contingent and unintended effect, and that his political conception of the person only concerns the way 'that the moral powers [of autonomy and a sense of justice] are exercised in political life and in basic institutions as citizens endeavour to maintain them and to use them to conduct public business' (1988: 272 n. 28). But what does it mean to exercise our capacity for autonomy 'in political life'? The capacity for autonomy is quite different in this respect from the capacity for a sense of justice, although Rawls treats them together in this passage. The capacity for a sense of justice is exercised by 'assessing the justice and effectiveness of laws and social policies', and hence is primarily concerned with, and exercised in, political life. The capacity to form and revise a conception of the good, on the other hand, is primarily concerned with what Rawls calls our 'non-public identity'—with our comprehensive, rather than our political, identity. As Rawls himself puts it, 'liberty of conscience and freedom of association enable us to develop and exercise our moral powers in forming, revising, and rationally pursuing our conceptions of the good that belong to our comprehensive doctrines, and affirming them as such' (1989: 254). Hence the capacity for justice is about evaluating *public* policies and institutions; while the capacity to form/revise a conception of the good is about evaluating the comprehensive religious and moral doctrines that define our *private* identity. But then what does it mean to say that the exercise of this latter capacity can be restricted to political life, without it impinging on our private identity? Since the capacity involved just is the capacity to form and revise our comprehensive ends, it seems that any exercise of it necessarily involves our private identity.
10. The assumption that we can assess and revise our ends is also needed, I believe, to justify Rawls's claim that people 'are regarded as capable of taking responsibility for their ends', in the sense that they 'are thought to be capable of adjusting their aims and aspirations in the light of what they can reasonably expect to provide for' (1985: 243). Because people can adjust their aims, Rawls claims, we have no obligation to subsidize

those with expensive ways of life. I discuss this aspect of Rawls's theory in Kymlicka 1990: 73–7.

11. I discuss Rawls's recent views in more depth in Kymlicka 1992*b*. Rawls gives two arguments for freedom of conscience. On the first argument, religious beliefs are 'regarded as *given and firmly rooted*', and we need freedom of conscience because society contains 'a plurality of such conceptions, each, as it were, non-negotiable'. On the second argument, religious beliefs are 'seen as *subject to revision* in accordance with deliberative reason', and we need freedom of conscience because there 'is no guarantee that all aspects of our present way of life are the most rational for us and not in need of at least minor if not major revision' (Rawls 1982*b*: 25–9, my emphasis). Rawls thinks that these two arguments 'support the same conclusion' (1982*b*: 29)—i.e. that recognizing the *plurality* of conceptions of the good within society, each of which is seen as fixed and beyond rational revision, has the same implications for individual liberty as affirming the *revisability* of each individual's conception of the good. But they do not support the same conclusion on issues such as proselytization, which is an essential liberty on the second argument, but a futile and disruptive nuisance on the first argument. The fact that modern democracies are pluralistic generally means that it would be wrong for the state to impose one way of life on everyone. But that does not justify the freedom, not only to pursue one's existing conception of the good, but also to question and revise it. The latter requires a belief in the value of autonomy, not just a recognition of the fact of pluralism.
12. See Nickel 1990: 214. Rawls's fear that the Millian conception of autonomy is not widely shared depends on conflating this conception of autonomy with the other, more controversial, conceptions discussed in Ch. 5 n. 7. It is important to note that while Mill's conception is 'general', in applying to all areas of life, it is not 'comprehensive', since it does not define a set of final ends or intrinsic goods to be pursued by each individual. Rather, it concerns the capacity by which we deliberate and assess our final ends.
13. This criticism has been raised by Kukathas 1992*a*; Chaplin 1993; McDonald 1993; Williams 1994, amongst others. The quotation is from Kukathas 1992*a*: 121.
14. If female members marry outside the tribe, their children are denied membership. But if men marry outside the tribe, the children are members. This discriminatory rule was upheld in *Santa Clara Pueblo* v. *Martinez* 436 US 49 (1978).
15. Some liberals hope that the United Nations will someday command the authority to intervene forcibly in foreign countries on behalf of human rights. But at present international intervention is largely limited to cases of gross violations of basic human rights—e.g. slavery, genocide, ethnic cleansing—and most contemporary liberals have accepted this. In any event, virtually everyone today agrees that only an internationally

accepted body like the UN could have the authority to intervene forcibly. For example, a group of private citizens would have no legitimate authority to invade Saudi Arabia, even if they were motivated solely by a concern for human rights. Nor would a group of neighbouring states. No individual or state can simply declare itself the international protector of human rights, with the authority to forcibly intervene whenever and wherever it sees a government violating the rights of its citizens.

16. For the imposition of federal civil rights guarantees on Indian tribes, see Resnik 1989; Ball 1989; Tsosie 1994. For the imposition of both federal civil rights guarantees and federal court enforcement of them in Puerto Rico, see Aleinikoff 1994.
17. For a survey of the arguments against imposing liberalism on other countries, see Walzer 1977; 1980. I think that virtually all of Walzer's points also argue against imposing liberalism on national minorities, although Walzer himself does not always make this connection.
18. The ability of members to leave is a very important proviso. However, unlike some commentators (Svensson 1979: 437; Kukathas 1992*a*: 133), I do not think it is sufficient to justify internal restrictions, any more than racial segregation in the American South was made legitimate by the fact that blacks could move north (although some defenders of segregation did make this argument). Kukathas, for example, accords cultural groups very great powers over their own members (including the right to restrict their freedom of speech and association, or to discriminate in the provision of services on the basis of gender or religious belief). Indeed, cultural minorities have virtually unlimited power over their own members, so long as individual members have a right to exit the community (Kukathas 1992*a*: 133). Kukathas thinks that this should be sufficient for liberals, for while it does not include any principle of respect for autonomy, it is a liberal theory 'inasmuch as it does not sanction the forcible induction into or imprisoning of any individual in a cultural community' (1992*a*: 125). But this is too weak to count as a distinctly liberal theory. Very few conservatives, socialists, or communitarians would accept forcible induction into a community.

    Kukathas later adds that individuals must have a 'substantial' right of exit (1992*a*: 133), and that recognizing such a right will mean that 'the ethical balance between individual and group has shifted irrevocably in the individual's direction' (1992*a*: 128, quoting Mulgan 1989: 64). The threat of exit, he thinks, will give individuals the *de facto* ability to question communal authority. But he has a dubious view of what gives individuals a 'substantial' right to leave. He says that people have substantial freedom of exit even if they have been deprived of literacy, education, or the freedom to learn about the outside world, *so long as they have an open market society to enter into* (1992*a*: 134). In other words, one's freedom to leave is determined by the openness of the society one might enter, no matter how closed one's own community is. He seems to think that someone who has been denied an education (perhaps because she is female), and who is denied the right to associate with or speak to anyone outside her culture, none the less has a substantial freedom to leave, assuming she can enter a market society. Most liberals, I think, would argue that she does not have a substantial freedom to leave, since she lacks the preconditions for making a meaningful choice, and that any system of minority rights which gives cultural communities that much power over their individual members is seriously deficient from a liberal point of view. See also L. Green 1994; Kymlicka 1992*a*.

19. Some liberals have argued that tolerating these non-liberal groups can provide certain incidental benefits to the larger liberal society—e.g. a model of moral conviction that is difficult to sustain in modern societies (Macedo 1995; Galston 1995). I do not myself think this is an adequate reason for tolerating injustice.
20. Joseph Raz, for example, seems to assume that most indigenous cultures are inherently illiberal, and so incapable of liberalization. Speaking, *inter alia*, of indigenous communities which do not give their members the conditions of autonomous choice, he says we face the choice of 'taking action to assimilate the minority group', or of accepting their illiberal ways. He says that the 'break-up' of these communities is the 'inevitable by-product' of attempts to liberalize their institutions (Raz 1986: 423–4). But he gives no reason for thinking that indigenous cultures are less capable of liberalizing than other cultures. As I noted in Ch. 5, it is important to remember that existing liberal nations were all once quite illiberal. To assume that any culture which is now illiberal is therefore inherently illiberal, and incapable of reform, is ahistorical.
21. See e.g. the statement of the First Nations of Treaty 6 and 7, which said that applying the Canadian Charter to Aboriginal self-government 'is a subjection of a value system based on individual rights. Our governments are based on the paramountcy of collective rights' (*Globe and Mail*, 24 Sept. 1992, p. A5).

CHAPTER 9

1. According to Rawls, a society in which rights and claims 'depend on religious affiliation, social class, and so on . . . may not have a conception of citizenship at all; for this conception, as we are using it, goes with the conception of society as a fair system of cooperation for mutual advantage between free and equal persons' (Rawls 1989: 241; cf. Heater 1990: 285).
2. Galston 1991: 215–17, 244; Macedo 1990: 138–9. This may account for the recent interest in citizenship promotion amongst governments (see Britain's Commission on Citizenship, *Encouraging Citizenship* (1990);

Senate of Australia, *Active Citizenship Revisited* (1991); Senate of Canada, *Canadian Citizenship: Sharing the Responsibility* (1993)). For further references and discussion, see Kymlicka and Norman 1994.

3. According to a recent survey, only 12% of American teenagers said voting was important to being a good citizen. Moreover, this apathy is not just a function of youth—comparisons with similar surveys from the previous fifty years suggest that 'the current cohort knows less, cares less, votes less, and is less critical of its leaders and institutions than young people have been at any time over the past five decades' (Glendon 1991: 129; cf. Walzer 1992*a*: 90). The evidence from Great Britain is similar (Heater 1990: 215).
4. As Luis Fraga puts it, 'Any knowledgeable student of the Voting Rights Act . . . understands that the crucial fact of minority politics—whether that of African Americans, Latinos or other groups—is their exclusion from the mainstream of American political affairs in spite of their desire to be full participants in it . . . Their goals are basically to be assimilated into the body politic, and the Voting Rights Act has been a most effective means to that end' (Fraga 1992: 278). Some critics worry that, even if group representation does not undermine a sense of common solidarity amongst the general public, it might none the less produce legislators who are doctrinaire and unwilling to engage in the normal process of compromise for the greater good. The basis for this worry is unclear. As Boyle notes, 'Surely the political process would work very much as it does now, with a high premium being placed on ability to be effective and to work with other groups in order to achieve this' (Boyle 1983: 805; cf. Cain 1992: 272).
5. The desire of Sikhs to join the RCMP in Canada is in contrast to many Aboriginal communities, who, as part of their self-government, have been trying to remove the RCMP from their reserves, and replace it with a native police force.
6. Moreover, a proliferation of such demands is unlikely, since they usually involve clear and specific cases of unintended conflict between majority rules and minority religious practices. And since proof of historical oppression is neither necessary nor sufficient to claim polyethnic rights, there is little risk that they will promote a politics of grievance whereby group leaders devote their political energy to establishing a perception of disadvantage—rather than working to overcome it—in order to secure their claim to group-specific rights.
7. Marshall 1965: 101–2; cf. Parry 1991: 167. In places, Marshall implies that citizenship rights both foster a sense of community, but also presuppose it. On this view, providing common citizenship rights, by itself, might not ensure the integration of excluded groups whose identity falls entirely outside the existing conception of national identity.
8. For a discussion of how citizenship has been 'constructed from men's

attributes, capacities and activities', so that citizenship can only be extended to women 'as lesser men', see Pateman 1988: 252–3; James 1992: 52–5.

9. As I discussed in Ch. 2, this political community may be directly or indirectly controlled by the national minority, depending on how its boundaries are drawn. The Puerto Ricans, Inuit, and Québécois indirectly form political communities, by forming the majority within one of the territorial units of the federal system. Most Indian tribes/bands, however, directly form a political community, tied to the system of Indian reserves.
10. This is true of most claims grounded in claims of self-government. But one particular aspect of self-government—guaranteed representation at the federal or intergovernmental level—clearly serves a unifying function. The existence of such group representation helps reduce the threat of self-government, by reconnecting the self-governing community to the larger federation. It is a form of connection which remains, and which can be drawn upon, when other connections are being weakened. This is true, I think, of Quebec's representation on the Supreme Court, and of proposals for Aboriginal representation in the Senate.
11. For a comprehensive review of the moral issues raised by secession, see Buchanan 1991. The breakup of Czechoslovakia was also peaceful, although it is too early to tell how healthy the resulting democracies will be. There is significant potential for violence in the former Czechoslovakia, not between Czechs and Slovaks, but between Slovaks and Hungary, regarding the Hungarian minority in Slovakia. As I noted in Ch. 4, the potential for violence is profoundly affected by the existence of irredentist minorities.
12. My argument here draws heavily on an unpublished paper by my colleague Wayne Norman, entitled 'The Ideology of Shared Values'. See also Nickel 1990: 205–16. For a related discussion, see Paris 1991, who argues that, even if there is a consensus on political principles, this is too 'thin' a basis for social unity, since severe conflicts can arise over the interpretation or application of these vague principles. He suggests that social unity is based on shared beliefs about the 'thick' virtues appropriate to very specific and localized practices.
13. e.g. Sir John A. MacDonald is admired by most English Canadians as one of the Fathers of Confederation, but reviled by French Canadians for his role in the execution of Louis Riel. Similarly, most English Canadians take pride in their role in the world wars, but each war led to a conscription crisis which set English against French. Indeed, it is striking how rarely discussions of social unity in Canada appeal to history, compared with the omnipresent references in American discussions to the Founding Fathers and the spirit of Philadelphia (e.g. AASA 1987: 85; Glendon 1991: 12). On the divisive role of history in multination states, see Cairns 1993: 205; Brilmayer 1992.

14. This raises an important question about the nature of citizenship education. If governments wish to generate a shared identity on the basis of a shared history, they will have to identify citizenship, not only with acceptance of principles of justice, but also with an emotional-affective sense of identity, based on a veneration of shared symbols or historical myths. And most countries do in fact include a glorified history as part of their citizenship education. But at what point does the veneration of history become manipulation, and hence illegitimate?

    For example, it seems clear that the sense of pride and identity which Americans gain from their history is in part inculcated through a deliberate misrepresentation of that history. As William Galston puts it, 'rigorous historical research will almost certainly vindicate complex "revisionist" accounts of key figures in American history. Civic education, however, requires a nobler, moralizing history: a pantheon of heroes who confer legitimacy on central institutions and are worthy of emulation' (Galston 1991: 244). Similarly, Andrew Oldenquist argues that information about American history 'should be taught so as to provide grounds for developing pride and affection', and that children will 'not acquire affection for our country by being told that we exterminated Indians, lynched Blacks, and slaughtered Vietnamese' (quoted in AASA 1987: 26).

    This raises a number of troubling questions. First, this way of promoting a national identity may undermine another goal of citizenship education—i.e. the development of the capacity for independent and critical thought about society and its problems (Norman 1994). Second, the sanitized version of history that Galston and Oldenquist defend is itself increasingly a cause of disunity. An account of history that focuses on the 'pantheon of heroes', while ignoring the historical mistreatment of women, blacks, Indians, and others is essentially an account of the history of upper-class white men. And it is precisely this view of history which many minorities find so offensive. They are insulted by the way their struggles are rendered invisible in school-books.
15. European theorists are confronting these dilemmas as they seek to understand the nature of the European Community and the form of citizenship it requires. Habermas argues that European unity cannot be based on the shared traditions, cultures, and languages that characterized successful nation-states. Instead, European citizenship must be founded on a 'postnational' constitutional patriotism based on shared principles of justice and democracy (Habermas 1992; Berten 1992; Ferry 1992). Others, however, argue that shared values are not a sufficient basis for unity, and that attention must also be paid to issues of identity (Taylor 1992*b*: 61–5; A. Smith 1993; cf. Lenoble 1992).
16. As Taylor puts it in the Canadian case, to insist that Quebecers should put Canada first 'makes no sense to Quebec federalists . . . We belong to Canada by belonging to Quebec. If these allegiances get polarized to the

point where one has to be put first, then *our* Canada has already been lost' (Taylor 1991).

17. While accommodating both polyethnic and multinational differences complicates the situation, I do not believe that the presence of immigrant groups substantially affects the likelihood that a multination state will successfully deal with its national differences. The fact that Canada contains many more immigrants than Belgium or Czechoslovakia does not, I think, have much bearing on the likelihood of Quebec's secession. Hence I disagree with Walzer, who seems to think that states can either view themselves as polyethnic or as multinational, but not as both (Ch. 4, s. 4). The fundamental challenge facing multination states is resolving the relation between national groups, and the lineaments of this challenge are similar whether there is a high or low rate of immigration. The sort of 'deep diversity' which comes from adding polyethnic on top of multinational differences is not, I think, the real threat to social unity.
18. As I noted in Ch. 6, s. 3, there is no tight connection between accepting the value of diversity in general and accepting the political claims of the particular groups around one.

CHAPTER 10

1. On the age of migration, see Castles and Miller 1993; on the age of nationalism, see Pfaff 1993; Ignatieff 1993. On the 'politics of cultural difference', see I. Young 1990; West 1990; Minow 1990*a*.
2. For the distinction between eliminating and managing ethnic and national conflict, see McGarry and O'Leary 1994.

BIBLIOGRAPHY

AASA (1987)—see American Association of School Administrators

Abrams, Kathryn (1988), '"Raising Politics up": Minority Political Participation and Section 2 of the Voting Rights Act', *New York University Law Review*, 63/3: 449–531.

Abu-Laban, Yasmeen, and Stasiulus, Daiva (1992), 'Ethnic Pluralism under Siege: Popular and Partisan Opposition to Multiculturalism', *Canadian Public Policy*, 18/4: 365–86.

Ackerman, Bruce (1980), *Social Justice in the Liberal State* (Yale University Press, New Haven, Conn.).

—— (1992), *The Future of Liberal Revolution* (Yale University Press, New Haven, Conn.).

Acton, Lord (1922), 'Nationalism', in J. Figgis and R. Laurence (eds.), *The History of Freedom and Other Essays* (Macmillan, London), 270–300.

Adam, Heribert (1979), 'The Failure of Political Liberalism', in H. Adam and H. Giliomee (eds.), *Ethnic Power Mobilized: Can South Africa Change?* (Yale University Press, New Haven, Conn.), 258–85.

Addis, Adeno (1991), 'Individualism, Communitarianism and the Rights of Ethnic Minorities', *Notre Dame Law Review*, 67/3: 615–76.

Ahmed, Aftab (1993), 'Ethnicity and Insurgency in the Chittagong Hill Tracts Region: A Study of the Crisis of Political Integration in Bangladesh', *Journal of Commonwealth and Comparative Studies*, 31/3: 32–66.

Ajzenstat, Janet (1984), 'Liberalism and Assimilation: Lord Durham Revisited', in S. Brooks (ed.), *Political Thought in Canada: Contemporary Perspectives* (Irwin, Toronto), 239–57.

—— (1988), *The Political Thought of Lord Durham* (McGill-Queen's University Press, Kingston).

Aleinikoff, Alexander (1994), 'Puerto Rico and the Constitution: Conundrums and Prospects', *Constitutional Commentary*, 11: 15–43.

American Association of School Administrators (1987), *Citizenship: Goal of Education* (AASA Publications, Arlington, Va.).

Anderson, Benedict (1983), *Imagined Communities: Reflections on the Origin and Spread of Nationalism* (New Left Books, London).

Asch, Michael (1984), *Home and Native Land: Aboriginal Rights and the Canadian Constitution* (Methuen, Toronto).

—— (1990), 'Consociation and the Resolution of Aboriginal Political Rights', *Culture*, 10/1: 93–102.

Bader, Veit (1995), 'Citizenship and Exclusion: Radical Democracy, Community and Justice', *Political Theory*, forthcoming.

Baines, Beverley (1992), '"Consider Sir . . . on What Does your Constitution Rest?" Representational and Institutional Reform', in

Conversations among Friends: Proceedings of an Interdisciplinary Conference on Women and Constitutional Reform (Centre for Constitutional Studies, University of Alberta), 54–7.

BALL, MILNER (1989), 'Stories of Origin and Constitutional Possibilities', *Michigan Law Review*, 87: 2280–2319.

BARBALET, J. M. (1988), *Citizenship: Rights, Struggle and Class Inequality* (University of Minnesota Press, Minneapolis).

BARKER, ERNEST (1948), *National Character and the Factors in its Formation* (Methuen, London).

BARRY, BRIAN (1991), 'Self-Government Revisited', in *Democracy and Power: Essays in Political Theory*, i (Oxford University Press, Oxford), 156–86.

BARSH, RUSSEL (1983), 'Indigenous North America and Contemporary International Law', *Oregon Law Review*, 62: 73–125.

—— and HENDERSON, J. (1980), *The Road: Indian Tribes and Political Liberty* (University of California Press, Berkeley, Calif.).

—— —— (1982), 'Aboriginal Rights, Treaty Rights and Human Rights: Indian Tribes and Constitutional Renewal', *Journal of Canadian Studies*, 17: 55–81.

BEITZ, CHARLES (1989), *Political Equality* (Princeton University Press, Princeton, NJ).

BELL, DANIEL (1993), *Communitarianism and its Critics* (Oxford University Press, Oxford).

BERGER, THOMAS (1984), 'Towards the Regime of Tolerance', in S. Brooks (ed.), *Political Thought in Canada: Contemporary Perspectives* (Irwin, Toronto), 83–96.

BERTEN, ANDRÉ (1992), 'Identité européenne: une ou multiple?', in Lenoble and Dewandre (1992), 81–97.

BINDER, GUYORA (1993), 'The Case for Self-Determination', *Stanford Journal of International Law*, 29: 223–70.

BIRCH, A. H. (1964), *Representative and Responsible Government* (University of Toronto Press, Toronto).

BLACK, SAMUEL (1991), 'Individualism at an Impasse', *Canadian Journal of Philosophy*, 21/3: 347–77.

—— (1992), 'Revisionist Liberalism and the Decline of Culture', *Ethics*, 102/2: 244–67.

BLOED, ARIE (1994), 'The CSCE and the Protection of National Minorities', *CSCE ODHIR Bulletin*, 1/3: 1–4.

BOLDT, MENNO (1993), *Surviving as Indians: The Challenge of Self-Government* (University of Toronto Press, Toronto).

—— and LONG, J. A. (1984), 'Tribal Philosophies and the Canadian Charter of Rights and Freedoms', *Racial and Ethnic Studies*, 4/4: 479–95.

BOURNE, RANDOLPH (1964), 'Transnational America', in C. Resek (ed.), *War and the Intellectuals: Essays by Randolph S. Bourne, 1915–1919* (Harper & Row, New York), 107–23.

BOWLES, S., *et al.* (eds.), (1972), *The Indian: Assimilation, Integration or Separation?* (Prentice-Hall, Scarborough).

BOYLE, CHRISTINE (1983), 'Home-Rule for Women: Power-Sharing between Men and Women', *Dalhousie Law Journal*, 7: 790–809.

BRAUDE, BENJAMIN, and LEWIS, BERNARD (1982), 'Introduction', in B. Braude and B. Lewis (eds.), *Christians and Jews in the Ottoman Empire: The Functioning of a Plural Society* (Holmes & Meir, New York), 1–34.

BRILMAYER, LEA (1992), 'Groups, Histories, and International Law', *Cornell International Law Journal*, 25/3: 555–63.

BROTZ, H. (1980), 'Multiculturalism in Canada: A Muddle', *Canadian Public Policy*, 6/1: 41–6.

BROWN-SCOTT, WENDY (1994), 'Justice Thurgood Marshall and the Integrative Ideal', *Arizona State Law Journal*, 26/2: 535–60.

BRUBAKER, W. R. (1989), *Immigration and the Politics of Citizenship in Europe and North America* (University Press of America, Lanham, Md.).

BUCHANAN, ALLEN (1975), 'Revisability and Rational Choice', *Canadian Journal of Philosophy*, 5: 395–408.

—— (1989), 'Assessing the Communitarian Critique of Liberalism', *Ethics*, 99/4: 852–82.

—— (1991), *Secession: The Legitimacy of Political Divorce* (Westview Press, Boulder, Col.).

—— (1993), 'The Role of Collective Rights in the Theory of Indigenous Peoples' Rights', *Transnational Law and Contemporary Problems*, 3/1: 89–108.

BURNET, JEAN (1975), 'Multiculturalism, Immigration, and Racism', *Canadian Ethnic Studies*, 7/1: 35–9.

BURNHAM, JOHN (1985), *Is Democracy Possible? The Alternative to Electoral Politics* (University of California Press, Berkeley, Calif.).

CAIN, BRUCE (1992), 'Voting Rights and Democratic Theory: Toward a Colour-Blind Society?', in B. Grofman and C. Davidson (eds.), *Controversies in Minority Voting: The Voting Rights Act in Perspective* (Brookings Institution, Washington, DC), 261–77.

CAIRNS, ALAN (1991), 'Constitutional Change and the Three Equalities', in Ronald Watts and Douglas Brown (eds.), *Options for a New Canada* (University of Toronto Press, Toronto), 77–110.

—— (1993), 'The Fragmentation of Canadian Citizenship', in William Kaplan (ed.), *Belonging: The Meaning and Future of Canadian Citizenship* (McGill-Queen's Press, Montreal), 181–220.

—— (1994), 'The Charlottetown Accord: Multinational Canada vs Federalism', in C. Cook (ed.), *Constitutional Predicament: Canada after the Referendum of 1992* (McGill-Queen's Press, Montreal), 25–63.

—— (1995), 'Aboriginal Canadians, Citizenship, and the Constitution', in *Reconfigurations: Canadian Citizenship and Constitutional Change* (McClelland & Stewart, Toronto).

CAMPBELL, GORDON (1994), 'Language, Equality and the Charter: Collective versus Individual Rights in Canada and Beyond', *National Journal of Constitutional Law*, 4/1: 29–73.

Canada West Foundation (1981), *Regional Representation: The Canadian Partnership* (Canada West Foundation, Calgary).

Canadian Ethnocultural Council (1989), 'A Dream Deferred: Collective Equality for Canada's Ethnocultural Communities', in Michael Behiels (ed.), *The Meech Lake Primer: Conflicting Views of the 1987 Constitutional Accord* (University of Ottawa Press, Ottawa), 335–48.

CANEY, SIMON (1991), 'Consequentialist Defenses of Liberal Neutrality', *Philosophical Quarterly*, 41/165: 457–77.

CAPOTORTI, F. (1979), *Study on the Rights of Persons Belonging to Ethnic, Religious and Linguistic Minorities*. UN Doc. E/CN. 4/Sub.2/384 Rev. 1 (United Nations, New York).

CARENS, JOSEPH (1987), 'Aliens and Citizens: The Case for Open Borders', *Review of Politics*, 49/3: 251–73.

—— (1992), 'Democracy and Respect for Difference: The Case of Fiji', *University of Michigan Journal of Law Reform*, 25/3: 547–631.

—— (1994), 'Citizenship and Aboriginal Self-Government' (paper prepared for the Royal Commission on Aboriginal Peoples, Ottawa).

CARLSON, ROBERT (1975), *The Quest for Conformity: Americanization through Education* (Wiley, New York).

CASSIDY, FRANK, and BISH, ROBERT (1989), *Indian Government: Its Meaning in Practice* (Institute for Research on Public Policy, Halifax).

CASTLES, STEPHEN, and MILLER, MARK (1993), *The Age of Migration: International Population Movements in the Modern Age* (Macmillan, Basingstoke).

CHAPLIN, JONATHAN (1993), 'How Much Cultural and Religious Pluralism Can Liberalism Tolerate?', in John Horton (ed.), *Liberalism, Multiculturalism and Toleration* (St Martin's Press, New York), 32–49.

CHARTRAND, PAUL (1991), *Manitoba's Métis Settlement Scheme of 1870* (University of Saskatchewan Native Law Centre, Saskatoon).

—— (1993), 'Aboriginal Self-Government: The Two Sides of Legitimacy', in Susan Phillips (ed.), *How Ottawa Spends: 1993–1994* (Carleton University Press, Ottawa), 231–56.

—— (1995), 'The Aboriginal Peoples in Canada and Renewal of the Federation', in Karen Knop *et al.* (eds.), *Rethinking Federalism* (University of British Columbia Press, Vancouver), 119–31

CHAVEZ, LINDA (1991), *Out of the Barrio: Toward a New Politics of Hispanic Assimilation* (Basic Books, New York).

CHRISTOFFERSON, CARLA (1991), 'Tribal Courts' Failure to Protect Native American Women: A Reappraisal of the Indian Civil Rights Act', *Yale Law Journal*, 101/1: 169–85.

Citizen's Forum on Canada's Future (1991), *Report to the People and Government of Canada* (Supply and Services, Ottawa).

CLARKE, F. (1934), *Quebec and South Africa: A Study in Cultural Adjustment* (Oxford University Press, London).

CLAUDE, INIS (1955), *National Minorities: An International Problem* (Harvard University Press, Cambridge, Mass.).

CLAY, JASON (1989), 'Epilogue: The Ethnic Future of Nations', *Third World Quarterly*, 11/4: 223–33.

CLINTON, ROBERT (1990), 'The Rights of Indigenous Peoples as Collective Group Rights', *Arizona Law Review*, 32/4: 739–47.

COHEN, JOSHUA (1989), 'Deliberation and Democratic Legitimacy', in A. Hamlin (ed.), *The Good Polity* (Blackwell, New York), 18–27.

COLAS, DOMINIQUE, EMERI, CLAUDE, and ZYLBERBERG, JACQUES, (eds.) (1991), *Citoyenneté et nationalité: perspectives en France et au Québec* (Presses Universitaires de France, Paris).

CONNOR, WALKER (1972), 'Nation-Building or Nation-Destroying', *World Politics*, 24: 319–55.

—— (1973), 'The Politics of Ethnonationalism', *Journal of International Affairs*, 27/1: 1–21.

—— (1978), 'A Nation is a Nation, is a State, is an Ethnic Group, is a . . .', *Ethnic and Racial Studies*, 1: 377–400.

—— (1984), *The National Question in Marxist-Leninist Theory and Strategy* (Princeton University Press, Princeton, NJ).

COOK, RAMSAY (1969), *French-Canadian Nationalism: An Anthology* (Macmillan, Toronto).

COPP, DAVID (1992), 'The Concept of a Society', *Dialogue*, 31/2: 183–212.

CRAIG, GERALD (1963), *Lord Durham's Report: An Abridgement of* Report on the Affairs of British North America (McClelland & Stewart, Toronto).

CRAWFORD, JAMES (1988), 'The Rights of Peoples', in James Crawford (ed.), *The Rights of Peoples* (Oxford University Press, Oxford), 159–75.

CRÊTE, JEAN, and ZYLBERBERG, JACQUES (1991), 'Une problématique floue: l'autoreprésentation du citoyen au Québec', in Colas *et al.* (1991), 423–33.

CROWE, KEITH (1974), *A History of the Original Peoples of Northern Canada* (McGill-Queen's University Press, Montreal).

CUMMINGS, IAN (1980), *Marx, Engels and National Movements* (Croom Helm, London).

DA CUNHA, MANUELA (1992), 'Custom is not a Thing, it is a Path: Reflections on the Brazilian Indian Case', in Abdullah Ahmed An-Na'aim (ed.), *Human Rights in Cross-Cultural Perspective* (University of Pennsylvania Press, Philadelphia).

DAHL, ROBERT (1989), *Democracy and its Critics* (Yale University Press, New Haven, Conn.).

DAMROSCH, LORI (1989), 'Politics across Borders: Nonintervention and Nonforcible Influence over Domestic Affairs', *American Journal of International Law*, 83/1: 1–50.

DANLEY, JOHN (1991), 'Liberalism, Aboriginal Rights and Cultural Minorities', *Philosophy and Public Affairs*, 20/2: 168–85.

DAVIDSON, BASIL (1992), *The Black Man's Burden: Africa and the Curse of the Nation-State* (Times Books, New York).

DAVIDSON, CHANDLER (1992), 'The Voting Rights Act: A Brief History', in B. Grofman and C. Davidson (eds.), *Controversies in Minority Voting: The Voting Rights Act in Perspective* (Brookings Institute, Washington, DC), 7–51.

DAVISON, RODERIC (1982), 'The Millets as Agents of Change in the Nineteenth-Century Ottoman Empire', in Braude and Lewis (1982), 319–37.

DEGANAAR, J. (1987), 'Nationalism, Liberalism, and Pluralism', in J. Butler (ed.), *Democratic Liberalism in South Africa: Its History and Prospect* (Wesleyan University Press, Middletown, Conn.), 236–398.

DE LA GARZA, R., and TRUJILLO, A. (1991), 'Latinos and the Official English Debate in the United States', in D. Schneiderman (ed.), *Language and the State: The Law and Politics of Identity* (Les Éditions Yvon Blais, Cowansville), 209–26.

DE ONIS, JUAN (1992), *The Green Cathedral: Sustainable Development of Amazonia* (Oxford University Press, New York).

DIETZ, MARY (1992), 'Context is All: Feminism and Theories of Citizenship', in Mouffe (1992), 63–85.

DION, STÉPHANE (1991), 'Le Nationalisme dans la convergence culturelle', in R. Hudon and R. Pelletier (eds.), *L'Engagement intellectuel: mélanges en l'honneur de Léon Dion* (Les Presses de l'Université Laval, Sainte-Foy), 291–311.

—— (1992), 'Explaining Quebec Nationalism', in R. Kent Weaver (ed.), *The Collapse of Canada?* (Brookings Institute, Washington, DC).

DREYER, JUNE (1979), *China's Forty Millions: Minority Nationalities and National Integration in the People's Republic of China* (Harvard University Press, Cambridge, Mass.).

DUCHACEK, I. D. (1977), 'Federalist Responses to Ethnic Demands: An Overview', in Daniel Elazar (ed.), *Federalism and Political Integration* (Turtledove Publishing, Ramat Gan), 59–71.

DWORKIN, RONALD (1981), 'What is Equality? Part II: Equality of Resources', *Philosophy and Public Affairs*, 10/4: 283–345.

—— (1983), 'In Defense of Equality', *Social Philosophy and Policy*, 1/1: 24–40.

—— (1985), *A Matter of Principle* (Harvard University Press, London).

—— (1987), 'What is Equality? Part III: The Place of Liberty', *Iowa Law Review*, 73/1: 1–54.

—— (1988), 'What is Equality: Part IV: Political Equality', *University of San Francisco Law Review*, 22/1: 1–30.

—— (1989), 'Liberal Community', *California Law Review*, 77/3: 479–504.

—— (1990), 'Foundations of Liberal Equality', in Grethe Petersen (ed.), *The Tanner Lectures on Human Values*, 11 (University of Utah Press, Salt Lake City): 1–119.

EDWARDS, JOHN (1985), *Language, Society and Identity* (Blackwell, Oxford).

EISENBERG, AVIGAIL (1994), 'The Politics of Individual and Group Difference in Canadian Jurisprudence', *Canadian Journal of Political Science*, 27/1: 3–21.

ELAZAR, DANIEL (1987), *Exploring Federalism* (University of Alabama, Tuscaloosa, Ala.).

ELKINS, DAVID (1992), *Where Should the Majority Rule? Reflections on Non-territorial Provinces and Other Constitutional Proposals* (Centre for Constitutional Studies, University of Alberta, Edmonton).

ELTON, G. R. (1984), 'Introduction', in W. J. Shiels (ed.), *Persecution and Toleration*, Studies in Church History 21 (published for the Ecclesiastical History Society by Basil Blackwell, Oxford), pp. xiii–xv.

FALK, RICHARD (1988), 'The Rights of Peoples (in Particular Indigenous Peoples)', in James Crawford (ed.), *The Rights of Peoples* (Oxford University Press, Oxford), 17–37.

FERRY, JEAN-MARC (1992), 'Identité et citoyenneté européennes', in Lenoble and Dewandre (1992), 177–88.

FISHMAN, JOSHUA (1989), *Language and Ethnicity in Minority Sociolinguistic Perspective* (Multilingual Matters Ltd., Clevedon).

FITZGERALD, FRANCES (1986), *Cities on a Hill* (Simon & Schuster, New York).

FLERAS, AUGIE (1985), 'From Social Control towards Political Self-Determination: Maori Seats and the Politics of Separate Maori Representation in New Zealand', *Canadian Journal of Political Science*, 18/3: 551–76.

—— (1991), 'Aboriginal Electoral Districts for Canada: Lessons from New Zealand', in Robert A. Milen (ed.), *Aboriginal Peoples and Electoral Reform in Canada*, vol. 9 of the research studies of the Royal Commission on Electoral Reform and Party Financing (Dundurn Press, Toronto), 67–103.

—— and ELLIOT, JEAN LEONARD (1992), *The Nations within: Aboriginal–State Relations in Canada, the United States and New Zealand* (Oxford University Press, Toronto).

FRAGA, LUIS (1992), 'Latino Political Incorporation and the Voting Rights Act', in B. Grofman and C. Davidson (eds.), *Controversies in Minority Voting: The Voting Rights Act in Perspective* (Brookings Institution, Washington, DC), 278–82.

FRIEDMAN, L. (1969), *Argument: The Oral Argument before the Supreme Court in* Brown v Board of Education (Chelsea House, New York).

GAGNON, ALAIN-G. (1993), 'The Political Uses of Federalism', in Michael Burgess and Alain-G. Gagnon (eds.), *Comparative Federalism and Federation: Competing Traditions and Future Directions* (University of Toronto Press, Toronto), 15–44.

—— and GARCEA, JOSEPH (1988), 'Quebec and the Pursuit of Special Status', in R. D. Olling and M. W. Westmacott (eds.), *Perspectives on Canadian Federalism* (Prentice-Hall, Scarborough), 304–25.

GALENKAMP, MARLIES (1993), *Individualism and Collectivism: The Concept of Collective Rights* (Rotterdamse Filosofische Studies, Rotterdam).

GALEOTTI, ANNA (1993), 'Citizenship and Equality: The Place for Toleration', *Political Theory*, 21/4: 585–605.

GALSTON, WILLIAM (1989), 'Community, Democracy, Philosophy: The Political Thought of Michael Walzer', *Political Theory*, 17/1: 119–30.

—— (1991), *Liberal Purposes: Goods, Virtues, and Duties in the Liberal State* (Cambridge University Press, Cambridge).

—— (1995), 'Two Concepts of Liberalism', forthcoming in *Ethics*, 105/3.

GANS, HERBERT (1979), 'Symbolic Ethnicity: The Future of Ethnic Groups and Cultures in America', *Ethnic and Racial Studies*, 2/1: 1–20.

GARET, RONALD (1983), 'Communality and Existence: The Rights of Groups', *Southern California Law Review*, 56/5: 1001–75.

GELLNER, ERNEST (1983), *Nations and Nationalism* (Blackwell, Oxford).

GIBBINS, ROGER (1986), 'Citizenship, Political and Intergovernmental Problems with Indian Self-Government', in J. Rick Ponting (ed.), *Arduous Journey: Canadian Indians and Decolonization*, (McClelland & Stewart, Toronto), 369–77.

—— (1991), 'Electoral Reform and Canada's Aboriginal Population: An Assessment of Aboriginal Electoral Districts', in Robert A. Milen (ed.), *Aboriginal Peoples and Electoral Reform in Canada*, vol. 9 of the research studies of the Royal Commission on Electoral Reform and Party Financing (Dundurn Press, Toronto).

GLAZER, NATHAN (1975), *Affirmative Discrimination: Ethnic Inequality and Public Policy* (Basic Books, New York).

—— (1978), 'Individual Rights against Group Rights', in A. Tay and E. Kamenka (eds.), *Human Rights* (Edward Arnold, London), 87–103.

—— (1983), *Ethnic Dilemmas: 1964–1982* (Harvard University Press, Cambridge, Mass.).

GLEASON, PHILLIP (1982), 'American Identity and Americanization', in William Peterson, M. Novack, and P. Gleason (eds.), *Concepts of Ethnicity* (Harvard University Press, Cambridge, Mass.), 57–143.

GLENDON, MARY ANN (1991), *Rights Talk: The Impoverishment of Political Discourse* (Free Press, New York).

GOCHNAUER, MYRON (1991), 'Philosophical Musings on Persons, Groups, and Rights', *University of New Brunswick Law Journal*, 40/1: 1–20.

GORDON, MILTON (1964), *Assimilation in American Life: The Role of Race, Religion, and National Origin* (Oxford University Press, New York).

—— (1975), 'Toward a General Theory of Racial and Ethnic Group Relations', in N. Glazer and D. Moynihan (eds.), *Ethnicity, Theory and Experience* (Harvard University Press, Cambridge, Mass.).

—— (1978), *Human Nature, Class, and Ethnicity* (Oxford University Press, New York).

—— (1981), 'Models of Pluralism: The New American Dilemma', *Annals of the Academy of Political and Social Science*, 454: 178–88.

Government of Canada (1991*a*), *Shaping Canada's Future Together: Proposals* (Supply and Services, Ottawa).

—— (1991*b*), *Shared Values: The Canadian Identity* (Supply and Services, Ottawa).

Grand Council of the Crees of Quebec (1992), *Status and Rights of the James Bay Crees in the Context of Quebec's Secession from Canada* (submission to the United Nations Commission on Human Rights, 48th Session).

GREEN, LESLIE (1994), 'Internal Minorities and their Rights', in Judith Baker (ed.), *Group Rights* (University of Toronto Press, Toronto), 100–17.

GREEN, T. H. (1941), *Lectures on the Principles of Political Obligation* (Longman's, Green, & Co., London).

GROFMAN, BERNARD (1982), 'Should Representatives Be Typical of their Constituents?', in B. Grofman *et al.* (eds.), *Representation and Redistricting Issues* (D. C. Heath & Co., Lexington, Mass.).

GROSS, M. (1973), 'Indian Control for Quality Indian Education', *North Dakota Law Review*, 49/2: 237–65.

GUINIER, LANI (1991*a*), 'No Two Seats: The Elusive Quest for Political Equality', *Virginia Law Review*, 77/8: 1413–514.

—— (1991*b*), 'The Triumph of Tokenism: The Voting Rights Act and the Theory of Black Electoral Success', *Michigan Law Review*, 89/5: 1077–154

GURR, TED (1993), *Minorities at Risk: A Global View of Ethnopolitical Conflict* (Institute of Peace Press, Washington, DC).

GUTMANN, AMY (1993), 'The Challenge of Multiculturalism to Political Ethics', *Philosophy and Public Affairs*, 22/3: 171–206.

HABERMAS, JÜRGEN (1992), 'Citizenship and National Identity: Some Reflections on the Future of Europe', *Praxis International* 12/1: 1–19.

—— (1993), 'Struggles for Recognition in Constitutional States', *European Journal of Philosophy*, 1/2: 128–55.

HANCOCK, W. K. (1937), *Survey of British Commonwealth Affairs*, i: *Problems of Nationality 1900–1936* (Oxford University Press, London).

HANNUM, HURST (1989), 'The Limits of Sovereignty and Majority Rule: Minorities, Indigenous Peoples, and the Right to Autonomy', in Ellen Lutz, Hurst Hannum, and Kathryn Burke (eds.), *New Directions in Human Rights* (University of Pennsylvania Press, Philadelphia), 3–24.

—— (1990), *Autonomy, Sovereignty, and Self-Determination: The Adjudication of Conflicting Rights* (University of Pennsylvania Press, Philadelphia).

—— (ed.) (1993), *Basic Documents on Autonomy and Minority Rights* (Martinus Nijhoff, Boston).

HARLES, JOHN (1993), *Politics in the Lifeboat: Immigrants and the American Democratic Order* (Westview Press, Boulder, Col.).

HARTNEY, MICHAEL (1991), 'Some Confusions Concerning Collective Rights', *Canadian Journal of Law and Jurisprudence*, 4/2: 293–314.

HEATER, DEREK (1990), *Citizenship: The Civic Ideal in World History, Politics and Education* (Longman, London).

HIGHAM, JOHN (1976), *Send These to Me* (Atheneum, New York).

HINDESS, BARRY (1993), 'Multiculturalism and Citizenship', in Chandran Kukathas (ed.), *Multicultural Citizens: The Philosophy and Politics of Identity* (Centre for Independent Studies, St Leonards), 33–45.

HOBHOUSE, L. T. (1928), *Social Evolution and Political Theory* (Columbia University Press, New York).

—— (1966), *Social Development: Its Nature and Conditions* (George Allen & Unwin, London).

HOBSBAWM, E. J. (1990), *Nations and Nationalism since 1780: Programme, Myth and Reality* (Cambridge University Press, Cambridge).

HOERNLÉ, R. F. A. (1939), *South African Native Policy and the Liberal Spirit* (Lovedale Press, Cape Town).

HOROWITZ, D. L. (1985), *Ethnic Groups in Conflict* (University of California Press, Berkeley, Calif.).

HOWSE, ROBERT, and KNOP, KAREN (1993), 'Federalism, Secession, and the Limits of Ethnic Accommodation: A Canadian Perspective', *New Europe Law Review*, 1/2: 269–320.

HUDSON, JAMES (1986), 'The Philosophy of Immigration', *Journal of Libertarian Studies*, 8/1: 51–62.

HUMBOLDT, WILHELM VON (1988), *On Language: The Diversity of Human Language-Structure and its Influence on the Mental Development of Mankind* (Cambridge University Press, Cambridge, 1st pub. 1836).

HURKA, THOMAS (1994), 'Indirect Perfectionism: Kymlicka on Liberal Neutrality', *Journal of Political Philosophy*, forthcoming.

IGNATIEFF, MICHAEL (1993), *Blood and Belonging: Journeys into the New Nationalism* (Farrar, Straus & Giroux, New York).

ISAAC, THOMAS (1992), 'Individual versus Collective Rights: Aboriginal People and the Significance of *Thomas v Norris*', *Manitoba Law Journal*, 21/3: 618–30.

JAMES, SUSAN (1992), 'The Good-Enough Citizen: Citizenship and Independence', in Gisela Bock and Susan James (eds.), *Beyond Equality and Difference: Citizenship, Feminist Politics and Female Subjectivity* (Routledge, London), 48–65.

JANZEN, WILLIAM (1990), *Limits of Liberty: The Experiences of Mennonite, Hutterite, and Doukhobour Communities in Canada* (University of Toronto Press, Toronto).

JENSEN, ERIK (1993), 'American Indian Tribes and Secession', *Tulsa Law Review*, 29: 385–96.

JENSON, JANE (1993), 'Naming Nations: Making Nationalist Claims in Canadian Public Discourse', *Canadian Review of Sociology and Anthropology*, 30/3: 337–58.

—— (1995), 'Citizenship Claims: Routes to Representation in a Federal

System' in Karen Knop *et al.* (eds.), *Rethinking Federalism* (University of British Columbia Press, Vancouver), 99–118.

JOHNSON, GERALD (1973), *Our English Heritage* (Greenwood Press, Westport, Conn.).

JOHNSTON, DARLENE (1989), 'Native Rights as Collective Rights: A Question of Group Self-Preservation', *Canadian Journal of Law and Jurisprudence*, 2/1: 19–34.

JONES, KATHLEEN (1993), *Compassionate Authority: Democracy and the Representation of Women* (Routledge, London).

KALLEN, EVELYN (1987), 'Ethnicity and Collective Rights in Canada', in L. Driedger (ed.), *Ethnic Canada* (Copp Clark, Toronto), 318–36.

KALLEN, HORACE (1924), *Culture and Democracy in the United States* (Boni & Liveright, New York).

KARMIS, DIMITRIOS (1993), 'Cultures autochtones et libéralisme au Canada: les vertus médiatrices du communautarisme libéral de Charles Taylor', *Canadian Journal of Political Science*, 26/1: 69–96.

KARPAT, KEMAL (1982), 'Millets and Nationality: The Roots of the Incongruity of Nation and State in the Post-Ottoman Era', in Braude and Lewis (1982), 141–69.

KING, TIMOTHY (1983), 'Immigration from Developing Countries: Some Philosophical Issues', *Ethics*, 93/3: 525–36.

KLOSS, HEINZ (1977), *The American Bilingual Tradition* (Newbury House, Rowley, Mass.).

KNOPFF, RAINER (1979), 'Language and Culture in the Canadian Debate: The Battle of the White Papers', *Canadian Review of Studies in Nationalism*, 6/1: 66–82.

—— (1982), 'Liberal Democracy and the Challenge of Nationalism in Canadian Politics', *Canadian Review of Studies in Nationalism*, 9/1: 23–39.

KRISTEVA, JULIA (1993), *Nations without Nationalism*, trans. Leon S. Roudiez (Columbia University Press, New York).

KUKATHAS, CHANDRAN (1991), *The Fraternal Conceit: Individualist versus Collectivist Ideas of Community* (Centre for Independent Studies, St Leonard's).

—— (1992*a*), 'Are There any Cultural Rights?', *Political Theory*, 20/1: 105–39.

—— (1992*b*), 'Cultural Rights Again: A Rejoinder to Kymlicka', *Political Theory*, 20/4: 674–80.

—— (1993), 'The Idea of a Multicultural Society' and 'Multiculturalism and the Idea of an Australian Identity', in Chandran Kukathas (ed.), *Multicultural Citizens: The Philosophy and Politics of Identity* (Centre for Independent Studies, St Leonard's), 19–30, 145–57.

KYMLICKA, WILL (1989*a*), *Liberalism, Community, and Culture* (Oxford University Press, Oxford).

—— (1989*b*), 'Liberal Individualism and Liberal Neutrality', *Ethics*, 99/4; 883–905.

—— (1990), *Contemporary Political Philosophy: An Introduction* (Oxford University Press, Oxford).

—— (1991), 'Liberalism and the Politicization of Ethnicity', *Canadian Journal of Law and Jurisprudence*, 4/2: 239–56.

—— (1992*a*), 'The Rights of Minority Cultures: Reply to Kukathas', *Political Theory*, 20/1: 140–6.

—— (1992*b*), 'Two Models of Pluralism and Tolerance', *Analyse und Kritik*, 14/1: 33–56.

—— (1993*a*), 'Group Representation in Canadian Politics', in Leslie Seidle (ed.), *Equity and Community: The Charter, Interest Advocacy, and Representation* (Institute for Research on Public Policy, Montreal), 61–89.

—— (1993*b*), 'Reply to Modood', *Analyse und Kritik*, 15/1: 92–6.

—— (1995*a*), 'Misunderstanding Nationalism', *Dissent*, Winter 1995: 130–7.

—— (1995*b*), 'Dworkin on Freedom and Culture', in Justine Burley (ed.), *Reading Dworkin* (Blackwell, Oxford), forthcoming.

—— (1995*c*), 'Concepts of Community and Social Justice', in Fen Hampson and Judith Reppy (eds.), *Global Environmental Change and Social Justice*, forthcoming.

—— and NORMAN, W. J. (1994), 'Return of the Citizen', *Ethics*, 104/2: 352–81.

LACZKO, LESLIE (1994), 'Canada's Pluralism in Comparative Perspective', *Ethnic and Racial Studies*, 17/1: 20–41.

LAFOREST, GUY (1991), 'Libéralisme et nationalisme au Canada à l'heure de l'accord du Lac Meech', *Carrefour*, 13/2: 68–90.

LAMOUREUX, DIANE (1991), 'La Citoyenneté: de l'exclusion à l'inclusion', in Colas *et al.* (1991), 53–67.

LAPONCE, J. A. (1987), *Languages and their Territories* (University of Toronto Press, Toronto).

LARMORE, CHARLES (1987), *Patterns of Moral Complexity* (Cambridge University Press, Cambridge).

LAYTON-HENRY, ZIG (1990), *The Political Rights of Migrant Workers in Western Europe* (Sage, London).

LECA, JEAN (1992), 'Questions on Citizenship', in Mouffe (1992), 17–32.

LENIHAN, DONALD (1991), 'Liberalism and the Problem of Cultural Membership', *Canadian Journal of Law and Jurisprudence*, 4/2: 401–19.

LENOBLE, JACQUES (1992), 'Penser l'identité et la démocratie en Europe', in Lenoble and Dewandre (1992), 293–315.

—— and DEWANDRE, NICOLE (eds.) (1992), *L'Europe au soir du siècle: identité et démocratie* (Éditions Esprit, Paris).

LERNER, NATAN (1991), *Group Rights and Discrimination in International Law* (Martinus Nijhoff, Dordrecht).

LIJPHART, AREND (1984), *Democracies: Patterns of Majoritarian and Consensus Government in Twenty-One Countries* (Yale University Press, New Haven, Conn.).

LIJPHART, AREND (1991), 'Self-Determination versus Pre-determination of Ethnic Minorities in Power-Sharing Systems', in D. Schneiderman (ed.), *Language and the State: The Law and Politics of Identity* (Les Éditions Yvon Blais, Cowansville), 153–65.

LONG, DAVID (1992), 'Culture, Ideology and Militancy: Movement of Native Indians in Canada', in W. E. Carroll (ed.), *Organising Dissent: Contemporary Social Movements in Theory and Practice* (Garamond, Toronto), 118–34.

LONG, J. A. (1991), 'Federalism and Ethnic Self-Determination: Native Indians in Canada', *Journal of Commonwealth and Comparative Politics*, 29/2: 192–211.

LYON, NOEL (1984), *Aboriginal Self-Government: Rights of Citizenship and Access to Government Services* (Institute of Intergovernmental Relations, Kingston).

LYONS, DAVID (1981), 'The New Indian Claims and Original Rights to Land', in J. Paul (ed.), *Reading Nozick: Essays on* Anarchy, State and Utopia (Rowman & Littlefield, Totowa, NJ).

MACDONALD, IAN (1989), 'Group Rights', *Philosophical Papers*, 28/2: 117–36.

MCDONALD, MICHAEL (1991*a*), 'Question about Collective Rights', in D. Schneiderman (ed.), *Language and the State: The Law and Politics of Identity* (Les Éditions Yvon Blais, Cowansville).

—— (1991*b*), 'Should Communities Have Rights? Reflections on Liberal Individualism', *Canadian Journal of Law and Jurisprudence*, 4/2: 217–37.

—— (1992), 'Liberalism, Community, and Culture', *University of Toronto Law Journal*, 42: 113–31.

MACEDO, STEPHEN (1990), *Liberal Virtues: Citizenship, Virtue and Community* (Oxford University Press, Oxford).

—— (1995), 'Liberal Civic Education and Religious Fundamentalism', forthcoming in *Ethics*, 105/3.

MCGARRY, JOHN, and O'LEARY, BRENDAN (1994), 'The Political Regulation of National and Ethnic Conflict', *Parliamentary Affairs*, 47/1: 94–115.

MACINTYRE, ALASDAIR (1981), *After Virtue: A Study in Moral Theory* (Duckworth, London).

MCKEAN, W. (1983), *Equality and Discrimination under International Law* (Oxford University Press, Oxford).

MACKLEM, PATRICK (1993), 'Distributing Sovereignty: Indian Nations and Equality of Peoples', *Stanford Law Review*, 45/5: 1311–67.

MCLEAY, E. M. (1991), 'Two Steps Forward, Two Steps Back: Maori Devolution, Maori Advisory Committees, and Maori Representation', *Political Science*, 43/1: 30–46.

MCNEILL, WILLIAM (1986), *Polyethnicity and National Unity in World History* (University of Toronto Press, Toronto).

MCRAE, KENNETH (1979), 'The Plural Society and the Western Political Tradition', *Canadian Journal of Political Science*, 12/4: 675–88.

McRoberts, Kenneth (1988), *Quebec: Social Change and Political Crisis*, 3rd edn. (McClelland & Stewart, Toronto).

Majone, Giandomenico (1990), 'Preservation of Cultural Diversity in a Federal System: The Role of the Regions', in Mark Tushnet (ed.), *Comparative Constitutional Federalism* (Greenwood Press, New York), 67–76.

Makinson, David (1988), 'Rights of Peoples: Point of View of a Logician', in James Crawford (ed.), *The Rights of Peoples* (Oxford University Press, Oxford), 69–92.

Maré, Gerhard (1992), *Brothers Born of Warrior Blood: Politics and Ethnicity and South Africa* (Raven Press, Johannesburg).

Margalit, Avishai, and Halbertal, Moshe (1994) 'Liberalism and the Right to Culture', *Social Research*, 61/3: 491–510.

—— and Raz, Joseph (1990), 'National Self-Determination', *Journal of Philosophy*, 87/9: 439–61.

Marshall, T. H. (1965), *Class, Citizenship and Social Development* (Anchor, New York).

Mason, Andrew (1990), 'Autonomy, Liberalism and State Neutrality', *Philosophical Quarterly*, 40/160: 433–52.

—— (1993), 'Liberalism and the Value of Community', *Canadian Journal of Philosophy*, 23/2: 215–40.

Maybury-Lewis, David (1984), 'Living in Leviathan: Ethnic Groups and the State', in D. Maybury-Lewis (ed.), *The Prospects for Plural Societies* (American Ethnological Society, Washington, DC), 222–7.

Mazzini, Joseph (1907), *The Duties of Man and Other Essays* (J. M. Dent, London).

Megyery, Kathy (1991*a*), *Women in Canadian Politics: Toward Equity in Representation*, vol. 6 of the research studies of the Royal Commission on Electoral Reform and Party Financing (Dundurn Press, Toronto).

—— (1991*b*), *Ethno-Cultural Groups and Visible Minorities in Canadian Politics: The Question of Access*, vol. 7 of the research studies of the Royal Commission on Electoral Reform and Party Financing (Dundurn Press, Toronto).

Mendes, Errol (1991), 'Two Solitudes: Freedom of Expression and Collective Linguistic Rights in Canada: A Case Study of the *Ford* Decision', *National Journal of Constitutional Law*, 1: 283–313.

Mendus, Susan (1989), *Toleration and the Limits of Liberalism* (Humanities Press, Atlantic Highlands, NJ).

Mill, J. S. (1972), *Considerations on Representative Government*, in *Utilitarianism, Liberty, Representative Government*, ed. H. Acton (J. M. Dent, London).

—— (1982), *On Liberty*, ed. G. Himmelfarb (Penguin, Harmondsworth).

Miller, David (1988–9), 'In What Sense Must Socialism Be Communitarian?', *Social Philosophy and Policy*, 6/2: 51–73.

MILLER, DAVID (1989), *Market, State and Community: The Foundations of Market Socialism* (Oxford University Press, Oxford).
—— (1993), 'In Defense of Nationality', *Journal of Applied Philosophy*, 10/1 3–16.
MILLS, RICHARD (1974), *The Colonization of Australia 1829–42: The Wakefield Experiment in Empire Building* (Sydney University Press, Sydney).
Minority Rights Group (1991), *Minorities and Autonomy in Western Europe* (Minority Rights Group, London).
MINOW, MARTHA (1990*a*), *Making all the Difference: Inclusion, Exclusion and American Law* (Cornell University Press, Ithaca, NY).
—— (1990*b*), 'Putting up and Putting down: Tolerance Reconsidered', in Mark Tushnet (ed.), *Comparative Constitutional Federalism* (Greenwood Press, New York), 77–113.
—— (1991), 'From Class Action to Miss Saigon: The Concept of Representation in the Law', *Cleveland State Law Review*, 39: 269–300.
MODOOD, TARIQ (1992), *Not Easy Being British: Colour, Culture and Citizenship* (Trentham Books, Stoke-on-Trent).
—— (1993), 'Kymlicka on British Muslims' and 'A Rejoinder', *Analyse und Kritik*, 15/1: 87–91; 97–9.
—— (1994), 'Establishment, Multiculturalism, and British Citizenship', *Political Quarterly*, 65/1: 53–73.
MOON, DONALD (1993), *Constructing Community: Moral Pluralism and Tragic Conflicts* (Princeton University Press, Princeton, NJ).
MOORE, MARGARET (1993), *Foundations of Liberalism* (Oxford University Press, Oxford).
MORTON, DESMOND (1986), *The New Democrats, 1961–1986: The Politics of Change* (Copp Clark, Toronto).
MORTON, F. L. (1985), 'Group Rights versus Individual Rights in the Charter: The Special Cases of Natives and the Québécois', in N. Nevitte and A. Kornberg (eds.), *Minorities and the Canadian State* (Mosaic Press, Oakville): 71–85.
MOSS, WENDY (1990), 'Indigenous Self-Government and Sexual Equality under the Indian Act: Resolving Conflicts between Collective and Individual Rights', *Queen's Law Journal*, 15/2: 279–305.
MOUFFE, CHANTAL (ed.) (1992), *Dimensions of Radical Democracy: Pluralism, Citizenship and Community* (Routledge, London).
MULGAN, RICHARD (1989), *Maori, Pākehā and Democracy* (Oxford University Press, Auckland).
MUNCK, RONNIE (1985), 'Otto Bauer: Towards a Marxist Theory of Nationalism', *Capital and Class*, 25: 84–97.
MURRAY, STEPHEN (1979), 'Institutional Elaboration of a Quasi-ethnic Community', *International Review of Modern Sociology*, 9/2: 165–77.
NARVESON, JAN (1991), 'Collective Rights?', *Canadian Journal of Law and Jurisprudence*, 4/2: 329–45.

NETTHEIM, GARTH (1988), '"Peoples" and "Populations": Indigenous Peoples and the Rights of Peoples', in James Crawford (ed.), *The Rights of Peoples* (Oxford University Press, Oxford), 107–26.

NICKEL, JAMES (1990), 'Rawls on Political Community and Principles of Justice', *Law and Philosophy*, 9: 205–16.

—— (1994), 'Ethnocide and Indigenous Peoples', *Journal of Social Philosophy*, 25: 84–98.

—— (1995), 'The Value of Cultural Belonging: Expanding Kymlicka's Theory', forthcoming in *Dialogue*.

NIELSSON, GUNNAR (1985), 'States and "Nation-Groups": A Global Taxonomy', in Edward Tiryakian and Ronald Rogowski (eds.), *New Nationalisms of the Developed West* (Allen & Unwin, Boston), 27–56.

NIETSCHMANN, BERNARD (1987), 'The Third World War', *Cultural Survival Quarterly*, 11/3: 1–16.

NIMNI, EHPRAIM (1989), 'Marx, Engels and the National Question', *Science and Society*, 53/3: 297–326.

—— (1994), *Marxism and Nationalism: Theoretical Origins of a Political Crisis* (Pluto Press, London).

NORMAN, W. J. (1994), 'Towards a Normative Theory of Federalism', in Judith Baker (ed.), *Group Rights* (University of Toronto Press, Toronto), 79–99.

O'BRIEN, SHARON (1987), 'Cultural Rights in the United States: A Conflict of Values', *Law and Inequality Journal*, 5: 267–358.

OGBU, JOHN (1988), 'Diversity and Equity in Public Education: Community Forces and Minority School Adjustment and Performance', in R. Haskins and D. MacRae (eds.), *Policies for America's Public Schools: Teachers, Equity and Indicators* (Ablex Publishers, Norwood, NJ), 127–70.

OLIVER, MICHAEL (1992), 'Laurendeau et Trudeau: leurs opinions sur le Canada', in R. Hudon and R. Pelletier (eds.), *L'Engagement intellectuel: mélanges en l'honneur de Léon Dion* (Les Presses de l'Université Laval, Sainte-Foy).

ORDESHOOK, PETER (1993), 'Some Rules of Constitutional Design', *Social Philosophy and Policy*, 10/2: 198–232.

PALMER, HOWARD (1976), 'Mosaic versus Melting Pot? Immigration and Ethnicity in Canada and the United States', *International Journal*, 31/3: 488–528.

PAREKH, BHIKHU (1990), 'The Rushdie Affair: Research Agenda for Political Philosophy', *Political Studies*, 38: 695–709.

—— (1991), 'British Citizenship and Cultural Difference', in Geoff Andrews (ed.), *Citizenship* (Lawrence & Wishart, London), 183–204.

—— (1994), 'Decolonizing Liberalism', in Aleksandras Shtromas (ed.), *The End of 'Isms'? Reflections on the Fate of Ideological Politics after Communism's Collapse* (Blackwell, Oxford), 85–103.

PARIS, DAVID (1991), 'Moral Education and the "Tie that Binds" in Liberal Political Theory', *American Political Science Review*, 85/3: 875–901.

PARRY, GERAINT (1991), 'Paths to Citizenship', in Ursula Vogel and Michael Moran (eds.), *The Frontiers of Citizenship* (St Martin's Press, New York), 167–96.

PATEMAN, CAROLE (1988), 'The Patriarchal Welfare State', in Amy Gutmann (ed.), *Democracy and the Welfare State* (Princeton University Press, Princeton, NJ), 231–60.

PENZ, PETER (1992), 'Development Refugees and Distributive Justice: Indigenous Peoples, Land and the Developmentalist State', *Public Affairs Quarterly*, 6/1: 105–31.

—— (1993), 'Colonization of Tribal Lands in Bangladesh and Indonesia: State Rationales, Rights to Land, and Environmental Justice', in Michael Howard (ed.), *Asia's Environmental Crisis* (Westview Press, Boulder, Col.), 37–72.

PETERS, R., and DE VRIES, G. (1976), 'Apostasy in Islam', *Die Welt des Islams*, 17: 1–25.

PETERSON, WILLIAM (1975), 'On the Subnations of Europe', in N. Glazer and D. Moynihan (eds.), *Ethnicity: Theory and Experience* (Harvard University Press, Cambridge, Mass.), 117–208.

PFAFF, WILLIAM (1993), *The Wrath of Nations: Civilization and the Furies of Nationalism* (Simon & Schuster, New York).

PHILLIPS, ANNE (1991), *Engendering Democracy* (Pennsylvania State University Press, University Park. Pa.).

—— (1992), 'Democracy and Difference: Some Problems for Feminist Theory', *Political Quarterly*, 63/1: 79–90.

—— (1993), *Democracy and Difference* (Pennsylvania State University Press, Philadelphia).

—— (1994), 'Dealing with Difference: A Politics of Ideas or a Politics of Presence?', *Constellations*, 1/1: 74–91.

—— (1995), *The Politics of Presence: Issues in Democracy and Group Representation* (Oxford University Press, Oxford), forthcoming.

PHILLIPS, D. Z. (1993), *Looking Backward: A Critical Appraisal of Communitarian Thought* (Princeton University Press, Princeton, NJ).

PINKNEY, ALPHONSO (1976), *Red, Black and Green: Black Nationalism in the United States* (Cambridge University Press, Cambridge).

PITKIN, HANNA (1967), *The Concept of Representation* (University of California Press, Berkeley, Calif.).

POMERANCE, MICHLA (1982), *Self-Determination in Law and Practice: The New Doctrine in the United Nations* (Martinus Nijhoff Publishers, The Hague).

POOLE, ROSS (1993), 'Nationalism and the Nation State in Late Modernity', *European Studies Journal*, 10/1: 161–74.

PORTER, JOHN (1975), 'Ethnic Pluralism in Canadian Perspective', in N. Glazer and D. Moynihan (eds.), *Ethnicity, Theory and Experience* (Harvard University Press, Cambridge, Mass.), 267–304.

—— (1987), *The Measure of Canadian Society* (Carleton University Press, Ottawa).

POULTER, SEBASTIAN (1987), 'Ethnic Minority Customs, English Law, and Human Rights', *International and Comparative Law Quarterly*, 36/3: 589–615.

RAWLS, JOHN (1971), *A Theory of Justice* (Oxford University Press, London).

—— (1974), 'Reply to Alexander and Musgrave', *Quarterly Journal of Economics*, 88/4: 633–55.

—— (1975), 'Fairness to Goodness', *Philosophical Review*, 84: 536–54.

—— (1978), 'The Basic Structure as Subject', in A. Goldman and J. Kim (eds.), *Values and Morals* (Reidel, Dordrecht).

—— (1980), 'Kantian Constructivism in Moral Theory', *Journal of Philosophy*, 77/9: 515–72.

—— (1982*a*), 'Social Unity and Primary Goods', in A. Sen and B. Williams (eds.), *Utilitarianism and Beyond* (Cambridge University Press, Cambridge), 159–85.

—— (1982*b*), 'The Basic Liberties and their Priority', in S. McMurrin (ed.), *The Tanner Lectures on Human Values*, iii (University of Utah Press, Salt Lake City), 1–87.

—— (1985), 'Justice as Fairness: Political not Metaphysical', *Philosophy and Public Affairs*, 14/3: 223–51.

—— (1987), 'The Idea of an Overlapping Consensus', *Oxford Journal of Legal Studies*, 7/1: 1–25.

—— (1988), 'The Priority of Right and Ideas of the Good', *Philosophy and Public Affairs*, 17/4: 251–76.

—— (1989), 'The Domain of the Political and Overlapping Consensus', *New York University Law Review*, 64/2: 233–55.

—— (1993*a*), *Political Liberalism* (Columbia University Press, New York).

—— (1993*b*), 'The Law of Peoples', in S. Shute and S. Hurley (eds.), *On Human Rights: The Oxford Amnesty Lectures 1993* (Basic Books, New York), 41–82.

RAZ, JOSEPH (1986), *The Morality of Freedom* (Oxford University Press, Oxford).

—— (1994), 'Multiculturalism: A Liberal Perspective', *Dissent*, Winter: 67–79.

RCERPF—see Royal Commission on Electoral Reform and Party Financing.

RÉAUME, DENISE (1991), 'The Constitutional Protection of Language: Security or Survival?', in D. Schneiderman (ed.), *Language and the State: The Law and Politics of Identity* (Les Éditions Yvon Blais, Cowansville), 37–57.

REBICK, JUDY, and DAY, SHELAGH (1992), 'A Place at the Table: The New Senate Needs Gender Equality, Minority Representation', *Ottawa Citizen*, 11 September: A11.

REED, ADOLPH (1988), 'The Black Urban Regime: Structural Origins and Constraints', *Comparative Urban and Community Research*, 1: 138–89.

REITZ, JEFFREY, and BRETON, RAYMOND (1994), *The Illusion of Difference: Realities of Ethnicity in Canada and the United States* (C. D. Howe Institute, Ottawa).

RESNIK, JUDITH (1989), 'Dependent Sovereigns: Indian Tribes, States, and the Federal Courts', *University of Chicago Law Review*, 56: 671–759.

RICH, P. (1987), 'T. H. Green, Lord Scarman and the Issue of Ethnic Minority Rights in English Liberal Thought', *Ethnic and Racial Studies*, 10: 149–68.

RORTY, RICHARD (1991), *Objectivity, Relativism, and Truth: Philosophical Papers I* (Cambridge University Press, Cambridge).

ROSENBLUM, NANCY (1984), 'Moral Membership in a Postliberal State', *World Politics*, 36/4: 581–96.

ROSENFELD, MICHEL (1991), *Affirmative Action and Justice: A Philosophical and Constitutional Inquiry* (Yale University Press, New Haven, Conn.).

ROTHCHILD, DONALD, and OLORUNSOLA, VICTOR (eds.) (1983), *State versus Ethnic Claims: African Policy Dilemmas* (Westview Press, Boulder, Col.).

Royal Commission on Electoral Reform and Party Financing (1991). *Reforming Electoral Democracy: Final Report*, vols. i and ii (Supply and Services, Ottawa).

RUBINSTEIN, ALVIN (1993), 'Is Statehood for Puerto Rico in the National Interest?', *In Depth: A Journal for Values and Public Policy*, Spring: 87–99.

RUIZ, RICHARD (1983), 'Ethnic Group Interests and the Social Good: Law and Language', in Winston van Horne and Thomas Tonneson (eds.), *Ethnicity, Law and the Social Good* (University of Wisconsin System American Ethnic Studies Coordinating Committee, Madison, Wis.), 49–73.

RUNCIMAN, STEVEN (1970), *The Orthodox Churches and the Secular State* (Auckland University Press, Auckland).

RUSSELL, JOHN (1993), 'Nationalistic Minorities and Liberal Traditions', in Philip Bryden *et al.* (eds.), *Protecting Rights and Liberties: Essays on the Charter and Canada's Political, Legal and Intellectual Life* (University of Toronto Press, Toronto), 205–41.

SAID, EDWARD (1993), 'Nationalism, Human Rights and Interpretation', in Barbara Johnson (ed.), *Freedom and Interpretation: The Oxford Amnesty Lectures 1992* (Basic Books, New York), 175–205.

SANDEL, MICHAEL (1982), *Liberalism and the Limits of Justice* (Cambridge University Press, Cambridge).

—— (1984), 'The Procedural Republic and the Unencumbered Self', *Political Theory*, 12/1: 81–96.

—— (1990), 'Freedom of Conscience or Freedom of Choice', in James Hunter and O. Guinness (eds.), *Articles of Faith, Articles of Peace* (Brookings Institute, Washington, DC), 74–92.

SCHWARTZ, BRIAN (1986), *First Principles, Second Thoughts: Aboriginal Peoples, Constitutional Reform and Canadian Statecraft* (Institute for Research on Public Policy, Montreal).

SELASSIE, ALEMANTE (1993), 'Ethnic Identity and Constitutional Design for Africa', *Stanford Journal of International Law*, 29/1: 1–56.

SHARP, ANDREW (1990), *Justice and the Maori: Maori Claims in New Zealand Political Argument in the 1980s* (Oxford University Press, Auckland).

SIEGAN, BERNARD (1992), *Drafting a Constitution for a Nation or Republic Emerging into Freedom* (Locke Institute).

SIGLER, JAY (1983), *Minority Rights: A Comparative Analysis* (Greenwood, Westport, Conn.).

SKUTNABB-KANGAS, TOVE (1988), 'Multilingualism and the Education of Minority Children', in T. Skutnabb-Kangas and J. Cummings (eds.), *Minority Education: From Shame to Struggle* (Multilingual Matters Ltd., Clevedon), 9–44.

SMITH, ANTHONY (1986), *The Ethnic Origins of Nations* (Blackwell, Oxford).

—— (1993), 'A Europe of Nations—or the Nation of Europe?', *Journal of Peace Research*, 30/2: 129–35.

SMITH, JENNIFER (1993), 'Canadian Confederation and the Influence of American Federalism', in Marian McKenna (ed.), *The Canadian and American Constitutions in Comparative Perspective* (University of Calgary Press, Calgary), 65–85.

SOHN, L. (1981), 'The Rights of Minorities', in L. Henkin (ed.), *The International Bill of Rights: The Covenant on Civil and Political Rights* (Columbia University Press, New York), 270–89.

SOWELL, THOMAS (1990), *Preferential Policies: An International Perspective* (Morrow, New York).

Special Joint Committee on a Renewed Canada (1992), *Report of the Special Joint Committee on a Renewed Canada* (Supply and Services, Ottawa).

SPITZ, ELAINE (1984), *Majority Rule* (Chatham House Publishers, Chatham, NJ).

STARK, ANDREW (1992), 'English-Canadian Opposition to Quebec Nationalism', in R. Kent Weaver (ed.), *The Collapse of Canada?* (Brookings Institute, Washington, DC), 123–58.

STEINBERG, STEPHEN (1981), *The Ethnic Myth: Race, Ethnicity, and Class in America* (Atheneum, New York).

STEVENSON, GARTH (1986), 'A Critique of Provincialism', in John Richards and Don Kerr (eds.), *Canada: What's Left?* (NeWest Press, Edmonton), 141–6.

STONE, JOHN (1976), 'Black Nationalism and Apartheid: Two Variations on a Separatist Theme', *Social Dynamics*, 2/1: 19–30.

—— (1985), *Racial Conflict in Contemporary Society* (Harvard University Press, Cambridge, Mass.).

SUNSTEIN, CASS (1991), 'Preferences and Politics', *Philosophy and Public Affairs*, 20/1: 3–34.

SVENSSON, FRANCES (1979), 'Liberal Democracy and Group Rights: The Legacy of Individualism and its Impact on American Indian Tribes', *Political Studies*, 27/3: 421–39.

TAMIR, YAEL (1993), *Liberal Nationalism* (Princeton University Press, Princeton, NJ).

TAYLOR, CHARLES (1985), *Philosophy and the Human Sciences: Philosophical Papers 2* (Cambridge University Press, Cambridge).

—— (1991), 'Shared and Divergent Values', in Ronald Watts and D. Brown (eds.), *Options for a New Canada* (University of Toronto Press, Toronto), 53–76.

—— (1992*a*), 'The Politics of Recognition', in Amy Gutmann (ed.), *Multiculturalism and the 'Politics of Recognition'* (Princeton University Press, Princeton, NJ), 25–73.

—— (1992*b*), 'Quel principe d'identité collective', in Lenoble and Dewandre (1992), 59–66.

THERNSTROM, STEPHEN (1983), 'Ethnic Pluralism: the U.S. Model', in C. Fried (ed.), *Minorities: Community and Identity* (Springer-Verlag, Berlin), 247–54.

THORNBERRY, PATRICK (1980), 'Is There a Phoenix in the Ashes? International Law and Minority Rights', *Texas International Law Journal*, 15: 421–58.

—— (1991), *International Law and the Rights of Minorities* (Oxford University Press, Oxford).

TODOROV, TZVETAN (1993), *On Human Diversity: Nationalism, Racism and Exoticism in French Thought* (Harvard University Press, Cambridge, Mass.).

TOLLEFSON, JAMES (1989), *Alien Winds: The Reeducation of America's Indochinese Refugees* (Praeger, New York).

TOMASI, JOHN (1991), 'Individual Rights and Community Virtues', *Ethics*, 101/3: 521–36.

—— (1995), 'Kymlicka, Liberalism, and Respect for Aboriginal Cultures', *Ethics*, forthcoming.

TOMUSCHAT, C. (1983), 'Protection of Minorities under Article 27 of International Covenant on Civil and Political Rights', in R. Bernhardt *et al.* (eds.), *Volkerrecht als Rechtsordnung Internationale Gerichtsbarkeit Menschenrechte* (Springer, Berlin), 950–79.

TORRES, GERALD (1991), 'Critical Race Theory: The Decline of the Universalist Ideal and the Hope of Plural Justice', *Minnesota Law Review*, 75: 993–1007.

TRAKMAN, LEON (1992), 'Group Rights: A Canadian Perspective', *New York University Journal of International Law and Politics*, 24/4: 1579–650.

TRUDEAU, P. E. (1969), speech of 8 Aug. 1969, repr. as 'Justice in our Time', in Eldon Soifer (ed.), *Ethical Issues: Perspectives for Canadians* (Broadview Press, Peterborough, 1992), 295–7.

—— (1990), 'The Values of a Just Society', in Thomas Axworthy (ed.), *Towards a Just Society* (Viking Press, Toronto), 357–404.

TSOSIE, REBECCA (1994), 'Separate Sovereigns, Civil Rights and the Sacred Text: The Legacy of Thurgood Marshall's Indian Law Jurisprudence', *Arizona State Law Journal*, 26/2: 495–533.

TULLY, JAMES (1994), 'Aboriginal Property and Western Theory: Recovering a Middle Ground', *Social Philosophy and Policy*, 11/2: 153–80.

TURPEL, M. E. (1989–90), 'Aboriginal Peoples and the Canadian Charter: Interpretive Monopolies, Cultural Differences', *Canadian Human Rights Yearbook*, 6: 3–45.

—— (1993), 'The Charlottetown Discord and Aboriginal People's Struggle for Fundamental Political Change', in K. McRoberts and P. Monahan (eds.), *The Charlottetown Accord, the Referendum, and the Future of Canada* (University of Toronto Press, Toronto), 117–51.

VAN DEN BERGHE, PIERRE (1981*a*), *The Ethnic Phenomenon* (Elsevier, New York).

—— (1981*b*), 'Protection of Ethnic Minorities: A Critical Appraisal', in R. Wirsing (ed.), *Protection of Ethnic Minorities: Comparative Perspectives* (Pergamon, New York), 343–55.

VAN DYKE, VERNON (1977), 'The Individual, the State, and Ethnic Communities in Political Theory', *World Politics*, 29/3: 343–69.

—— (1982), 'Collective Entities and Moral Rights: Problems in Liberal-Democratic Thought', *Journal of Politics*, 44: 21–40.

—— (1985), *Human Rights, Ethnicity and Discrimination* (Greenwood, Westport, Conn.).

WALDRON, JEREMY (1989), 'Autonomy and Perfectionism in Raz's *Morality of Freedom*', *Southern California Law Review*, 62/3–4: 1097–152.

—— (1992*a*), 'Minority Cultures and the Cosmopolitan Alternative', *University of Michigan Journal of Law Reform*, 25/3: 751–93.

—— (1992*b*), 'Superseding Historic Injustice', *Ethics*, 103/1: 4–28.

WALKER, GRAHAM (1994), 'The New Mixed Constitution', *Polity*, 26/3: 503–15.

WALZER, MICHAEL (1977), *Just and Unjust Wars* (Basic Books, New York).

—— (1980), 'The Moral Standing of States', *Philosophy and Public Affairs*, 9/2: 209–29.

—— (1982), 'Pluralism in Political Perspective', in M. Walzer (ed.), *The Politics of Ethnicity* (Harvard University Press, Cambridge. Mass.), 1–28.

—— (1983*a*), *Spheres of Justice: A Defence of Pluralism and Equality* (Blackwell, Oxford).

—— (1983*b*), 'States and Minorities', in C. Fried (ed.), *Minorities: Community and Identity* (Springer-Verlag, Berlin), 219–27.

—— (1990), 'The Communitarian Critique of Liberalism', *Political Theory*, 18/1: 6–23.

—— (1992*a*), 'The Civil Society Argument', in Mouffe (1992), 89–107.

—— (1992*b*), *What it Means to Be an American* (Marsilio, New York).

—— (1992*c*), 'The New Tribalism', *Dissent*, Spring: 164–71.

WALZER, MICHAEL (1992*d*), 'Comment', in Amy Gutmann (ed.), *Multiculturalism and the 'Politics of Recognition'* (Princeton University Press, Princeton, NJ), 99–103.

WARD, CYNTHIA (1991), 'The Limits of "Liberal Republicanism": Why Group-Based Remedies and Republican Citizenship Don't Mix', *Columbia Law Review*, 91/3: 581–607

WEAVER, SALLY (1985), 'Federal Difficulties with Aboriginal Rights in Canada', in M. Boldt and J. Long (eds.), *The Quest for Justice: Aboriginal Peoples and Aboriginal Rights* (University of Toronto Press, Toronto), 139–47.

WEINSTEIN, BRIAN (1983), *The Civic Tongue: Political Consequences of Language Choices* (Longman, New York).

WEINSTEIN, J. (1986), *Aboriginal Self-Determination off a Land Base* (Institute for Intergovernmental Relations, Kingston).

WEST, CORNEL (1990), 'The New Cultural Politics of Difference', in R. Ferguson *et al.* (eds.), *Out There: Marginalization and Contemporary Cultures* (MIT Press, Boston), 19–36.

WESTON, WILLIAM (1981), 'Freedom of Religion and the American Indian', in R. Nichols (ed.), *The American Indian: Past and Present*, 2nd edn. (John Wiley & Sons, New York).

WHITAKER, REG (1992), *A Sovereign Idea: Essays on Canada as a Democratic Community* (McGill-Queen's University Press, Montreal).

WILLIAMS, MELISSA (1994), 'Group Inequality and the Public Culture of Justice', in Judith Baker (ed.), *Group Rights* (University of Toronto Press, Toronto), 34–65.

WILSON, V. SEYMOUR (1993), 'The Tapestry Vision of Canadian Multiculturalism', *Canadian Journal of Political Science*, 26/4: 645–69.

WOODSWORTH, J. S. (1972), *Stranger within our Gates* (University of Toronto Press, Toronto).

YALDEN, ROBERT (1989), 'Liberalism and Language in Quebec: Bill 101, the Courts and Bill 178', *University of Toronto Faculty of Law Review*, 47 (Supplement), 973–94.

YOUNG, IRIS MARION (1989), 'Polity and Group Difference: A Critique of the Ideal of Universal Citizenship', *Ethics*, 99/2: 250–74.

—— (1990), *Justice and the Politics of Difference* (Princeton University Press, Princeton, NJ).

—— (1993*a*), 'Together in Difference: Transforming the Logic of Group Political Conflict', in Judith Squires (ed.), *Principled Positions: Postmodernism and the Rediscovery of Value* (Lawrence and Wishart, London), 121–50.

—— (1993*b*), 'Justice and Communicative Democracy', in Roger Gottlieb (ed.), *Radical Democracy: Tradition, Counter-tradition, Politics* (Temple University Press, Philadelphia), 123–43.

—— (1995), 'Communication and the Other: Beyond Deliberative Democracy', in Seyla Benhabib (ed.), *Democracy and Difference:*

Changing Boundaries of the Political (Princeton University Press, Princeton, NJ), forthcoming.

YOUNG, LISA (1994), *Electoral Systems and Representative Legislatures: Consideration of Alternative Electoral Systems* (Canadian Advisory Council on the Status of Women, Ottawa).

YUVAL-DAVIS, NIRA (1993), 'Gender and Nation', *Ethnic and Racial Studies*, 16/4: 621–32.

ZIMMERN, ALFRED (1918), *Nationality and Government* (Chatto & Windus, London).

INDEX